Praise for
Where the Wild Winds Are

' *Where the Wild Winds Are* is full to the brim with
learning, entertainment, description, scientific fact and
conjectural fiction. It is travel writing *in excelsis*.'
Jan Morris, *Literary Review*

'A quest both quixotic and entertainingly escapist.'
Financial Times, Books of the Year

'A thrilling and gorgeous tale, packed
with meteorological wonder.'
Amy Liptrot, author of *The Outrun*

'There are poignant moments of calm amid the tumult,
insights that capture the joy of walking alone.'
The Times Literary Supplement

'It's damned hard to describe the invisible. Hunt,
on his journey through landscape and legend,
science and superstition, proves more than equal
to the challenge. He dares, and he wins.'
Daily Telegraph, Books of the Year

'Hunt's contribution to travel writing has at its epicentre
not places at all but winds – five European zephyrs, whose
characteristics, styles, legends, beauties and varied awfulnesses
he exploits to compelling and entertaining effect.'
Spectator, Books of the Year

Where the Wild Winds Are

Also by Nick Hunt

Walking the Woods and the Water

Where the Wild Winds Are

Walking Europe's Winds from the Pennines to Provence

NICK HUNT

NICHOLAS BREALEY
PUBLISHING

London • Boston

This paperback edition first published in 2018 by Nicholas Brealey Publishing
First published in hardback by Nicholas Brealey Publishing in 2017
An imprint of John Murray Press

An Hachette company

1

Maps drawn by Rodney Paull

British Library Cataloguing-in-Publication Data
A catalogue record for this book is available from the British Library.

ISBN 978-1-47366-575-0
eBook ISBN (UK) 978-1-47365-975-9
eBook ISBN (US) 978-1-47365-880-6

Typeset by Hewer Text UK Ltd, Edinburgh
Printed and bound by Clays Ltd, St Ives plc

John Murray Press policy is to use papers that are natural, renewable and
recyclable products and made from wood grown in sustainable forests.
The logging and manufacturing processes are expected to conform
to the environmental regulations of the country of origin.

Nicholas Brealey Publishing
John Murray Press
Carmelite House
50 Victoria Embankment
London, EC4Y 0DZ, UK
Tel: 020 3122 6000

Nicholas Brealey Publishing
Hachette Book Group
Market Place Center, 53 State Street
Boston, MA 02109, USA
Tel: (617) 263 1834

www.nicholasbrealey.com
www.nickhuntscrutiny.com

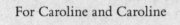
For Caroline and Caroline

Contents

My eyes already touch the sunny hill
going far ahead of the road I have begun.
So we are grasped by what we cannot grasp;
it has its inner light, even from a distance –

and changes us, even if we do not reach it,
into something else, which, hardly sensing it, we already are;
a gesture waves us on, answering our own wave . . .
but what we feel is the wind in our faces.

'A Walk', Rainer Maria Rilke (trans. Robert Bly)

May the road rise to meet you,
May the wind be always at your back . . .

Anon.

PROLOGUE
BLOWN AWAY

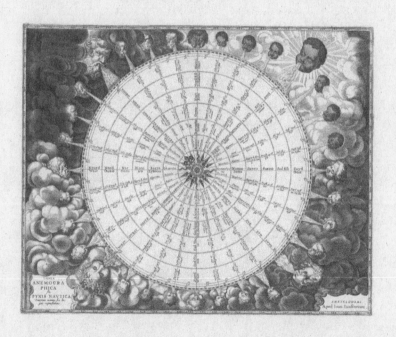

The wind almost blew me away for the first time in 1987, when the Great Storm hit the British Isles. I was six years old. It was on the mountainside of Ynys Enlli, the holy island off the coast of North Wales, where my mother took me every year to volunteer for the local trust and hear the seals sing at night. Now the storm had stranded us there, for the weekly boat was cancelled. There was no shop on the island, and food supplies were running low; one of my most vivid memories is of my mother, by the glow of a paraffin lamp, inexpertly skinning a rabbit the farmer had shot for stew. I remember hugging the cottage wall on trips to the outhouse in the yard, and my fear of slates zipping off the roof to brain me if I ventured far. But what I remember above all else is standing on the mountainside and the wind filling the coat I was wearing – many sizes too large for me – and my feet actually leaving the ground before my mother grabbed my legs and dragged me back to earth. We laughed about it afterwards. It became one of those stories. Could it have actually blown me away, across the foam-flecked Irish Sea? I'm not sure, but for years part of me secretly wished it had, and I imagined being borne through the sky to Ireland, France, America, Iceland, the Arctic Circle or any of the other wonderful places waiting in the world. I'd only travelled a foot off the ground. Nevertheless, I couldn't help feeling slightly blessed.

Despite being moved by the wind in this way I did not grow up to be a glider pilot, a windsurfer, a paraglider or a wind turbine engineer. My attempts with kites mostly ended in dismal tangles of string. I did not become a meteorologist, one who understands weather as a science, as I'm sure this book will make only too clear. What I did become, however, was someone with an urge to travel, and especially to travel by walking, which allows you to follow paths not dictated by road or rail, paths not marked on any map, or to follow no path at all; to wander and to wonder as freely as your feet can take you. But every journey has a logic, even if it's an invisible one. All travelling, I came to understand, is an act of following something: whether a coastline, an ancient migration, a trade route, a border or someone else's footsteps. Scanning the travel section of a bookshop, it appeared that everything had been followed that it was possible to follow. There seemed to be no trails left that hadn't been traversed.

And then one day I saw a map with paths I hadn't seen before. It was a map of Europe transfigured by coloured lines, marauding arrows like troop advances that ploughed across borders, over land and sea, connecting regions and cultures that seemed quite separate in my mind: Latin with Slavic, continental with coastal, North African with southern European. These mysterious corridors had names every bit as tantalising as the Silk Road or the Camino de Santiago: the Mistral, the Tramontana, the Foehn, the Sirocco, the Bora. There was even one in the north of England, more brusquely named the Helm. The map showed the routes of local winds, which blow with tremendous force at specific times of year – normally at the transitions between seasons, such as when winter turns to spring – and, I was intrigued to discover, they were said to influence everything from architecture to psychology. The fact that these invisible powers had names, rather than simply compass directions that described where they were from, gave them a sense of majesty, even of personality. They sounded like characters I could meet. Those swooping, plunging arrows suggested routes I might follow, trails that had not been walked before. As soon as I saw that map I knew: I would follow the winds.

But where do winds come from, and where do they go? Can they be said to 'go' at all, in the sense that a walker goes, or a road, from one location to another? And if they can, what happens to them once they have got there?

What, in fact, *is* wind? Before asking that it is better to begin with a more fundamental question: what is air? Ashamed as I am to admit it, until I started this book I assumed – as I suspect many people do – that air isn't really anything, that it doesn't exist in the same way that earth or water does. I thought of it as an absence, a nothing waiting to be filled with something, so it was a revelation to learn that air is something in its own right.

Air is a gas, or a mixture of gases: mostly nitrogen and oxygen, with tiny amounts of carbon dioxide, argon and water vapour. Like every gas it is made of molecules, which are made of atoms. So air not only has substance, but weight – that was my next revelation – and the proper term for the weight of the air, its billions of molecules combined, is 'atmospheric pressure'. Just as pressure at the bottom of the ocean is greater than at its surface, because of the volume of water above, atmospheric pressure is higher at low altitudes – because there is more weight pressing down – and lower at high altitudes, where the weight pressing down is less. Pressure is dependent on temperature: when the weather is warm air rises, creating areas of low pressure, and when the weather is cool it descends, with the opposite effect. When neighbouring 'parcels' of air find themselves at different pressures the atmosphere must equalise, so air is forced from high pressure areas to low pressure areas to balance things out. It is sucked rather than blown: that was my third revelation.

That is our culture's answer, at least. Other cultures have answered differently, providing tales as twisting and varied as the winds themselves. The ancient Greeks gave wind its place at the very beginning of time: when the goddess Eurynome, mother of all things, emerged naked out of Chaos and separated the sea from the sky, her dancing set the air in motion and created the north wind, which became the serpent Ophion (appearing in a later incarnation as the god Boreas). Eurynome coupled with this flowing, sinuous snake of wind and afterwards, in the form of a dove, laid the universal egg from which all life hatched.

Wind and life: the two are connected at the deepest level of language. The words for 'wind', 'breath' and 'spirit' are the same in many tongues, including the Hebrew *ruach* and the Arabic *ruh*. The Greek word for wind, *anemos*, is the root of the Latin *anima*, 'soul', the force that animates, or gives life, to breathing creatures: animals. Another Latin word, *spirare*, which means 'to breathe' or 'to blow', is the source of 'spirit' as well as 'respiration'. And to the Greeks, in the words of writer and translator Xan Fielding, 'breezes used to be called *zoogonoi*, life-begetters, and *psychotrophoi*, soul-nurturers; and the mythical ancestors of the human race who were worshipped in Athens . . . were wind-spirits as well as ancestors, breaths as well as souls.'

I wanted to follow these breaths, these souls, but where to begin? In ancient times an aspiring wind-walker might have consulted an aeromancer or, even better, an austromancer, the former being a weather diviner, the latter specifically a wind diviner (from the Latin *auster*, 'south', suggesting an emphasis on powerful southerlies). Wind was rendered visible in clouds of dust or seeds thrown in the air, the blown patterns of which were interpreted like language; in sacred groves Hellenic seers made predictions from the percussion created by gongs struck by wands swinging in the breeze. Such blasphemous divinations were condemned by later Christians, and the science, or magic, of aeromancy was excoriated by the medieval theologian Albert of Cologne; though he may have confused it with necromancy, a far more sinister hobby.

Today our forecasts might be shaped with the aid of satellite images and fantastically complex computer models, but the assumption is the same: that the invisible patterns of wind can be interpreted to understand the future. From an aesthetic point of view the results are beautiful; to look at an online weather map is to see an ever evolving world of gorgeous psychedelic design, a shifting spectrum of purples, greens, yellows, blues and oranges, punctuated by the jabbing blue triangles and red half-hemispheres of cold fronts and warm fronts. Wind becomes a topography of dizzying, concentric whorls: the contours of isotachs and isobars – which represent lines of equal wind speed and atmospheric pressure – and wind-barbs, directional lines which branch at five-knot increments, swirling through the atmosphere like clusters of musical notes. They have the appearance of runes, illegible to those without knowledge to read them. They are a kind of alphabet, as wind is a kind of voice.

In the summer of 2015, before the first of my wind-walks, I went to find a building in Athens called the Tower of the Winds.

Constructed 2,000 years ago by the astronomer Andronicus of Cyrrhus, in the ancient neighbourhood known as the Roman Agora, it's an octagonal marble tower about the height of a three-storey house. It depicts, on each of its eight sides, the Anemoi: gods of the wind.

To say they were gods *of* the wind is perhaps inaccurate, suggesting that one controlled the other. To the ancient Greeks – and to many other cultures, as I was to discover – the gods and the winds were indivisible, as they were from the compass directions from which they arrived. Xan Fielding puts it well in *Aeolus Displayed*: 'Since wind was identified with breath, breath with life, life with soul, and soul with divinity, it is hardly surprising that the winds became personified as gods.' The carvings on the Tower of the Winds portray them as winged men, some in sandals, some barefoot, horizontally in flight, bearing symbolic objects that represent their power. From the north comes Boreas, the ferocious old man who unleashes winter – scowling incarnation of the lustful wind-serpent Ophion – clasping a conch that signifies the howling of his voice. From the south comes Notus, destroyer of crops, holding an upturned vase that represents rain. From the east comes Eurus, the unlucky, associated with dark skies and storms. From the west comes gentle Zephyrus – from whom we get the word 'zephyr', 'breeze' – whose mantle is filled with spring flowers (though his sweet reputation is somewhat tarnished by his murder of the hero Hyacinth, whom he jealously killed by blowing a discus into his head). These are the cardinal deities, sandwiched between their ordinal brothers: north-westerly Skiron tilting his urn of hot ashes over the world, north-easterly Kaikias with his shield full of hailstones, south-westerly Lips with the stern of a ship – which he has either saved or destroyed – and south-easterly Apeliotes, clean-shaven and bearing fruit, like the perfect dinner guest.

Once topped by a weather vane in the form of the merman god Triton, which spun to indicate which of these deities was ascendant at any given moment, the tower was an early blend of religion and science. As well as being a sacred place it served as a 'wind-rose', a representation of wind direction of a type used for navigation long before the magnetic compass, and the same basic design – a circle divided into four, eight, sixteen or thirty-two segments radiating from a central point – was copied by cartographers for hundreds of years. On medieval maps the cardinal winds were depicted as furious faces puffing out blasts of air – 'Blow, winds, and crack your cheeks!' as Lear cries on the blasted heath – and in more elaborate examples Boreas blows out ice and snow, dark-skinned Eurus fiery suns, Zephyrus blossoming flowers and 'unhealthy' winds emit showers of human skulls.

But under the iconography wind-roses were practical devices, early attempts at mapping something that might seem unmappable. 'A wind-rose tames the air,' writes Alexandra Harris in *Weatherland*, 'each wind has its section of the compass, each is neatly and helpfully labelled with a polyglot list of names, and each blows from the mouth of a puff-cheeked face. The wind-rose looks like an astronomical clock and it soothes the mariner by making the air seem to run like clockwork.'

The wind-roses used today follow this managerial logic, resembling organisational charts more than depictions of the divine. Gone are the baleful cherubic faces, gone the puffing cheeks; instead wind speed and direction are shown by computerised spokes in bright, friendly colours, the varying lengths of which denote wind frequency. But nonetheless, their basic design resembles what I was looking at now, near the base of the Acropolis. The aesthetics might have changed, but the concept remains the same.

I had made my pilgrimage to this tower in order to orientate myself, imagining it as an epicentre from which to begin my search. Instead I found it meshed in scaffolding, the deities hidden under a veil of flapping green gauze; as bad luck would have it, the Tower of the Winds was closed for restoration. A notice informed that the ancient carvings had been damaged not only by bullets from hundreds of years of wars but ironically by the winds themselves: Notus had lost most of his features to carbon and nitrogen pollution wafted into his face from the south, while Apeliotes was crumbling from humidity blown from the south-east. If the gods and the winds were one and the same, then the tower's sorry condition suggested a long drawn-out suicide.

Having walked across the city to get there, I took a seat at its base all the same. It was a hot day in June. Athens was blinding and buzzing, a pinkish smog hanging in the sky above the Parthenon, the sunlight dazzling off the mirrors of passing scooters. But there was a slight breeze, so I took out the compass I had brought to see where it was coming from. It was blowing from the north-east, the domain of Kaikias. As I watched, glad of the cooling air, the breeze strengthened and shifted direction to become a northerly − Boreas − making the dark cypresses wriggle and an olive tree expose one side then another of its leaves, flashing green and silver. Tourists squinted against blown dust. Grasses and flowers cast flickering shadows. Then its course shifted again and a counter-wind welled in the south, from the realm of Notus. It wasn't as strong but its flow was consistent; the grasses smoothed in a different direction, and fur rippled on the coat of a stray cat prowling in the bushes. Then the gauze that covered the tower itself began to ripple and roll, undulating in liquid waves, giving the structure an expressiveness it had not possessed before. That inanimate thing came to life; there was no other way to see it.

Suddenly everything was transformed. I couldn't see the winds in stone, as I had expected to, but the way that veil was billowing now, fluctuating in minute articulation of each twist of air, revealed the faces of the gods better than marble ever could. As surely as an austromancer reading patterns of blown seeds, or a meteorologist scanning isotachs and isobars, I realised I could *see* the wind. Now I just had to follow it.

The Meltemi, the Halny, the Sirocco, the Tramontana, the Levanter, the Košava, the Marin: Europe has dozens of named winds but I decided to follow four, a nod to the proverbial four winds and the four points of the compass. The Helm would take me to the north of England, over the highest point of the Pennines that form the country's backbone. The Bora would take me from Italy south-east down the Adriatic coast, through Slovenia and Croatia, between the mountains and the sea. The Foehn would take me on a meandering journey through Switzerland, passing through tiny Liechtenstein, into the heart of the Alps. And the Mistral would lead down the Rhône Valley in the south of France, finishing at the Mediterranean that is the source, and the terminus, of many other winds. These four invisible arrows provided the paths I walked on the map, but the Jugo, the Tramontana and the Bise were to make their appearances, as well as innumerable minor breaths too small to merit names. It was clear that to follow the wind meant following uncertainty, allowing myself to be carried along by the unknown and the inferred, the guessed-at and the half-imagined. Chasing the invisible was in many ways a quixotic quest, which appealed to my romantic side; I would be less an aeromancer than an air-romancer.

Nevertheless I went prepared, as best I could. My equipment comprised a rucksack, a tent – I couldn't resist a Zephyrus 2 – a sleeping bag, walking boots and clothes for every type of weather: these journeys would lead through rain and fog, blizzards, storms and sunshine. For my head I packed a waterproof sou'wester I'd bought on a Norwegian ferry, and for my body a fleece-lined vest to serve as a windcheater. My smartphone provided online forecasts when I needed them, but inevitably the best information came from the people I encountered – whose experience of local winds was better than any weather chart – communicating in whatever spoken or unspoken language we could. I carried a compass, the successor to the wind-rose, and a piece of wool to use as an impromptu weather vane. I also carried a device that measures the speed of the wind: an anemometer, from 'Anemoi', which I took to thinking of as my 'god-meter'.

My walks took me from a lonely bothy on the fells to a cabinet of bottled airs in the backstreets of Trieste, from a howling blizzard on a Balkan mountain to the stony desolation of western Europe's only steppe. These were journeys into wild wind, but also into wild landscapes and the people who inhabit them; they were also, inevitably, journeys into myself. As anthropologist Tim Ingold writes, we live inside a 'weather-world', and internal mental climates often reflect the external. The various characters of the winds would at times exhilarate me, at times transport me to a different mind, and at times plunge me into depression or even fear. Finally and unexpectedly, they became journeys into what I can only describe as animism – the root of the word should be clear by now – an understanding of the world as a living, breathing body.

The act of walking was essential to the quest, and to the writing. Borrowing from Ingold again, it is no coincidence that the word 'wind' has more than one meaning: it can refer to the movement of air, or to 'wind your way' through the world, to travel in the meandering manner of the wind itself. But most importantly, it is only by walking that you can feel its hand at your back, or stagger and lose your footing as it ambushes you at the top of a hill, or pause for breath and truly hear its hollow boom in your ears.

HELM

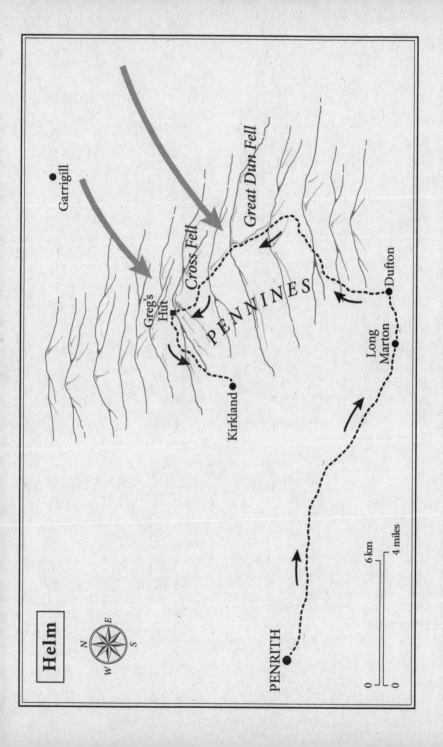

Helm

Garrigill

Great Dun Fell

Cross Fell

Greg's Hut

PENNINES

Kirkland

Dufton

Long Marton

PENRITH

0   6 km

0   4 miles

To walk up the fellside against it is an unforgettable experience, and, while I don't object to wind, I don't recommend going up in a 'helm' for pleasure. One stoops against it with everything buttoned up as tight as it can be, and slogs wearily up the hill with this steady roaring torrent of air pressing against one, sometimes at fifty or sixty miles per hour, even on a 'fine day' . . . it is bitterly cold.

Gordon Manley

It was a twelve-mile slog from Penrith, where I'd stepped off the train, to the village of Long Marton, which lies below the bleak escarpments of the Northern Pennines. I carried three days' worth of food, a tent and a camping stove on my back, and already the rucksack was chafing my shoulders and the impact of the road was jarring the bones in my feet; but it was important to walk in, an opening flourish. Having endured the unsympathetic rubbernecking of drivers in passing cars, I turned off the busy A6 and on to a smaller, shabbier road more promisingly named Wetheriggs, past drystone walls and flocks of birds grounded in distant fields. Ahead the great wall of the Northern Pennines evolved in bulk and detail, a whaleback of brown and grey rising to the summit of Cross Fell, the desolate plateau that forms a springboard for the only named wind in Britain.

If the Pennines are the 'backbone of England', running for almost 300 miles from Derbyshire to the Scottish Borders, the Helm blows over just a couple of its gritstone vertebrae. It forms when wind from the north-east pours at a right angle over Cross Fell – the highest point of the range, and the highest in England outside the mountains of the Lake District – and rushes down the steep western slope with enough force to uproot trees and tear the roofs off houses. It is a truly local phenomenon, affecting about a dozen villages in the Eden Valley below, and my first wind-walk reflected that – from Long Marton, where I planned to spend the night, I would walk to the village of Dufton to follow the Pennine Way to Cross Fell, a journey of only eleven miles – but I aimed to sleep several nights up there, waiting for the right conditions to form. Notoriously barren and exposed, Cross Fell is 'a surly beast, often in a black mood', in the words of Alfred Wainwright's *Pennine Way Companion*. 'In all respects . . . a force to be reckoned with.' The crest looked serene for now, but its menacing reputation was enough to produce a pleasant tingle of apprehension.

All morning I'd been checking the forecasts like someone trailing through entrails for signs, and had seen the wind swing from the west to the east, as had been predicted. Now I could turn my attention to the raw data of the sky itself – marbled, milky, mottled and smeared – but found its code too hard to decipher, its messages obscure. The telltale sign of a coming Helm is the long white cloud, polished smooth on the under-side, that wallows above the top of the range in an otherwise empty sky. It is called the Helm Bar, and its resemblance to a helmet – an armoured cap for the mountain's head – is probably where the wind got its name, perhaps a term that appeared with the encroaching Saxons. In 1797 a travelling lawyer called William Hutchinson described the Bar as exhibiting 'an awful and solemn appearance, tinged with white by the sun's rays that strike the upper parts, and spreading like a gloom below, over the inferior parts of the mountains, like the shadows of night'. As I walked I kept a hopeful eye on a cloud that seemed to be developing that way – growing more awful and solemn by the minute – but disappointingly it lost form and dissolved back into the general mush of the sky. Twice I thought I heard a roar that might be the wind picking up, but in this I was disappointed too: the first turned out to be an HGV on the A66, and the second a black bull bellowing in a field.

I arrived in Long Marton at lamp-lighting time. Woodsmoke was rising from red sandstone cottages, October leaves dropped from the trees, and a raucousness of crows was settling in the branches. A key was waiting for me under a flowerpot outside an old farmhouse, where I had booked a bed for that night, so I would be fresh to tackle Cross Fell in the morning. As it was, marching down roads had left me more battered than I'd anticipated – I'd forgotten how much tarmac hurts – and I just had the energy for some carbohydrates and a pint at the nearby Masons Arms before hauling myself to bed. In the pub I read accounts of the Helm as another visitor might study a guidebook of local sights. Newspapers have recorded its visitations for hundreds of years: blowing a countryman from his horse in 1815, howling for fifteen days without pause in 1843, uprooting a tree that crushed a man to death in 1859 – he left behind a wife and five children – and in 1866 demolishing the only remaining tower of Haresceugh Castle near Renwick.

Many other observations appeared to have come from clergymen, combining Victorian amateur zeal with Old Testament awe. The Reverend William Walton, from the village of Allenheads, wrote that it produced 'a loud noise like the roaring of distant thunder; and is carefully avoided by travellers in that district . . . as being fraught with considerable danger'. The Reverend J. Watson of Cumrew described its psychological impact: 'when we find it blowing and roaring morning, noon and night, for days together, it makes a strong impression on the mind . . . it has been compared to the noise made by the sea in a violent storm, or that of a large cotton mill when all the machinery is going.' The *Ipswich Journal* reported the case of a Cumberland vicar 'greatly afflicted with a spasmodic asthma' who was forced to abandon his house, which stood in the brunt of the wind: 'When he was at the communion-table, his lungs were so much affected by the helm-wind that he fell down. He was unable to reside in that place, and therefore he removed from thence by the advice of his physician . . . if he had continued to reside there, suffocation was unavoidable.' Some believed the Helm caused rheumatism and other ailments, though Reverend Watson, with bracing faith in the power of restorative airs, thought it exhilarated the spirits and gave 'buoyancy to the body'. Buoyancy to the body was right: throughout the centuries, everyone agreed that the Helm could propel a person through the air, hurl sheep about like pieces of wool, overturn heavy carts and destroy stone barns. As the *Leeds Times* put it: 'desolation follows in the train of this devastating wind'.

As I left the pub, two voices drifted from the hubbub of a table by the door: 'That wind last night, I couldn't believe . . .' 'Aye, that's a windy ridge all right . . .' It seemed the signs were everywhere; good omens for a bad wind.

In order to time my first wind-walk correctly I had sought advice from Geoff Monk, a former Met Office meteorologist who now ran a private forecasting business. We had met the previous week in the crypt café under the church of St Martin-in-the-Fields, a stroll from Trafalgar Square; a windowless brick dome like an ecclesiastical bomb shelter, protected from all natural elements. Geoff's eyes were the blue of a stormy sky, his eyebrows touched by frost. For the next two hours we talked of nothing but the weather.

It was a meeting between two ways of understanding the world: my own romantic wonderings versus his meticulous science, which brought me down to earth. 'The principles are easy,' he said, 'but beyond that, whether you like it or not, it's all complex maths and physics.' On his laptop he clicked between computer-generated maps of migrating colour and shape, the invisible world above our heads rendered in swarming pixels. As an artwork it was beautiful, but as a guide to finding the Helm, and understanding why it occurred, it looked unfathomable.

His wife Cath leaned over his shoulder. 'It's just coloured splodges to me,' she said with a smile, and went to see the paintings at the National Gallery.

Geoff zoomed into the Northern Pennines; the outline of Cross Fell was visible, with the contours of isotachs and isobars superimposed on top. Clicking forward in three-hour units of time, he showed me how the flowing lines morphed, twisted and expanded over the next few days as different areas of pressure interacted. 'Got that?' he would often ask. 'I'm going to show you something more complicated in a minute,' and, just as frequently, 'There's one other thing I haven't added to the mix,' before introducing a new factor that confounded me once again. When it came to explaining the Helm, he resorted to wargaming with tableware: 'This saucer is Cross Fell – it's the summit of an eight-mile ridge, with no gaps, cols or passes for the wind to get through.' He picked up a teaspoon. 'This is the wind . . .'

With the help of cutlery and crockery, my understanding increased. The Helm occurs when a steady flow of air from the north-east and north-north-east, bottled up behind the Pennines, breaks over Cross Fell and rushes down the other side, like liquid suddenly released; its force is due to the sudden drop in height as it descends. I followed this easily enough, but there was more: the crucial thing is an 'inversion' at the top of the plateau – where the normal air profile is reversed, being warmer higher up, and cooler nearer the ground – which causes a 'hydraulic jump' as the wind accelerates downslope. A hydraulic jump is when fast-moving air discharges into station-ary air, manifesting in a wave formation known as a 'standing wave'. No teacup or cake fork could represent this. I was lost again.

'Think of it like this,' said Geoff. 'If you fill the bath, and stick in a hosepipe emitting a jet of coloured water, where that coloured water flows into the tub it will break into vortices.'

'Vortices being . . . like spirals?'

'Exactly. The Helm is one of those spirals. Got that? Now there's one other thing I haven't added to the mix . . .'

Eventually, these things were distilled into three critical factors: a constant easterly or north-easterly at more than twenty miles per hour; high pressure over the Pennines; and a temperature gradient that favours an inversion. It was clear that trusting to luck and blindly charging the fells would not work; the timing of my walk must align with these conditions. Geoff checked his weather maps one more time, and the colours and contours on the screen swirled like smoke in a crystal ball. 'It's all westerlies now, but next week things will start to change. You'll get cold winds from the north-east. The pressure looks promising. October's about the right time of year. In weather nothing is guaranteed – but you might just get a Helm then.'

Cath came back to collect her husband. I had time to ask Geoff one more question: what had started him down the road to this complex, beautiful realm of knowledge? 'I was secluded as a child,' he said, after thinking for a while. 'I found it hard to relate to people. But I always loved the weather. Weather was everything to me. I was always looking at the sky . . .'

I was looking at the sky as I stepped out the next morning. Cloud was smeared haphazardly across the lower atmosphere, as if abstractly painted on the air, in no particular pattern that I could see. There was nothing resembling the Bar, and certainly no distant roar. But the wind was nipping from the east, and its taste was cold.

The lady who had trustingly left me her home had also left a note on the kitchen table, advising that if I was walking alone I should give my route to her neighbours in case of accident. Anne and Peter Brown lived across the road from the pub, in a house surrounded by trees. The stove had just been lit, and coffee was brewing. They were both ex-police officers, and knew the area inside out; Peter had lived all his life in the region, and his dad had been a country bobby too. 'Also a fell-walker,' he said, passing me a steaming mug. 'He could never be bothered to take his hands out of his pockets to get out the map. But he could tell the way he was going from the angle of the wind.' I asked what it had been like, growing up in the path of the Helm. 'As a teenager I thought it raged for two months without stopping. Of course it didn't – that's just how you remember things, like thinking it was always sunny in the summer. But it did seem fiercer then – the weather is milder these days. I haven't had to scrape the frost off the windscreen for a long time, or sweep the snow off the drive. There is a change.'

Both of them agreed, however, that the sky today looked promising. They were going walking themselves, and were happy to give me a lift to Dufton a couple of miles down the road, where I would join the Pennine Way to climb into the fells. Dufton was another red sandstone village, built to house the families of miners working for the London Lead Company; two centuries ago the sloped moorland above, empty now but for sheep and birds, was in the booming, belching throes of the Industrial Revolution.

'I remember an open-air service here,' said Anne as we passed through the village. 'It was in the middle of summer and the temperature dropped ten degrees, the tables and chairs got hurled across the lawn. The trees were bending all over the place. It can come when you least expect it.'

'Once I was sitting on Knock Fell,' said Peter. 'The atmosphere suddenly changed. I'm not a man who normally gets frightened, but I just threw myself on the ground. The pressure was unbelievable. I thought I was going to get sucked up into the sky.'

'After three days of it you go mad, don't you?'

'Something like that.'

They showed me the squat Methodist chapel, built to preach temperance to the workers – 'You can tell which side of the chapel is east, because the gutters and tiles are all stove in' – and then Peter pointed out another, much older church, not situated in the village itself but seemingly cowering out of sight behind a stand of trees. 'You know why they built that there, don't you? To be out of view when the reivers came. They'd hide all their women and cattle in there.'

'No,' corrected Anne, 'they'd hide their cattle in there, and if there was room they'd hide the women.'

They walked me as far as the Pennine Way, threading unobtrusively past the outlying cottages into wider, wilder terrain. There we said goodbye and I continued down an avenue of twisted hazel trees, on a carpet of butter-yellow leaves, past dilapidated farmhouses and fields in which docile cows sprawled lazily, like seals.

My mind was on the reivers Peter had mentioned: border raiders who terrorised this part of the country for hundreds of years. For much of its history Cumbria was the disputed frontier between the kingdoms of England and Scotland, and thought of itself as belonging to neither; with an identity all of its own, and even a separate language, Cumbric – deriving from the Celtic tongue of the Britons who lived here in pre-Roman times – this region bore the marvellous name of 'the Debatable Lands'. In the absence of centralised government powerful clans such as the Eliots, Armstrongs, Grahams and Musgraves carved out private fiefdoms here, and lived by raiding – or 'reiving' – livestock, often pursuing bloody vendettas that lasted for generations. Centuries of pillaging, cattle-rustling, raping and murdering left their architectural legacy in the construction of sturdy pele towers, fortified against invasion much as stone barns were built to defend against the wind; the village of Milburn nearby is said to have been constructed on similar defensive principles, with alleyways that could be barricaded against both perils. The reivers grew to be such a problem that in 1525 Archbishop Gavin Dunbar of Glasgow issued his vengeful Monition of Cursing, circulated and read from pulpits throughout the blighted borderlands:

I CURSE their head and all the hairs of their head; I CURSE their face, their eyes, their mouth, their nose, their tongue, their teeth, their skull, their shoulders, their breast, their heart, their stomach, their back, their womb, their arms, their legs, their hands, their feet, and every part of their body, from the top of their head to the sole of their feet, before and behind, within and without. I CURSE them going, and I CURSE them riding; I CURSE them standing, and I CURSE them sitting; I CURSE them eating, I CURSE them drinking; I CURSE them walking, I CURSE them sleeping; I CURSE

them rising, I CURSE them lying; I CURSE them at home,
I CURSE them from home; I CURSE them within the
house, I CURSE them without the house . . .

This most unchristian of rants runs to over 1,000 words, ending
with the raiders' souls condemned to the deepest pit of hell, and
their bodies to be hanged, 'then torn apart with dogs, swine,
and other wild beasts, abominable to all the world'. The bloody
malediction, however, only seemed to lend them greater power;
the reign of terror continued for almost another century. It took
the Union of the Crowns to finally break the reivers' strength;
when James Stuart ascended the throne of England in 1603 he
issued a proclamation against 'all rebels and disorderly persons'
and poured troops into the region. The brutality of the campaign
surpassed even that of the reivers themselves; hundreds of
clansmen were executed, their fortified houses destroyed, and
prominent families such as the Grahams banished to Ireland.
The Borders were renamed the 'Middle Shires', regarded as
frontier lands no longer, but a newly pacified province between
two united kingdoms.

The folk memory, however, has never gone away. Raiding
season traditionally started around this time of year – when the
animals were still plump from summer and the nights were
growing long – and it was easy to imagine the inhabitants of
these villages anxiously straining their ears for a warning of the
destructive forces rushing down upon them. The thought of
these fearsome horsemen sweeping from the high places to
devastate the farmlands of the Eden Valley – smashing down
buildings, throwing men from their horses, scattering sheep and
cows – sounded much like the Helm itself, manifested in human
form. This was my first intimation of what would become a
strong theme on these walks: highlands have always been the
home of wild winds and wild people.

Having skirted the range for a mile or so, stalking its long flank, the Pennine Way turned sharply towards the fell and started climbing. The padded fields dropped away and the landscape rapidly grew bleaker. I studied my route. The dialect terms for many of the natural features scattered across the map – becks, ghylls, tarns, fosses and the mighty fells themselves – derive from an age when these lands were settled by raiders even more infamous than reivers. These words spring from Old Norse – *bekr*, 'stream'; *gil*, 'ravine'; *tjorn*, 'small mountain lake'; *fors*, 'waterfall'; *fjallr*, 'mountain' – testifying to the presence of the Vikings, from whom many Cumbrians proudly claim descent. Another layer of language was laid in the eighteenth and nineteenth centuries: the map indicated disused quarries, shakeholes, spoil heaps and shafts, many of the surrounding hillsides fatally compromised by the mines that lay beneath my boots. Peter had warned me of the dangers of this riddled ground, and I soon passed a notice with a further warning of conditions deteriorating beyond this point – 'Be prepared with weatherproof clothing' – that served as another sign of crossing a certain threshold. I was leaving gentle Eden for the wilderness.

Now the climb got heavier as the fields gave way to moors, peat-holes rainbow-hued with dark oils, reeds indicating patches of bog and carpets of squelchy sphagnum. Even the sheep got hardier, the white woollies of below replaced by black-faced Swaledale ewes with tapered horns and calculating eyes, who held their ground and returned my stare as I climbed towards them. It was warm enough to break a sweat. After the third hour of walking I had achieved a state of swinging exhilaration that felt like it could go on for ever, the secret of perpetual motion, as I traced a stream called Knock Hush towards the summit of Knock Fell, home of Knock Old Man.

Knock Old Man was a currick – a tall cairn, intricately constructed, resembling a beehive made of stone – below which sat a real old man, brewing tea on a Primus stove. He turned out to be a Mancunian window cleaner called Jim, and actually he wasn't that old, but decades of tramping the fells had given him a suitably weathered appearance and the garrulousness peculiar to people used to spending long days alone; his only companion was a tiger-striped bull terrier named Boston. This pair, it turned out, were making for the same shelter as me: the bothy underneath Cross Fell, where I planned on setting up my base-camp for the Helm. He offered me some of his brew, but neither of us suggested joining forces; there was an implicit understanding that we'd both come to be alone. I let him and his dog walk on until they were moving specks in the land, and then followed in the same direction, by a slightly different route.

By mid-afternoon I had reached Great Dun Fell, the second highest point in the Pennines, home to an important radar and meteorological station. In *Pennine Way Companion* the gloriously subjective Wainwright heaps invective on this peak – 'so defaced, so debased' – in language that wouldn't be out of place in Dunbar's Monition of Cursing. 'A monstrous miscellany of paraphernalia, most conspicuous being four tall masts, disgraces it. Additionally there are wind and sunshine recorders, other grotesque contraptions, and several squat buildings of no charm whatsoever . . . quite the ugliest of all summits.' Personally I rather liked it: bristling with instruments, dominated by the white segmented orb of a bulging radome, accompanied by mushroom-shaped towers and sentinel antennae, it looked like a futuristic mosque, almost deliberately channelling the architecture of a place of worship. Something about this location – that peculiar marriage of science with the aesthetics of a temple – turned my mind unexpectedly back to the Tower of the Winds. From the bottom of my rucksack I dug out my 'god-meter', the anemometer I had brought to gauge the speed of the wind, and held it up. Numbers flickered on the digital display as the vane purred in the breeze.

The results were disappointing. The wind was wafting tepidly at four or five miles per hour, scarcely more than walking pace; worse, as I established with my compass, it was blowing from the south, where the lowlands languished in a smear of greens and greys. The frigid easterly I needed seemed to have vanished altogether. I looked towards the sky for help, but there was only haze.

I was not the first to stand in this place and scan the air for signs. The original weather station here – no more than a lonely wooden hut – was established in 1937 by the climatologist Gordon Manley, who was drawn to the Northern Pennines as 'the most extensive area of bleak uncompromising upland that England possesses'. Most famous for his work on the Central England Temperature record, which used historical accounts to compile average air temperatures from the seventeenth to the twentieth centuries – the longest unbroken record for any region in the world – his story is also intimately bound up with the Helm. Manley did more than anyone else to apply a scientific understanding to the force that rattled his hut. He was the first to recognise the pattern as a standing wave – a regular wave formation caused by two masses of air moving against one another – and determined the conditions needed for the Helm to occur. Climbing to Great Dun Fell through gales, blizzards and rain, it was a fascination that surely bordered on obsession. In winter months he needed an ice-axe to open the door of the Stevenson screen that housed his instruments. A photograph from January 1939 resembles a scene from the Antarctic: the little hut encased in ice, a pair of skis jutting from the snow like a flagpole.

Though writing as a scientist he had a knack for engaging prose, describing the Helm's effects on the Eden Valley below:

[T]he farmer's wife shivers in the brilliant sun and finds her heavy blankets stretched horizontally from the wire on which they are strung to dry, or flapping and tearing at their edges when the wind in its retreat becomes gusty. The farmer looks gloomily at the roofs of his Dutch barns, at the dusty plough-land, the cowering sheep and shrivelled pasture and the snowy slopes above.

These two types of observation – the statistical combined with the visual – say a lot about the deeper history of reading the weather. Ancient Babylonian, Indian and Chinese forecasting relied on studying the clouds and the colours of the sky, as well as paying careful attention to animal behaviour. Theophrastus of Eresus, a student of Aristotle – whose seminal treatise *Meteorologica*, written in 350 BC, identified wind as a 'dry exhalation' emanating from the earth – listed natural clues to weather in his *Book of Signs*. A breeze, he wrote, could be predicted by a heron screaming from over the sea, while a dog rolling on the ground is the sign of a violent wind. Some observations are obvious – cobwebs in motion portend a storm – and some much more esoteric: if the upper horn of a crescent moon is bent, westerly winds will prevail, while if the lower horn is bent, the wind will come from the south. 'The behaviour of the hedgehog is also significant: this animal makes two holes wherever he lives, one towards the north, the other towards the south: now whichever hole he blocks up, it indicates wind from that quarter, and, if he closes both, it indicates violent wind.'

It's hard to pinpoint exactly when these systems of natural observation – largely dismissed in later centuries as mere 'weather lore' – were supplanted by hard science. In the thirteenth century Arab scholars translated the works of Aristotle, which had been forgotten in Europe, into Arabic and Latin, and theoretical understandings of weather developed throughout the Middle Ages; first through philosophy, and increasingly through the use of instruments and devices. Sundials had been in use for at least 4,000 years, playing an important role in Egyptian astronomy, weather vanes were ancient tools, and traditional 'weather sticks' were used in the Americas to gauge humidity in the air. (Knots, the unit of speed at sea and also the speed of the wind, came from the nautical measure of trailing a knotted rope behind a ship and counting the knots that passed through a sailor's fingers as the line played out.) But it wasn't until the fifteenth century that more precise technologies appeared: Leonardo da Vinci invented the first hygrometer, which measures atmospheric moisture, the first standardised rain gauges were deployed in royal Korea, and the Genoan polymath Leon Battista Alberti designed an anemometer that worked on similar principles to the one in my hand. The seventeenth century introduced the barometer and Galileo's thermoscope – which prefigured the thermometer – and as the eighteenth century gathered heat Daniel Gabriel Fahrenheit and Anders Celsius developed their respective temperature scales, part of the Enlightenment drive to fix the world in numbers. In 1802 Luke Howard drew on the work of Carl Linnaeus to propose a taxonomic system for the classification of clouds, which were ranked by Latin names – *cirrus*, *stratus*, *cumulonimbus* – and winds were ordered into place by Francis Beaufort's wind force scale:

0. Calm: Smoke rises vertically
1. Light Air: Direction shown by smoke drift, but not by wind vanes
2. Light Breeze: Wind felt on face; leaves rustle; wind vane moved by wind
3. Gentle Breeze: Leaves and small twigs in constant motion; light flags extended

4. Moderate Breeze: Raises dust and loose paper; small branches moved
5. Fresh Breeze: Small trees in leaf begin to sway; crested wavelets form on inland waters
6. Strong Breeze: Large branches in motion; whistling heard in telegraph wires; umbrellas used with difficulty
7. Near Gale: Whole trees in motion; inconvenience felt when walking against the wind
8. Gale: Twigs break off trees; generally impedes progress
9. Strong Gale: Slight structural damage (chimney pots and slates removed)
10. Storm: Seldom experienced inland; trees uprooted; considerable structural damage
11. Violent Storm: Very rarely experienced; accompanied by widespread damage
12. Hurricane: Devastation

Theophrastus might have observed similar clues 2,000 years before, but Beaufort's use of numbers places him squarely in the rational age. The era of colonial expansion brought an increasing emphasis on classification, charts, calculations; a rarefied, abstracted realm above the untidy natural world, where science was pure and undisturbed by past superstitions.

Partly through technology, and partly through technological thinking, the habits of herons and hedgehogs came to be seen as old wives' tales. Time-worn adages – 'When the wind is in the east, 'tis neither good for man nor beast' – were fine for farmers and fishermen, but not regarded as serious thought; much empirical folk observation was dismissed as nursery rhyme. Taking a giant leap into the space age, 1960 saw the launch of the first weather satellite, which provided, for the first time, a forecast from data gathered from space. It is hard to think of a clearer symbol of the distancing process mankind has embarked on: looking down on the weather-whipped world from above, discomforted by no wind, in clinical isolation. Such remote observations are vital to forecasting today – there are over 1,000 satellites now in orbit around Earth – feeding into supercomputers of vast complexity and power, their processes made possible by advances in numerical prediction, fluid dynamics, thermodynamics and chaos theory.

It all felt a long way from Gordon Manley's wooden hut. I wondered what had happened to it. Perhaps it had been dismantled when the radar station was built, or perhaps the wind had blown it away.

Turning my back on the gleaming radome, busy with its sensors and antennae, I found a comfortable seat on the grass and assembled my camping stove. It took some minutes for the water to boil, and then with a mug of coffee cupped in my hands I picked up reception on my smartphone and checked the latest forecasts. Numbers tracked, isobars whorled, but it all felt very abstract. Tired, I closed my eyes for a while. I felt the currents of the air playing on my face and hands, the back of my neck, my lower arms. My right cheek was getting cold. After several minutes my ear was numb. It took me a moment to understand: the wind was shifting to blow from the east.

For the next couple of hours I traversed the boggy saddle between Great Dun Fell, Little Dun Fell and the rising hump of Cross Fell to the north. The Pennine Way was paved in some sections with enormous granite slabs leading through swathes of sucking black peat, blanket bog and cotton grass sporting wispy white tufts like spurts of pale flame. My destination took shape as a great horseshoe-shaped ridge, vaster and bleaker than it had looked from below, a crest of variegated brown worn threadbare at its western seam to expose raw grey rock, dropping steeply like a wave. The wind lifted as I climbed, skipping from five miles per hour to ten – finally moving faster than me – fifteen, sometimes touching on twenty, swinging between the east and north-east, occasionally the north. The clouds thickened from a vaporous mash into two distinct bands, forming a fluffy white wall above the fells. There was a new chill in the air. Ascending, my hopes grew.

Perhaps because my attention was focused as much on the sky as the earth, the climb was imperceptible, and I found myself on the summit without realising how it had happened. Cross Fell, while technically a mountain, is peculiarly hard to comprehend, being at once too huge to take in – eight bleak miles from end to end – and almost entirely devoid of features. There is no top, no resolution, only a vaguely sloping expanse of heather, curdled black peat and pale rocks lying here and there resembling butchered chunks of meat, strangely notched and pitted. At 2,930 feet it felt more like being on a headland high above a desolate coast, the Eden Valley dim below, like a beach at its lowest tide. I turned a slow circle: there was nothing but unchanging brown moorland stretching on every side, majestic in its way, but far from pretty. I was starting to see the Northern Pennines as the ugly, unromanticised cousin of the Lake District twenty miles to the west, the peaks of which I could distantly glimpse beyond the intervening haze. William Wordsworth, Samuel Taylor Coleridge, Thomas De Quincey, Percy Bysshe Shelley, Walter Scott, Alfred Lord Tennyson, Arthur Ransome, Beatrix Potter: writers have flocked to the Lakes for generations to be inspired by its views, but most have remained revealingly silent on the subject of Cross Fell. The only one who came to mind was the poet Simon Armitage, who travelled the length of the Pennine Way for his book *Walking Home*; he called it a 'truly terrible place . . . illegitimate and monstrous', and experienced an existential crisis lost in fog.

In the middle of this emptiness I caught up with Jim, halfway through another brew. He and Boston were hunkered below a strange piece of architecture: a solid igloo made of stone, with four long radial arms ending in right-angled crosspieces, which had the appearance, from above, of a Celtic cross. It was a shelter built to break the wind from every angle, and as the frigid gusts picked up, blasting the easterly side of my face, I was grateful for its protection. The experience of being cold had a transformative effect on my thoughts, and suddenly the wind felt more like something to hide from than actively seek. The daylight was beginning to die; there was still no sign of the Helm. We drank the tea, shared a biscuit or two, and then walked on together.

Our refuge was Greg's Hut on the far side of the fell, situated snugly in the lee of a spoil heap left behind by a long-vanished mining operation. It wasn't a hut, as the name suggested, but a slate-roofed cottage with strong stone walls containing two rooms, with a sleeping platform and a blackened iron stove. We arrived to find it occupied by a young man called Callum, who had hiked up from Garrigill earlier that day; a cheerful loner who, like Jim, spent his weekends wandering the moors. 'My mates are into drinking and going to clubs,' he said, as Boston stood guard at the door and Jim prepared yet another brew. 'All them flashing lights, I can't stand it. Saturday night I'd rather be up here. You always meet good people.' The first time he'd come to Greg's Hut he'd been lost in the dark, had waded knee-deep through bogs, frozen to the bone. 'And then I stumbled on this place and there were still hot embers in the fire, wet bootprints leading out the door. They'd left food and everything. It was like a fairy tale.'

As night closed in the three of us pressed close around the stove, feeding in split pine logs, drawn together in its warmth. A sweet, slightly awkward companionship developed, the conversation revolving almost exclusively around the weather, whose turn it was to prepare the next brew, and the status of the fire, the health of which obsessed us all, our happiness directly dependent on the brightness of its flames and the ferocity of its roaring in the flue. By ten o'clock it was time for bed. My tent seemed a cosier option than the bare stone room, for the fire wouldn't last the night, so I struggled with pegs and poles by torchlight in the buffeting wind. Throughout the night the wind coursed in black jets, shaking and tugging the walls of the tent, twanging the ropes and sometimes partially lifting the groundsheet on which I lay. I drifted to sleep with tentative hopes for meeting the Helm at dawn.

Instead I woke to sodden cloud squatting on the land. I could hardly see the bothy, let alone the surrounding fells; visibility was reduced to metres rather than miles. Moorland birds croaked like frogs. Becks burbled under the peat. There was not the slightest hint of wind. I felt like I'd been tricked.

Inside the bothy Jim and Callum were sitting up in sleeping bags sucking pensively on e-cigarettes, each surrounded by his own scented vapour cloud. Boston impatiently paced the room, anxious to be leaving. Soon my companions took the dog's cue, each bound on his separate path, and I sensed they were mildly concerned that I was staying. Jim gave me his mobile number. Callum gave me a spare gas canister and a serrated blade from his penknife, so I could saw some kindling. 'Just leave it here when you're done. Someone else'll have use of it.' We shook hands, and they vanished in the fog. Boston lingered, staring at me as if I were something left behind by mistake, and then his master called for him, and he vanished too.

It was alarmingly quiet. The only sounds came from myself, shuffling in multiple jumpers round the bothy, clattering saucepan and tin cup, my boots tapping on the flagstone floor. Every ten minutes, neurotically, I went outside to check the conditions and saw nothing, heard nothing, felt nothing move against my skin. It was a form of sensory deprivation, like being wrapped in felt. Outside lay impenetrable whiteness and a vast, wallowing silence that I was almost panicked by, if I listened to it too hard. I had come here to be alone with the wind; in the absence of the wind, I was simply alone.

I sat in the dim light from the window – another Norse-origin word, from *vindauga*, which means 'wind-eye' – and spent half an hour leafing through the visitors' book. 'A welcome refuge from wind and rain and awful conditions on Cross Fell' read a typical entry, along with 'Happy to escape the wind' and 'Gave shelter from the terrible wind.' None mentioned the Helm by name; either from some superstition or, more probably, because when it was actually blowing no fool would come up here.

But who would come in these conditions either? And having come, who would stay? Venturing on top of the spoil heap with my phone held up in the air I managed to get the latest forecast, and saw – both with relief and foreboding – that easterlies would rise through the night, and by the next afternoon would be pouring at a steady thirty miles per hour. With twenty-four hours ahead, it felt like laying siege. In the spirit of digging in, I checked the supply of wood and found that every log had been burned, leaving only splinters and twigs that wouldn't last ten minutes. The thought of spending the night alone in that room, with nothing but whistling darkness outside, was too ghastly to contemplate; I needed wood, but trees haven't grown on the fells for hundreds of years. Iron axes chopped them down, and the ravages of sheep – not to mention the wind itself – have prevented them from coming back, along with oozing blanket bog that nothing can take root in. A couple of long-suffering pines struggled outside the bothy door, literally the only trees from horizon to horizon. Using Callum's blade I worked some spindly branches off, but felt too guilty to go on; those trees had enough to deal with, in this godforsaken location.

I scoured the bothy's surroundings in vain and then widened my search to the moor, following a wire fence that divided one area of nothingness from another. I must have walked for half a mile before noticing the sturdy wooden posts driven into the ground every few metres. One of those would be a job to chop with the blunt axe chained by the bothy's door, but the thought of those square-cut logs crackling inside the stove filled my heart with happiness. There was the moral aspect, however, which I couldn't quite get past. I thought about the coming night, and the misery of having no fire. Then I thought about wandering sheep, and I thought about people reading this book, and decided against wrenching one out; but only just.

There was nothing else for it but to walk the seven miles to Garrigill, a round trip of about five hours, in the hope of finding something combustible in the village. The Pennine Way ran north-east, deeper into the heart of the fells; I set off just before midday, into the white, featureless world, splashing through slicks of carbon-rich water that dribbled in rivulets from the sodden peatlands above. Becks were gurgling in their scores, swollen by the saturated air, producing a liquid symphony of varying tone and volume. Apart from the occasional bird – the comical, mechanical gobble of grouse startled from the heather – it was the only thing I could hear. Sheep swam in and out of focus, wet wool merging with wet fog. The land's contours revealed themselves shyly and swiftly slunk away as the cloud swooped back and forth, as if patrolling the hills. This path, I later learned, followed the route of the ancient Corpse Road, along which Garrigill's dead would be hauled for burial in the consecrated ground of the Eden Valley.

After I had walked for an hour, lulled almost senseless by the quiet, there was a sudden intervention: on the dirt track ahead appeared a convoy of military-looking four-wheel-drive vehicles revving determinedly through the mud, tall antennae swaying. I stood aside to let them pass. They contained not soldiers, as I expected, but a boozy contingent of red-cheeked squires in flat caps, tweeds and Barbour jackets, on their way to blast living hell out of the grouse population. They rolled down their windows to exchange loud comments about the weather, commanded me to have a good walk, and were gone. Further on a teenage beater with a flag made from ripped plastic sheeting loitered at the edge of the moor, his hoodie pulled up against the cold. 'Tell the lad down there to sit on the fence when the guns set off. Cheers, pal,' he called, indicating another beater a hundred yards down the trail. Their job was to drive the fleeing grouse back into range of the guns, should any escape the initial bombardment, and their accents contrasted starkly with the plummy, self-assured tones of the visiting gentry. Soon the muffled percussion of shotgun blasts started up behind me.

That, of course, was the other reason trees don't grow on the fells: the moors are kept deliberately barren – and deliberately free from birds of prey, foxes, weasels and other life forms – by the owners of grouse estates, who make a fortune breeding these hapless birds for the wealthy to shoot. I remembered what Peter Brown had said: 'When my dad was a country bobby there were one hundred and five farms. Now there's barely a quarter of that – all cleared for grouse. There's big money in grouse.' Much of Peter's own career as a policeman had been spent in trying to safeguard breeding pairs of peregrine falcons, a highly protected species, from the gamekeepers trying to kill them. It was always an uphill struggle; the birds were invariably shot or poisoned, their nests found and destroyed.

There is a rich history of conflict between walkers and the grouse industry, which, until the Countryside and Rights of Way Act was passed in 2000, aggressively prevented access to highland areas. The long campaign for the right to roam began in 1932 with the mass trespass of Kinder Scout, the highest point of the Peak District – at the southernmost end of the Pennine Way that I was following now – which is considered one of the most successful acts of civil disobedience in British history. Four hundred militant ramblers, mostly working-class youths from Manchester, engaged in a 'wilful trespass' of the peak, scuffling with gamekeepers and risking arrest. Five were subsequently jailed, but public opinion was on their side; the action led directly to legislation that established the first National Parks and, indirectly, seven decades later, to the introduction of the ramblers' rights that I was now enjoying. The event is commemorated by a jaunty, irreverent song by the folk-singer Ewan MacColl, 'Manchester Rambler', celebrating the freedom of the moor as an escape from wage slavery in the working week. It made me think of Jim, a modern-day Manchester rambler.

By mid-afternoon the fog had cleared enough to see shreds of blue sky, the clouds as clean and fluffy white as if they'd been tumble-dried. My shadow appeared for the first time, leading the way downhill. The grasses shimmied electrically in an unexpected breeze, and when the air streamed over my face it was as if the fells and everything on them had been released from a padded cell. Garrigill appeared below – its fields glowing green, its grey stone cottages neatly arranged – a tempting target for marauding reivers, or for a woodless man. After the formless opacity I'd just been groping through, descending to this pretty village felt like my eyes coming back into focus after blindness.

The George & Dragon was closed, and entering the post office and general store was like stepping into a shop from the

1950s. 'Logs? No, we don't sell those. Candles? Oh no, not any more. Firelighters – we're out of them. Kindling? Not these days, everyone has electric fires now . . .' This quite evidently wasn't true – woodsmoke was rising from chimneys outside, and logs were stacked invitingly against the houses in the street – but I didn't argue. Denied at the only shop, I went door to door.

The first door on which I knocked was opened by a tousle-haired, bearded man, who turned out to be an artist called Lionel Playford. I couldn't have made a better choice: without hesitation he led me to a yard containing stacks of broken furniture, offcuts and smashed picture frames. 'Help yourself. It should burn well, it's been drying for a hundred years.' As I filled my rucksack with wood, I told him what I was doing on Cross Fell. It sounded strange – staked out in the bothy, waiting for the wind to come – but he happened to be a dedicated chronicler of weather himself. When he offered to show me his work I felt a slight pang of anxiety – what if it was terrible? – but within seconds I was enthralled. The walls were hung with studies of the sky, of swirling clouds lit by sun and swollen heavy with rain, which seemed as much examinations of psychology as weather. Sketchbooks bulged with Pennine landscapes rendered in dark peat from the moors, a palette of blacks, ochres, browns, and tracings of the land itself, rubbings obtained from weathered rock, which he explained to me as a type of map. He had bored into thousand-year-old peat bog to extract ancient pollen samples perfectly preserved by its oils – from a time when deforesting Saxon farmers and Vikings had walked the moors – and made his own paper from a pulp of grass and moss. Most beautifully, he had used this paper to create two-dimensional clouds that were suspended from the ceiling, rotating in the thermals of the room, casting shadows on the walls: an internal weather system to mirror the one outside.

Despite this fascination with weather, he had never experienced the Helm. He lived on the 'wrong' side of Cross Fell, to the east and not the west. It revealed how truly parochial the phenomenon was.

Lionel thought of his art as field work, much as scientists undertake. The task of artists and scientists was basically the same, he said: to gather raw information from the world, whether with meteorological instruments or with sketchbooks bent by wind, splashed with mud and streaked with rain, before returning to laboratory or studio to work that information into shape, to give the data meaning. 'That's what you're doing too,' he said. 'Isn't that why you're camped out on the fell?' We talked for over an hour – conveniently, during the time it took for a downpour to scour the village and disperse, leaving the sky a dazzling blue – and then I left him to his work. Garrigill sparkled in the sun, its slate roofs gleaming. A tottering wall of rain-streaked cloud retreated towards Great Dun Fell as I returned with my cargo of wood, back towards the sky.

The paintings I'd seen in Lionel's studio followed a long tradition of artists responding to the weather. In English art, the most famous of these are undoubtedly John Constable and J.M.W. Turner, painting around the same time in the early nineteenth century. The two men were bitter rivals – Constable dismissed Turner's work as 'just steam and light' – perhaps because their obsessions mirrored each other's so closely. Both were drawn to weather at its grandest, its wildest and least civilised; both embarked on the Romantic quest to capture the sublime. In chemistry, sublimation is the process by which a solid object converts directly into a vapour, bypassing the liquid stage, which seems a perfect metaphor for work so obsessed with natural vapours of every kind: mists, fogs, hazes, smogs and especially clouds. Constable was greatly influenced by the taxonomies of Luke Howard, who had organised the clouds into Latin classifications, and he regarded the sky as the 'chief organ of sentiment' in all landscape painting; throughout his life he chronicled the firmament in its changing moods, noting times and dates with scientific exactitude, even inventing a new word, 'skying', to describe this process.

Turner's meticulous studies of light – which he regarded as an emanation of the power of the divine – were really examinations of how light diffuses through weather, whether through storms at sea or London's notorious smogs. His early work focuses on classical and historical scenes, common subjects for the period, but, increasingly, natural forces came to dominate the canvas. His 1812 masterpiece *Snow Storm: Hannibal and his Army Crossing the Alps* demonstrates this shift of focus: the struggling soldiers in the foreground are almost irrelevant, while the surging black cloud above, the blizzard and the glowering orange sun contain the true life, and the true menace, of the painting. The later part of his career sees human figures, or ships at sea, reduced to incidental specks, or elbowed out of the frame altogether; such mortal distractions were really just excuses for painting the weather. In *Snow Storm: Steam-Boat off a Harbour's Mouth*, the ship itself is merely hinted at with a few smudged lines. The weather is not the background, but the subject: the waves below and the storm above merge to become one element, a fearful swirling entity of inhuman strength and size. It is an intensely religious painting, though it contains no reference to God. Today we would describe such a vision as 'ecocentric'. The work was inspired by Turner's experience of a violent gale near Harwich; the story goes that the famous painter, sixty-seven years old, asked to be tied to the steamship's bridge to gain full exposure to the storm, like a nineteenth-century Odysseus, and endured its fury for four hours. This account may not be true – it is perhaps just a feature of Turner's self-mythologising – but, like all apocryphal tales, what it *says* is true. Turner, like Constable, worshipped the power of weather.

Beyond Britain's windy shores, other artists have plunged into weather as a subject in itself, rather than simply a framing device or a backdrop for human affairs. The Japanese print-maker Katsushika Hokusai depicted the effects of wind in *A Gust of Wind at Ejiri* – leaves and scattered papers flying, conical hats tumbling – as well as in his most famous work, *The Great Wave off Kanagawa*. Impressionists and Post-Impressionists including Claude Monet, Paul Cézanne and Pierre-Auguste Renoir – not to mention Vincent Van Gogh, whose mental landscapes I would traverse six months later on the last of these wind-walks – painted weather as pure sensation, capturing the movement of air through thrashing trees, tormented skies and swirling clouds. The French inventor Étienne-Jules Marey, whose work with chronophotography prefigured the development of cinema, spent three years photographing movements of air through the patterns observed in wisps of smoke. The Australian artist Cameron Robbins designed a series of mechanical 'Wind Drawing Machines' that harness the wind to create works of art, ranging from intricate ink patterns to transitory arcs of light. But perhaps the purest example of weather-centric art, abstracted entirely from the earthbound world, are James Turrell's 'Skyspaces': enclosed rooms consisting of a bench and a hole in the ceiling – some round, some square, some ovular – which act as a simple frame for the troposphere above. The sky and the weather passing through it is an artwork in itself. Turner and Constable would surely have approved.

Returning steeply up the hill, weighted with my bag of wood, it was easy to forget to watch the sky myself. But suddenly I glanced up – my view framed by the fells – and what was happening above was enough to stop me in my tracks. Since I had left Garrigill the clouds had performed a magic trick, and

without me being aware of it had stealthily assembled themselves into a long, chubby band stretching the length of Cross
Fell. It matched every description I'd read of the Helm Bar –
glowering grey on the underside, white on top, polished marble-
smooth – and when I checked my god-meter the wind was
streaming from the north-east at twenty-five miles per hour.
The air had the taste of iron. Could this be the start of the
Helm? But even as I allowed the thought to form the top of
the cloud broke ranks, cauliflowering upward into plumes and
engorged turrets. Within minutes the promising structure had
heaved into separate bergs, tearing apart and drifting away, leaving only wispy mozzarella strands above. I watched, frustrated,
as the composition atrophied into abstraction again; the canvas
of the sky was incomprehensible once more.

That night, sipping whisky from my hip-flask, I toasted
thanks to Lionel as the hundred-year-old frames caught light,
bellowing in the grate and kicking out heat so intense it drove
me from the stove. The stillness of the morning was gone;
the wind blew loose and wild outside, hammering against the
door, sucking from the chimney in great draughts like a thirsty
drinker. I woke at dawn, under an orange sky, to my third day
on the fells.

The view resembled a different country to the one I'd seen the
morning before. There was no sodden murk; the land was bright
and loud again, the weather vane of the topmost pines twitching
to the west. I made coffee in a pan, cowboy style – a mouthful
of grits and a mule-kick to the heart – and as I was thinking of
going out, the door banged open.

It was a cheerful pink woman who had hiked up from
Kirkland. 'You can hear the Helm up there,' she announced

breathlessly. 'It's horrible, howling and moaning and groaning. I was too scared to go up.' I was already pulling on my boots, fumbling with the laces. 'You know why it's called Cross Fell?' she continued, taking out her sandwiches. 'It used to be called Fiends Fell. People thought that demons lived there, so they sent a holy man to bless it. He exorcised the evil spirits, built a cross to drive them away. But I don't think it worked. It still sounds like it's cursed . . .' I was halfway through the door. I didn't want to miss them.

It certainly looked like the home of fiends, despite the bright sunshine. Dramatic events were occurring above, in the fathom-less workings of the clouds; it seemed that opposing weather systems were engaged in epic warfare. To the north and west a ragged mass scoured the lower slopes of the fell – Grey Scar, Black Doors, Man at Edge, said the place-names on my map – hazing the air with a smudge of rain, leaving shreds of itself behind. Autonomous mists of water vapour travelled in long vertical trails high above the Eden Valley, and grandiose crepus-cular rays poured down on the mountains of the Northern Lakes, where Ullswater distantly shone as bright as a mirror. The Helm Bar was not in place, but developments were moving so rapidly it seemed that anything might happen. Scattering Swaledale ewes, I hurried on the Pennine Way, up the long, deceptive rise that led towards the summit.

Who was this mysterious holy man? I wondered as I climbed. Unsurprisingly, research suggests that no one really knows; some say a bishop, some say a saint, some say a wandering monk. Another local clergyman, the Reverend Robinson of Ousby, wrote in 1709 of the

> evil Spirits which are said in former Times to have haunted the Top of this Mountain; and continued their Haunts and Nocturnal Vagaries upon it, until St. Austin, as is said, erected

a Cross and built an Altar upon it, whereon he offered the Holy Eucharist, by which he countercharm'd those Hellish Fiends, and broke their Haunts. Since that time it has had the Name of Cross-Fell, and to this day there is a heap of stones which goes by the name of the Altar upon Cross-Fell.

St Austin, I later discovered, is the Anglicised name for St Augustine of Canterbury, the 'Apostle to the English', a Benedictine monk from Rome sent to convert the pagan Saxons in 597. After baptising King Aethelbert and Christianising the people of Kent he established several bishoprics and continued his missionary work, though he failed to impress the native Britons, who were Christians already. Did his evangelising zeal carry him to the top of Cross Fell? Sadly it seems unlikely: 'as far as we know he never came nearer to the North than the Cotswolds,' according to David Uttley, a local neurosurgeon who published *The Anatomy of the Helm Wind* in 1998. '[I]ndeed he was separated from it by several independent kingdoms, and considering his other responsibilities he had much more on his plate to worry about than an obscure wind plaguing a pagan land three hundred miles away.' Uttley suggests that St Augustine may have been confused with St Paulinus, another Roman missionary, who travelled to Northumbria in 627 in the retinue of a Kentish princess sent to be a bride to the pagan King Edwin. After converting Edwin's kingdom, Paulinus remained in the north for five years as the first Bishop of York.

But did he ever cross the Pennines to exorcise the fiends? Again history suggests otherwise, although Uttley can't resist comparing the rebranding of the fell to 'an early example of Political Correctness, occurring as a result of well-meaning, but essentially ill-considered, European interference in our every day affairs'. He ends his account with a vague suggestion that it might have been St Ninian, Apostle to the Southern Picts – a meddling monk from Britain rather than the continent – who drove the demons away, but evidence is circumstantial at best: he was influential in the region, and many local churches bear his name. The identity of the holy name-changer, if such a character even existed, will probably never be known. Whatever original truth there was is lost in layers of myth.

Leaving the path, I traced level ground until I reached the edge of the fell, where the escarpment plunged steeply towards the Eden Valley. It was a vertiginous view, like the drop-off point of a coastal shelf, below which mica-gleaming gritstone lay in a jumbled scree. This precipitous descent is the cause of the hydraulic jump, the wind rapidly picking up speed as it rushes downslope, and I had a moment of giddiness imagining the force of the flow, an invisible tidal wave breaking against the stone-walled cottages far below. I stuck my god-meter in the air: thirty miles per hour. The Helm Bar had not come but the cold still chapped my lips and numbed my mittened hands, and the sou'wester on my head rattled against my ears.

Scarfing up my lower face, I turned and waded east again, against the current of the air, up the imperceptible slope towards the summit. Away from that dramatic view, which at least gave the prospect depth, the moorland was desolate and intensely lonely. In reaction to this emptiness my mind started playing tricks: the upright, stupa-like structures of curricks tracking past on the horizon looked like distant figures approaching, making the moorland seem oddly populated. I kept catching them out of the corner of my eye and thinking they were closing in. But apart from these interventions on the skyline there was only whistling blankness. It felt like somewhere an Old Testament prophet might come to hear the voice of God, looking for answers in the sky, for the land had lost all meaning.

What had the woman from Kirkland meant, talking about howling and moaning? Alone in that empty place I soon found out. Something must have shifted in the air, for the aural landscape suddenly changed: above the buffeting blows of gusts that banged recurrently on my ears, flatlining like microphone distortion, rose an unearthly whispering like dozens of tiny voices. It was a mischievous chattering accompanied by a hissing that suggested branches and spirals, complex patterns being woven in the air, and under it all a low moan, like an animal in distress.

> Voiceless it cries,
> Wingless flutters,
> Toothless bites,
> Mouthless mutters

The riddle from Tolkien's *The Hobbit* popped into my mind. The resemblance to language was uncanny – I could almost make out individual words – and once or twice, in paranoia, I actually turned my head. No wonder people had once thought that demons lived here. The cacophony made me wish for shelter, and there was only one in sight: near the summit, marked by the lonely obelisk of a concrete trig point, and so I hurried towards the stone-walled windbreak where I'd shared a brew with Jim.

'The belief that the air harboured demons was already widespread in antiquity and was especially favoured by Plato and his disciples,' writes the historian Lucian Boia in *The Weather in the Imagination*. In Plato's cosmology demons could either be evil or good – morally ambiguous, much like the Greek deities from which they were distantly derived – and acted as intermediaries between the realms of gods and men; as gods lived in heaven and men lived on earth, demons naturally occupied the air that lay between them. Later Christian theology kept the belief in demons intact – and the recognition of the air as their natural habitat – but stripped them of any possible goodness. Demons became purely evil beings, intermediaries not between men and God, but between men and Satan. The work of St Augustine of Hippo – misleadingly, a different Augustine from the one linked to Cross Fell, though the coincidence of names might partly explain the confusion – incorporates Plato's concept of demons into Christian thinking. 'God banished the rebel angels to the lower regions of the air,' explains Boia. Caught between heaven and hell, the vanquished host remained in the atmosphere, waging irregular warfare on God through a proxy war on mankind. Indeed, Satan is sometimes called the 'Prince of the Power of the Air'. The thirteenth-century theologian

> Thomas Aquinas also took the airborne nature of demons into consideration. The existence of creatures who delighted in tormenting humans could explain the vagaries of the weather: 'Atmospheric disturbances and the permanent conflicts of water and wind were thus the sign of demonic life, as opposed to the serenity of the skies. They prevented souls from ascending to heaven and hovered above the Earth, intent upon the destruction of human beings.'

It wasn't just Christian cultures that envisaged an atmosphere alive with the supernatural. The *djinni*, or 'genies', of Arabian and early Islamic belief – which, along with angels and humans, were seen as creations of Allah – were associated with the elements of air, water, earth and fire; some resembled snakes and dogs, some travelled ceaselessly, and some had wings to propel them through the air. In his book *Heaven's Breath: A Natural History of the Wind*, anthropologist Lyall Watson recounts how cultures across the world have regarded winds and spirits as indivisible entities – much like the ancient Anemoi – and have taken action to drive the malevolent ones from their homes. The Inuit of the Canadian Arctic beat the wind with seaweed whips, or else threw urine into the fire to repel its visitations. In Alaska 'it was the women who drove the offending wind spirit toward the fire with clubs, while the men waited there with a bowl of water, to make the demon manifest in steam, and a large flat stone, to crush it to death.' The Kai people of New Guinea attached spears to their roofs 'in order to pierce the wind's belly', and the Xhosa of South Africa summoned a priest-diviner to spit potion into its eye 'while directing a mass demonstration of communal rage'. In Scotland, meanwhile – fifty miles north of where I shivered now – it was believed that hurling your left shoe was an effective deterrent.

The link between winds and spirits filters into language. There's an obvious connection between a 'gust' and a 'ghost', as there is with 'breeze' and 'breath', and in Ireland the Gaelic *sídhe* – the invisible fairy-folk, or gentry, of the countryside – were one with the *sídhe gaoithe*, 'fairy-wind', which might arise to punish humans failing to show respect. The cultural ecologist David Abram expands on this interrelationship, flipping 'civilised' preconceptions on their heads: 'whenever indigenous, tribal persons speak (often matter-of-factly) about "the spirits," we moderns mistakenly assume, in keeping with our own impoverished sense of matter, that they're alluding to a supernatural set of powers unrelated to the tangible earth.' It may be more accurate, he suggests, to understand spirits not as ghosts – and not merely as 'primitive' explanations from pre-scientific cultures, which is how they are often dismissed – but rather as another title for the winds themselves. As the Greeks conflated winds and gods, many indigenous cultures conflate winds and spirits. They might be seen as different words for the same elemental force.

I had reached the cross-shaped windbreak now, my shelter from the spirits. The wind was pouring from the north-east so I huddled in the crook between its western arms, crouching low and huffing on my fingers to keep them warm. The whispering voices stopped at once, as if at a command, and suddenly everything went still; I stuck my head above the parapet and they started up again. Now that demons were in my mind the cruciform nature of those walls took on a new significance. It all connected in a flash: somewhere in the mists of time that mythical saint had erected a cross and built an altar from a heap of stones, 'countercharm'd the Hellish Fiends, and broke their Haunts'. This windbreak was a crucifix breaking the currents of the air, constructed in the exact location where the altar must have stood. The totem of a new god attempted to banish the forces of the old, those untamed, unchristian powers raising hell in the parishes below. The saint had exorcised the demons as the bishop had excommunicated the reivers: 'I CURSE them at home, I CURSE them from home; I CURSE them within the house, I CURSE them without the house . . .'

Could it have been that those early believers were not attempting to expel demons, but the wind itself?

Despite the protection of the cross my body was thoroughly chilled now. I got to my feet, and in the minutes that I'd sheltered behind the walls the easterly wind had dropped and limbo had claimed the land: the horizon had been smudged away and fog was sneaking low. As I walked the curricks blinked out one by one, like beacons at sea, and soon I found myself in an insubstantial twilight. Solid objects flattened to silhouettes, silhouettes faded to nothing. The dense vapour stirred like soup in which occasional shapes swam past, but no breath stirred the air and cloud clogged the space. My compass was back in the bothy, the Pennine Way had disappeared, and it took almost an hour to navigate off the fell. It illustrated a basic point, which would serve me well on these walks: without the spirits to clear a path I was unable to find my way. Without them I was lost.

The bothy was deserted again, and darkness closed in quickly. I sat by guttering candlelight as the last picture frames crackled in the grate, alone with my frustration. The delicate alignment of factors had been agonisingly close. If only the wind had nudged a little more to the north or north-east, if only the air flow had been more constant . . . But the forecasts showed westerlies now; the window had closed, the chance was gone. I had failed to find my first wind. Would I find the others?

Peter Brown picked me up from Kirkland, below the western shoulder of the fell, at ten o'clock the next morning for the ten-mile drive to Penrith. 'How'd you get on?' he asked, as Cross Fell shrank in the rear-view mirror. 'Didn't come, did it? Never mind. We'll call you when it does. You'll get a message – "the Bar is up" – and then you can jump on the next northbound train.' He was silent for a while as he drove. 'It'll come again, that's for sure.'

BORA

It blows a *bora* twice a week, and a high wind on the
other five days. I call it a high wind when I hold onto
my hat and a *bora* when I am in danger of breaking my
arm.

Stendhal

It took a day and a night and a day to travel from London St
Pancras to Trieste Centrale. I changed trains at Paris and Venice,
and shared my *couchette* with a bony Frenchman and a chubby
Italian computer programmer, communicating awkwardly in a
mixture of all our tongues. I woke in the night to ice on the
windowpane and a vision of frosted pines – an update on my
phone informed me that this was Switzerland – and later to
vineyards and cypresses, pink snow on distant mountains.
Bowling through Italy as the sun climbed, I felt Switzerland was
a secret dream; a country only glimpsed at night, deep under
snow and darkness.

Trieste is nestled in the extreme north-easterly corner of Italy,
on the Balkan and not the Italian side of the Adriatic Sea. The
train crept into its outskirts at dusk, after tracing the narrow
coastal strip that umbilically connects the city with the body of
Italy proper; without which, it would be enclaved within
surrounding Slovenia. On my map, the province resembled
something that had been left behind, an anomalous historical

appendage waiting to be snipped off by a pedantic cartographer with a dislike of loose ends. 'Trieste is like a peninsula settlement, on a spit protruding out of western Europe into the sea of the Balkans,' writes Jan Morris in *Trieste and the Meaning of Nowhere*, going on to quote the writer François-René de Chateaubriand in 1806: 'The last breath of civilization expires on this coast where barbarism starts.' Even 200 years later, the journey produced the distinctive sense of going out on a limb.

The final twenty miles of travel were squeezed between the mountains and the sea: the Gulf of Trieste lay on my right, gleaming as smooth as wax in the sunset, while on my left towered the imposing wall of the Karst plateau, the brutalist limestone wedge that abuts the city. These dominating natural features – the stark highlands and the soft sea – create the crucial conditions for the wind I was seeking.

Trieste was grander than I'd expected, and oddly un-Italian in tone; it was as if I'd taken the wrong train and ended up in central Europe rather than the south. In the gathering gloom of the streets I caught glimpses of neoclassical buildings that wouldn't have looked out of place in Vienna, tramlines and granite-clad boulevards with the self-important and faintly stuffy air of Mitteleuropa. If it didn't feel like an Italian city, that's because for much of its history it was run by Austrians; formerly the principal port of the Habsburg Empire, and one of the great trading hubs of the world, it enjoyed huge wealth and global importance before the shifting tides of history robbed it of its purpose. Annexed by the Italian state at the end of the First World War, as the imperial centre collapsed, it lost its lifeline to the continent; when Mussolini came to power irredentist Fascist attacks on Slovenes, German-speakers and Jews put an end to its tradition of multiculturalism. During the Second World War it enjoyed a brief spurt of importance again, as conquest expanded Italian territory deep into Yugoslavia, but Italy's withdrawal from the war was followed by Nazi occupation, and soon after that the city was seized by the victorious Slavs. After briefly becoming a Free Territory under international protection Trieste was returned to Italy almost as an afterthought in 1954 – with chunks of its hinterland stranded within communist Yugoslavia – exhausted, broke and abused, its glory days long gone. The imperial architecture, looking slightly dog-eared now, remains the only clue to its grand past.

Despite the majestic style of the streets, my first meander through the city exposed the unhurried atmosphere and rather reassuring dullness of a small provincial town. When I stopped to ask directions a courteous shopkeeper walked me practically halfway to my destination, and a short stroll brought me to the room I'd booked on the Via della Pietà. Thirty hours on trains across Europe had given my body a rail-sick sway, and I collapsed gratefully into bed. The city, and its wind, could wait until the morning.

I woke to golden January light and breath-in-the-air cold-ness. Children filed their way to school in gloves, scarves and bobble hats, and sausage dogs on leads wore coats. Cars were driving courteously and stopping to let pedestrians cross. After macchiato in the nearest café to remind myself this was Italy, and not some central European city somehow drifted south of the Alps, I made my way towards the sea to get a sense of orienta-tion. The architecture grew ever huger the closer I got to the quay, opening on to the cobbled expanse of the Piazza Unità d'Italia, which Triestines proudly call the largest sea-facing square in Europe. One side of the square was dominated by the statued façade of what looked like a palace, but turned out to be the former head office of the Lloyd Triestino shipping company – previously Österreichischer Lloyd, with a fleet of over sixty ships – a kind of temple to the city's mercantile past. Near the sea two absurdly tall flagpoles, topped with halberds, menaced the sky. And in the middle of this space stood the Fountain of the Four Continents, a quartet of female statues representing Europe, Africa, Asia and America, surrounded by four reclining males – avatars, I presumed, of the winds – three of them scowling and bearded, and one with a sinisterly veiled face, perhaps to shield him from the spindrift lashing off the sea.

It was a good place to pause and consider the route ahead; it would be a longer stretch than the journey to Cross Fell. From Trieste I planned to walk north, over the Slovenian border – across the barren Karst plateau into the Slovene Littoral – and then to swing south-east again to follow the coastline of Croatia, through the ports of Rijeka and Senj, crossing to the islands of Rab and Pag, and finally venturing into the mountains of the Velebit range, which form part of the Dinaric Alps that shadow the Adriatic. It was a couple of hundred miles, and the wind I was hunting might strike at any time during the journey.

Today was an utterly windless day, but I discovered a clue to my quest a few minutes' walk away. Protruding from the end of the piazza into the glassy waters of the gulf ran a stone jetty called the Molo Audace – long enough for sailboats and steamers to anchor in their scores in times past, but entirely deserted now – and at its terminus I found my direction-giver. At first it looked like an oversized compass, with a bronze face on a plinth of stone, but was in fact a wind-rose indicating the principal Mediterranean winds – the north-easterly Greco, the south-easterly Sirocco, the south-westerly Libeccio and the north-westerly Maestro – whose names derive from the Latin-inflected *lingua franca* used by sailors in medieval times. Such a representation might be seen anywhere from Istanbul to Gibraltar. But this one displayed an additional presence, like an uninvited guest: from the east-north-east, a demented cherubic face puffed out a wintry blast, the only one to have the honour of anthropomorphisation. This furious character was my quarry, *enfant terrible* of the Adriatic: the Bora, whose name comes from Boreas, the ice-bearded god of winter.

The Bora is a dry, frigid wind that forms when cold air from the north-east bottles up behind the Karst plateau, and on the continental side of the mountains that run along the coast. When the pressure is high enough the air is dragged, with enormous violence, through a handful of passes and cols to equalise in the warmer, lower pressure zone above the sea; it can reach hurricane strength, sink ships, smash houses, topple trucks, close motorways, uproot trees, blow fish from the sea and cover everything in its path in crystalline ice formations. Its range extends perhaps 500 miles the length of the Adriatic, from Italy to Albania, but several locations are worse hit than others, and these are known as the Bora's 'mouths': the gaps in the mountain wall through which the air is forced. Rijeka and Senj are two of these. Trieste is another.

Trieste, as that wind-rose suggests, takes peculiar pride in that status. Every guidebook I'd read, every article, every internet travel forum, mentioned the Bora as a kind of local celebrity, invariably listed alongside the city's other famous visitors – Casanova, Rainer Maria Rilke, Sigmund Freud, Italo Svevo, Stendhal, James Joyce – but far more wild, melodramatic and frequently returning. Much is made of the ropes and chains slung along pavements at intersections for people to cling to on Bora days – many have been removed, as people kept stealing them for souvenirs – and shops sell postcards of flying hats, uplifted skirts and pedestrians bent at forty-five degrees. The Bora is, as Morris says, 'fundamental to Trieste's self-image'.

I waited a full week, but the Bora didn't come. The days were mild and serene, with no sense of urgency; strollers drifted in the streets with a dreamlike lack of purpose. Basing myself in the room on the Via della Pietà I checked the forecasts every few hours, watched Italian TV news and pestered everyone I met for information about the wind. I wandered the piazzas and boulevards, struck up conversations in bars, and made a daily pilgrimage to the wind-rose on the Molo Audace, falling into leisurely pace with promenading Triestines who brought to mind Morris's description of the city as an 'allegory of limbo'. Everyone seemed strangely lost: African migrants sat motionless on stone benches near the quay, old men gazed into the water, and a solitary teenage boy practised a mournful trumpet dirge, mindlessly repeating the same few bars as if caught on a loop. 'Melancholy is Trieste's chief rapture,' Morris writes affectionately:

> In almost everything I read about this city, by writers down the centuries, melancholy is evoked. It is not a stabbing sort of disconsolation, the sort that makes you pine for death (although Trieste's suicide rate, as a matter of fact, is notoriously high). In my own experience it is more like our Welsh *hiraeth*, expressing itself in bitter-sweetness and a yearning for we know not what.

Elsewhere she notes that the name of the city is onomatopoeic with the French *tristesse*. This sadness, it seemed to me, this aura of wistfulness and displacement, contrasted so absolutely with what I'd heard about the Bora's interventions – knocking pedestrians off their feet, blasting hats off people's heads – that the city suffered from a kind of split personality disorder. No wonder the locals made so much of their celebrity wind; those violent bursts of clarity must jolt them back to life. Looking at the grand, pointless buildings of the Piazza Unità, built to honour what was once one of the world's greatest ports – now a provincial backwater, pensioned and nostalgic – I wondered if the wild wind might fill a certain vacuum.

In its absence, though, I discovered a cave of wonders. One night I found my way to the Museo della Bora, which wasn't marked on any map, after a man's voice on the phone had directed me to a certain door on a backstreet called the Via Belpoggio, somewhere in the tangle of alleyways near the docks. 'I can show you a curious collection of curious things relating to Bora. You must come at eight o'clock tonight.' The set-up was clandestine, and suitably eccentric.

The museum was housed in the ground-floor flat of a crumbling apartment block. Its curator Rino Lombardi, an energetic balding man with thick-framed designer glasses, welcomed me as a fellow fanatic, guiding me around the exhibits at a phenomenal pace. His career had started with a gimmick, creating his *Bora in Scatola* – a Canned Bora, a tub of air listing record Triestine wind speeds – and gone on to collect hundreds of wind-related artefacts, from a library of meteorological books to an archive of Trieste newspaper cuttings: black and white photographs of blown-over automobiles and trams, tumbling trilbies and smashed umbrellas, policemen escorting old ladies across boulevards turned into battlefields of flying shrapnel. There were windmills, kites, antique anemometers, a Slovenian windpowered device called a *klopotec* that produced a clop-clop sound to frighten birds off the crops, a collection of wind warning signs, and an original Bora rope. But by far the strangest and loveliest thing was the glittering display cabinet full of 'captured winds' sent by enthusiasts from around the world. He had over 150, like a meteorological BFG: bottles, jars, phials, tins, flagons, flasks and Tupperwares stacked in disorderly rows, each with its label of origin, including a Sirocco from Rome, a Mistral from

Provence, a Tramontana from Tuscany, an unnamed but undoubtedly holy wind from Lourdes, and even one from Darfur with a sprinkle of red desert sand. Each contributor was rewarded with a certificate proclaiming them an *ambasciatore eolico*, 'ambassador of winds'. He didn't yet have a Helm. I promised I'd find him one.

It was all very kitsch, but deeper down, in mythological terms, this eccentric Italian collector was playing the role of Aeolus. In Greek mythology Aeolus is the Keeper of the Winds, who kept the world's gales and breezes chained in a cave on the island of Aeolia until the arrival of Odysseus, returning from Troy. The hero was given the captive winds – with the exception of gentle Zephyrus, primed to carry his ship safely home – stuffed inside an ox-hide sack, with instructions not to open it; but his greedy crew did just that, thinking there was treasure inside, unleashing a storm that drove Odysseus away from Ithaca for ten long years. The archetype of a Master of Winds – whether a man, a god or a demon, often depicted clasping a sack or a shawl with both hands – is common to ancient cultures from Europe to the Far East. One theory says that the myth of Aeolus was carried east along the Silk Road by the armies of Alexander the Great, who conquered as far as the Indus River and mingled Greek with Buddhist beliefs; Aeolus entered the pantheon as the Greco-Buddhist god Wardo, later evolving into the Chinese Feng Po, the kindly 'Uncle Wind', and finally ending up as the fearsome green-skinned demon Fūjin in Japanese Shinto. It wasn't the first time I would find classical Greek and Roman myths folded into local cultures, transplanted in different soils. Myths are as migratory as the winds they represent.

Zooming outward from Eurasia, Lyall Watson lists similar wind-hoards – part of an 'ancient and common code' – in cultures across the world, from the Maori to the Mayan: 'Caves, sacks, bags, baskets, calabashes, gourds and coconuts are only thinly veiled symbols for the womb in which the winds wait for release ... They are, however, no ordinary children, but wayward, somewhat rowdy, progeny over which there is little or no possibility of control.' These words were echoed by Signor Lombardi as he ushered me through the door, having concluded his hurricane tour: 'Wind is disorder. In this room I try to make order – it's a crazy idea. I am happy I will never succeed.'

And then, more cryptically: 'This is a museum that does not exist. To show something that is invisible is not easy, not easy at all. You will discover this, I think.' Before I could ask any more questions he wished me *buon vento*, 'good wind', and I found myself back on the street.

But the forecasts predicted no *vento* – *buon* or *male* – on the horizon. Every day dawned hushed and still, with a haze lying over the sea. Trieste's most famous visitor was on a long sabbatical, so I waxed my boots and packed my rucksack in advance of the journey over the Karst; if the wind wouldn't come to the walker, the walker would go to the wind. The afternoon before I left I had lunch with Guy Bristow, an Englishman who lived in the Slovenian port of Koper – just a few miles over the border, an industrial sister-city to Trieste – with whom I'd been in touch over the past few months. He and his Slovene girlfriend Mara traded war stories of the wind: the time it had blown a Turkish truck on its side by the Piazza Unità, blocking both traffic lanes, or stripped the tiles off their roof, or torn their olive tree up by the roots and hurled it across the garden. Despite this outrageous behaviour, Mara's face glowed when she talked about it. 'It's a healthy wind. It cleans the air, makes everything clear, and the cold makes you feel good. People feel better when it comes. It makes everything alive.'

'All the locals love it,' said Guy. 'For us foreigners it's hard to get used to. Tell him about your hands.'

Looking ever so slightly embarrassed, Mara rubbed her palms together. 'I can predict it with my hands. When it's coming my palms go dry, because it is such a dry wind . . .'

'How dry are they now?'

She considered. 'Yes, they're a little dry. I don't want to promise anything. But if you're lucky, you might meet it in the next few days.'

With this hope in mind, early next morning I caught the old-fashioned funicular tram that hauled itself, with enormous strain, past the steeply stacked streets and houses on the northern edge of the city and up a seemingly impossible gradient to the monument of Obelisco. On the chapped lip of the Karst plateau, 1,000 feet above the sea, I lingered to look back at Trieste, a wind's-eye view of the city. Its piazzas basked in golden light, its waters were unruffled by the slightest perturbation; I was happy to leave it to its nostalgic dreaming. Southwards, beyond the gantries of a sprawling industrial zone, was the distant smear of the Istrian peninsula, where Slovenia ends and Croatia begins. And somewhere in the other direction, up the coast towards Italy proper – though it was too far to see – stood the castle of Duino, where Rilke's famous elegies were inspired directly by the Bora, so the story goes. In 1912, as he watched the sea during a violent storm, the poet heard the lines emerge, intact, from the voice of the wind: 'Who, among the orders of angels, would hear me if I screamed? . . . Every angel is terrible.'

Poetry being inspired by wind should come as no surprise; the Latin *spirare* is, of course, the root of 'inspiration'. 'Be thou, Spirit fierce,/My spirit! Be thou me, impetuous one!' Shelley exhorts in his ode to the wind. And Joyce must have been similarly stirred when he described the Bora's effects in a letter to his brother in 1905:

I went out yesterday for a walk in a big wood outside Trieste. The damned monotonous summer was over and the rain and soft air made me think of the beautiful (I am serious) climate of Ireland. I hate a damn silly sun that makes men into butter. I sat down miles away from everybody on a bench surrounded by tall trees. The Bora (the Trieste Wind) was roaring through the tops of the trees. I sniffed up all the fragrance of the earth and offered up the following prayer . . .

O Vague Something behind Everything!

Making a similar invocation, I turned inland. The long straight road ahead cut through the suburb of Villa Opicina, and from there to the Slovenian border. It felt good to be walking.

Already the signs looked promising. The mildness and haze had dropped at this higher altitude; a chill had come to the air, and it was bitter enough for mittens. Olive trees trembled in the breeze, torn posters rattled on marble walls, and the fur trim on an old lady's coat rippled like a living pelt. Collars were up, hat brims down, and people stooped forward as they walked. I passed a war memorial emblazoned with a communist red star and a ribbon in Slavic white, blue and red – the first hint I was leaving western Europe for the former Yugoslavia – and continued north-east, into the Bora's mouth.

The border slipped past quietly, without any flags or fuss; the only clue was the bilingual road signs suddenly flipping the other way, with Slovenian on top and Italian on the bottom, like water draining in reverse when you cross the Equator. Everything seemed a little more rustic, a little less manufactured. The villas felt more like cottages, with wells in the gardens and much evidence of digging and planting, the logs more jealously hoarded than on the Italian side. The first village I reached hosted a bizarre Nativity scene, though it was many weeks past Christmas: a host of child-sized mannequins dressed in aprons and rubber boots, gardening gloves and knitted hand-me-downs, their papier-mâché faces frozen in curiously horrified expressions, as if caught in a moment of shock. Jesus, Mary and Joseph were not given centre stage in this tableau but shunted to one side in a shed, surrounded by sly-looking sheep. The emphasis was clearly not on them but on the members of the village, the ordinary men and women gathered round to visit. It was naïve, communal art with a distinctly peasant feel. The civic grandeur of Trieste already felt quite distant.

The wind had a new name in this land: when I crossed the border it had changed from the Bora to the Burja (the 'ja' pronounced as a 'ya', flicking the word upward at the end) and I practised it as I walked, the first item of a new vocabulary. The linguistic shift fitted the more calloused, rough-and-ready style of the country. In the last few miles Italian's rococo adornments had been pruned, lopped off to produce an earthier tongue with a typically Slavic disdain for vowels: Slovenes call Trieste Trst, the region's famous prosciutto *pršut*, and the Karst over which I walked – which Italians prettily term the Carso – is vulgarised to the Kras, a name better suited to the harshness of the land.

The term 'karstic' is generic, applying to arid limestone and dolomite topographies riddled by networks of underground caves. My first impression was of desiccation, of drystone walls criss-crossing enclosures of hissing yellow grass and dead oak leaves quivering on branches, rattling like maracas. The pale karstic rock itself, ineffectually covered by the meanest tissue of vegetation, broke from the thin soil everywhere to form irregular heaps and cairns, as bleached and brittle as clay left far too long in the oven. The forest either side of me, consisting of scrubby oaks and black pines, was planted in the last two centuries to mitigate the Bora's effects – a domesticating campaign initiated by the Austrians – but it had done little to soften the land. A regular testimony to this was the symbol of the local municipality on signs along the road: the silhouette of an olive tree bent violently by wind.

Back in Trieste I'd come across a legend about the Karst's origin. It was a twisted retelling of the original Aeolus myth: the Master of Winds had a beautiful daughter named Bora – surely a sister to Boreas – who fell in love with Tergesteo, one of the Argonauts returned from the quest for the Golden Fleece. When Aeolus discovered the pair, shacked up in a cave for seven days and nights, he murdered Tergesteo in his rage; when Bora wept her tears turned to stone, creating the rubble of the Karst. The dried tears of Bora clattered beneath my boots as I walked, following the E61, on the trail of her namesake.

I started to become aware of a steady frigid current. It was subtle but unmistakable, and though it never rose as high as anything approaching a strong wind, it signalled that I'd entered another climate zone. The coast lay smothered in milky haze; up here in the hinterland, it was a different season.

Soon I diverted north, off the main road. A one-armed man in a purple shell-suit directed me down a rutted farm track he said would lead to the village of Tomaj, halfway to Štanjel, where I planned to spend the night. Jays scattered as I crashed off the highway on to a carpet of dry leaves, and what looked very much like an eagle lifted from a fencepost and soared away. For the rest of the day I walked through oak woods, tracing pale drystone walls laid haphazardly, as if they had been sprinkled. I met no one, and heard nothing but the explosive crunch of ice when my boots hit frozen puddles. Occasionally the trees opened up to allow glimpses of mountains ahead, and in those moments I was reminded of the approach to the Northern

Pennines from the Eden Valley, a geographical *déjà vu* that almost fooled me into thinking I was heading back to Cross Fell. But then I would see hayricks stacked in a style that England hasn't seen in a century, and vineyards instead of muddy cow fields, and be snapped back to Slovenia and the thrill of unknown horizons.

There was one affinity, though, between the Debatable Lands and this Balkan littoral: for much of their respective histories both were unpoliced frontier zones between the civilised and the wild, plagued by bandits. Warfare between the imperial Habsburgs – who ruled the region as Inner Austria between the fourteenth and seventeenth centuries – and the rival empires of the Ottomans and the Venetians recurrently swept the land, along with peasant uprisings from the Slavic underclass, leaving an outlaw legacy that continued long after the territory was won. An observer in 1777 described frequent piles of embers in the nearby Planina region, 'the remains of fires lately kindled, as we were informed, by robbers, many of whom infest the neighbouring forests'. In 1802 a German architect called Karl Friedrich Schinkel, on his way to Italy, claimed that 'From Turkey and Istria whole bands of gypsies and mamelukes enter the country, and one hears daily of robberies and murders.' And as late as 1851 John Murray's *Handbook* warned: 'Highway robbery, though less frequent than formerly, is by no means unknown, and military posts are established for the protection of travellers on the great road from Laibach to Trieste' (using the old German name for the capital, Ljubljana). This endemic lawlessness left its mark on architecture, as it did in the borderlands of Cumbria: each small village, perched on a hill like an island in a sea of trees, commanded a sweeping view of the terrain, with the steeples of the churches in constant visual contact with their neighbours. It gave the country a feeling of alertness, of protective watchfulness, that was entirely at odds with the drowsy air of the villages themselves. No one moved in the streets, cars seldom stirred the dust, and often the only motion I saw came from the brightly painted windmills in the forms of ducks and aeroplanes, with whirling wooden wings and propellers: folk technology for harnessing the Bora.

Life hardly became more peaceful after the nineteenth century. During the Second World War, Yugoslavia was occupied and the Slovenian part trisected – divided into three zones controlled by Fascist Italy, Nazi Germany and Hungary – plunging the region into violence worse than all the centuries of banditry combined. The Karst saw fierce resistance from the communist Partisans, leading to savage reprisals against the civilian population: mass executions, the destruction of ethnically Slovene villages, and the deportation of tens of thousands to concentration camps. The Partisans responded with their own atrocities against the Italians, killings that became known as the 'foibe' massacres. A *foiba* is a deep natural sinkhole in the surface of the Karst – there are hundreds throughout the region, riddling the porous rock from the Slovene Littoral to Istria – and into these chasms disappeared countless thousands of bodies, many thrown in alive. These brutal disappearances continued long after the war, as the communists settled old scores and purged unwanted elements from Josip Broz Tito's new Socialist Federal Republic of Yugoslavia. Corpses continue to be exhumed from one forgotten shaft or another – in 2005 the remains of 130 were discovered – but many of them will never be found. Their skeletons will become part of the Karst, another strata of its myth; Bora's dried tears.

Reaching the village of Križ I saw my first *golobica*, 'little doves', the heavy rocks laid on roofs to prevent their tiles being blown away. In this region, researchers can chart the Bora's path by measuring the density of stone on rooftops, and – as in the Eden Valley – walls are bricked thicker to the north and east.

Even the chimneys resembled miniature fortresses. There was another clue: in the window of an inn hung a row of *pršut* hams, a delicacy flavoured by the Bora. After being cleaned and salted the meat is cured in the frigid air, which gives it its distinctive taste and preserves it for years; in the wars and famines of centuries past, it must have been a lifeline. When I paused to take off my mittens I had the unsettling realisation that my hands had partially cured as well – the skin was parched and starting to crack, resembling hunks of ham themselves – and thought back hopefully to Mara's prediction of the palms. A weather vane in the shape of a pig's head swung its snout to the south-west. Walking on, I tried not to think of my body as drying meat.

'This is not Burja, not yet. You will know it when it comes,' said Erika, the luminous-eyed woman who let me into a cosy room in a guest-house in Kobdilj. I'd emerged from the woods into this small village as the temperature plunged, and was glad to find a welcoming door. She was delighted that I'd walked, and ferreted out a pile of maps, geological pamphlets and local histories to teach me about the area, though most were in German. 'Burja is a healthy wind,' she said, echoing Mara's words. 'People who live on the Kras are strong. In the wind, people grow thick skins.'

That night was very cold and clear, stippled with stars that looked bigger than normal, eerily magnified. By the light of the moon, just shy of full, I climbed the hill to Štanjel, the older and more ancient village looming above Kobdilj, the former feudal seat of the Habsburg counts of Coblenz. It was dominated by a curious church with a steeple like an elongated lemon, or something specifically designed for aerodynamism, as if the architecture were shaped by the flow of air. Its streets were deserted, its windows black – the population of the village, said Erika, was just twenty-six – and wandering down cobbled alleyways, under fallen arches and up broken steps, I neither saw nor heard any signs of life. The massive walls, built to defend against Ottoman invasion, had proved no protection in later years: half the houses were in ruins, partly destroyed by Allied bombs trying to dislodge the Germans who were headquartered there in the war, and partly ravaged by weather and time, returning their stones to the land. In the distance, above grey slopes descending in waves towards the Vipava Valley, a tiny light flickered on the crest of a black silhouette. This was the radar and meteorological station on the summit of Nanos, another day's walk away, and I imagined the resident aeromancer diligently checking dials, scanning pressure and temperature, a wizard in a purple robe festooned with crescent moons. The moonlit ghost town around me encouraged such fairy-tale thinking.

The geographer Strabo knew Nanos as the 'last peak of the Alps', but my interest in the mountain stemmed from a different title. The curator of the Museo della Bora had referred to it – along with Snežnik, a smaller mountain to the south – as one of two 'doorposts of the Bora', through the open threshold of which the wind sweeps on to the Karst. I zeroed in on that winking light. My path led to that peak.

Not for another day, however. I woke to a glittering silver morning, the vineyards trembling with frost, and the frozen beauty of the land coupled with Erika's hearty breakfast – fried eggs, *pršut*, cheese and bread – convinced me to stay another night. On a borrowed bicycle I set out to explore the Karst, tracing unpaved roads alongside walls of lichen-flecked stone, making a meandering loop between the scattered villages of Kosovelje, Pliskovica and Krajna Vas. Again nobody stirred in the streets, though woodsmoke drifted from the fortified chimneys and wallowed in the troughs of the land. Everything was bitter, bone-dry. The trees were stunted, their crowns lopsided, permanently skewed to the south. Gnarled karstic rocks decorated gateposts and boundary walls, and vulnerable tiles on every roof were weighted with little doves. Louvred shutters and protruding beams were bleached and cracked in the manner of driftwood, though they were far from the sea; the Bora's aridity cured wood as it cured flesh. The countryside had a desolate feel despite the surface prettiness, and when ice peppered from the sky in a popping mist, I turned for home. I wheeled back down the rattling road past shrines where candles glowed softly, and only the Virgin Mary stayed warm, behind soot-blackened glass.

Back in the guest-house Erika asked if I'd met anyone on the way. When I said I'd hardly seen a soul, she nodded without surprise. 'That's because people in this region are all in their territories. They do not like to go far. They stay inside. They keep close to the home.'

'Is that because of the wind as well?'

'Perhaps! Most things are.'

I started to see the connection now between the Bora's bitterness and these thick-walled villages, with their thick-skinned people. The sense of autonomy, of reluctance to venture as far as the next village, let alone the world beyond, is borne out by the amazing number of dialects that Slovenia harbours: over thirty, some mutually unintelligible, in a country of 2 million people. This parochialism filters down to the flimsiest of borders: the inhabitants of Štanjel were nicknamed *špagarji* by their neighbours, 'those who hold up their trousers with rope', while people down the road in Kobdilj – a ten-minute walk away – were called *rogovilci*, 'horned ones', because they caused so many fights. Only a day from Italy, the Balkans were already living up to their tribal reputation; but also, after Erika's welcome, for their warmth and kindness too.

The history of Slovenia, and its southern neighbour Croatia, has followed a slightly different path from that of other Balkan countries, owing to the vagaries of geopolitics. While the Slavic peoples of Serbia, Bosnia and Bulgaria spent centuries under

Ottoman rule, the Slovenes and Croats to the west found themselves in the Habsburg sphere, effectively isolating them from
their linguistic cousins. Until the late nineteenth century the
region acted as a buffer between the two empires; and when,
a hundred years later, another empire fell apart – that of the
USSR – the collapse of Yugoslavia exposed some of that old
divide. As Slobodan Milošević pursued the irredentist dream of
a Greater Serbia, Slovenia and Croatia declared independence
in 1991, the first of the former socialist republics to break away.
Their fates were very different though: Croatia faced full-scale
invasion from Serbian and Montenegrin forces and was plunged
into years of ethnic conflict that saw its economy destroyed,
its cities mercilessly shelled, tens of thousands of its people
displaced and thousands killed. Slovenia, on the other hand –
bordered by Italy and Austria, and with no significant Serb
population of its own – gained its freedom after a war that
lasted just ten days. The chain reaction of the Yugoslav Wars
became progressively bloodier the further east and south they
rolled, culminating in the killing fields of Bosnia and Kosovo.
This westernmost fringe of the Balkans was spared the worst, at
least; although you wouldn't want to look too deep inside its
sinkholes.

The following day dawned colder still. The leaves were furred
with thick hoar frost, the earth rutted as hard as iron, and icicles
as slender as needles hung from shadowed rocks. The trail
onwards from Kobdilj led over a forested hill and dropped
steeply on the other side, out of the stony heartland of the Karst
and towards the valley of Vipava. I descended through a colour
spectrum shifting from frozen to temperate: below the level
exposed to the wind, out of the refrigerated air flow, the trunks
turned from frosted white to damp and dingy brown. Reaching
the sheltered valley floor was like crossing an invisible border
into a warmer country. Villages rose from lagoons of woodsmoke,

and I saw more people in their streets than I'd seen across the expanse of the Karst. Workmen were repairing walls, farmers hacking the earth with spades and trundling battered wheel-barrows, and in place of little doves the roofs were yellow with drying corncobs.

This mildness belied the fact that Vipava, just a few miles ahead, is a notorious Bora channel, with wind speeds of almost 200 miles per hour recorded in Ajdovščina. Yet another, much more ancient, imperial power struggle took place here, one in which the wind played a starring role. That small town is one contender for the site of the Battle of the Frigid River, which has also been called the Battle of the Bora, fought in 394 between the divided halves of the Roman Empire: the Eastern Emperor Theodosius I, who was Christian, and the Western usurper Eugenius, whose sympathies leaned towards the old gods. More than a mere civil war, it represented the last stand of the Greco-Roman pantheon against the rise of monotheism; the last time a major pagan army opposed the Christianisation of Rome. Different sources give different accounts: either the Bora blew clouds of dust into the eyes of Eugenius's troops, who were facing to the east, or its howling demoralised his men, or their arrows were turned in the air like boomerangs and directed back at them, causing panicked retreat. Theodosius triumphed, and Eugenius had his head cut off and displayed. The victory meant not only that Rome was back in the hands of a single emperor – though he died just a few months later – but that the new religion spread rapidly throughout Europe.

This wasn't the only time a wind has altered the course of history. The Japanese Kamikaze, the 'divine wind' that destroyed an invading Mongol fleet in 1281, is the most famous example; there is also the Gregale, another gust credited with assisting the Christian faith. When the apostle Paul was being shipped to Rome to stand trial for his subversive beliefs this cold north-easterly – which the Bible calls the Euroclydon – wrecked his ship on the coast of Malta, allowing him to escape. Paul swiftly proceeded to convert the island's Roman governor, and Malta became, by some definitions, the first Christian nation in Europe. But in the case of the Frigid River, the divine intervention seemed the wrong way round. It was ironic that the wind that swung the war against paganism took its name from a pagan god; Boreas smiting the last of the polytheists seemed a suicidal move, relegating him to the dustbin of history with the rest of his pantheon. If only the armies had drawn their battle lines the other way – Theodosius to the west and Eugenius to the east, with the wind at his back – things could have turned out differently. I might be seeing painted temples instead of churches in these villages, and scowling men with ice in their beards, not Virgin Marys, in the roadside shrines.

The valley gradually widened out, and I found myself back on country roads threading between checkerboard fields. But the gentle lowlands came to an end: after half a dozen miles I turned a corner to see the snow-striped flank of Nanos ahead, lounging north to south across the land like an enormous slug, the erect antennae of its weather station blinking on the summit. The bells were tolling midday as I arrived in the square, or *trg*, of Podnanos – literally 'Under Nanos' – a village of solid stone houses whose roofs were dense with little doves. Stopping for coffee in the first open establishment I had seen for three days, I made enquiries of the Bora as if asking for a mutual acquaintance. 'You're looking for Burja?' said the barmaid, without particular surprise. 'You're in the right place, but it's not here today. Burja is leaving us alone at the moment, I don't know why.' I asked if she approved of it, expecting to hear the usual claims of good health and clean air, but her answer was vehement. 'Oh no! It destroys the houses, throws trucks over on their sides. Sometimes we can't go out in the street, and the school can be closed for days. Burja makes our life very hard – I would like to live somewhere else.'

Not far down the road a marked trail branched upward to the mountain. Three hours to the summit, said the sign; I judged that I'd have just enough daylight to make it down the other side, to the village of Razdrto where a bed awaited that night. I ascended through steep woods, leaving the valley far below – the gravelly roar of the H4 motorway zooming to Italy in the west – and at the end of the second hour I found myself in snow. I hadn't been expecting this; the whiteness had been hidden from below and the transition was alarming, especially when I started to see climbers equipped much better than me – telescopic hiking poles, lurid ski-wear and even snowshoes – dotted up the slopes. The trail led south along the ridge, on the brink of a savage drop that plunged as steeply as a waterfall into the valley below, and for once I was relieved that no wind was blowing. Nestled below the peak was a snowbound little church, its shoulders hunkered against the cold, where I stopped to catch my breath before going on.

Looking back at the distance I'd walked, I saw that a curious thing had occurred. The sky had been starkly bisected into two neat halves by a perfectly horizontal line, divided between bright blue and sickly pinkish-grey. Two hikers walking an enormous hound saw me staring, and offered the explanation: it was a pall of smog drifting from Italian cities, driven northwards on the breath of a different wind, the Jugo.

Jugo: this was the first mention of a name that would haunt me for weeks. The local variant of the Sirocco, it wafts warm air from Africa across the Mediterranean (*jugo*, pronounced 'yugo', is the Slavic word for 'south'; as in Yugoslavia, 'the country of the South

Slavs'). Appropriately for a force with such a huge geographical range – it can affect weather systems as far north as the British Isles – the Sirocco goes by many names: south of the Mediterranean it is called the Khamsin in Egypt, the Ghibli in Libya and the Sharav in Israel, while on the other side of the sea it becomes the Marin in France, the Leveche in Spain and the Xaloc in Catalonia. Italians call it the Scirocco, with an extra 'c'. It begins as a dry desert wind, but by the time it reaches Europe it has become sultry with moisture, driving in humidity that is known for causing headaches. It is notorious for picking up Saharan sand, transporting it over vast distances and dumping it over unsuspecting cities, coating everything in a layer of orange dust. Also – judging by the noxious colour of the sky – heavy particle pollutants.

Throughout history this many-named wind has been associated with 'blood rain', when water stained with reddish sand has poured from the sky and run in torrents through the streets. Understandably these ghastly happenings were seen as portents of disaster – Viking invasion, outbreaks of plague and the untimely deaths of kings – and the historian Gregory of Tours claimed that when blood fell over Paris in 582, people 'were so stained and spotted that they stripped themselves of their clothing in horror'. Xan Fielding writes that 'Renaissance philosophers identified each cardinal wind not only with an element but with its corresponding humour; Boreas with earth and black bile, Notos with air and blood, Euros with fire and yellow bile, Zephyros with water and phlegm.' As the avatar of the south, Notos (Notus) is yet another of the sand-bringer's appellations; perhaps the link between air and blood reflects those incarnadine rains.

No blood fell on the snows of Nanos, but the cast of the sky was ominous. It looked like a grey blanket being dragged across the atmosphere, closing the land below like a lid, blobbing the horizon. 'We say it is like someone squashing you, sitting on your head,' said one of the hikers, knocking snow from her boots. 'The Jugo makes you feel very bad. It's an unhealthy wind. That is why we need the Burja to blow the bad air away.'

'But what is away?' asked the other. 'The badness still has to go somewhere.'

'The Italians can have it back! We don't want it here!'

Leaving them to argue the matter, I climbed on towards the peak. The Jugo's appearance troubled me; already my head felt slightly squashed at the sight of it. Those comments about unhealthy wind, industrially polluted or not, sounded something like miasma theory: the medieval belief that epidemics were caused by the stench of decomposing matter carried on the breeze. Before the discovery of germs it was thought that everything from cholera to the Black Death resulted from this 'bad air', and attempts to get upwind of it determined centuries of town planning: in European cities affected by prevailing westerlies, foul-smelling industries – tanneries, factories, sewage works – were often built in the east, so the miasmas would be carried away from the populous centre. In the case of the Jugo, or Sirocco, Europeans have always feared the 'miasmatic and sticky south wind packed with infectious particles' thought to waft over the Mediterranean, according to Vladimir Janković, a Croatian weather researcher whose papers I happened to have stuffed at the bottom of my rucksack. The eighteenth-century epidemiologist Joseph Browne, writes Janković, identified warm southerlies as the cause of Europe's plagues, reasoning that as the winds passed over the deserts of Egypt they became 'loaded with putrid emanations exhaled from the animal and vegetable substances' decomposing in the cemeteries of the Nile Delta. 'Thus impregnated, the wind "blasted" the inhabitants of the Mediterranean and their northern neighbours.'

If Italy was substituted for Egypt, and factories for cemeteries – and carbon monoxide and sulphur dioxide, perhaps, for the Black Death – the 'unhealthy wind' of the Jugo was regarded much the same by those hikers: a miasma of ill health wafting from dirty southern neighbours, which needed a northerly counterattack to clear the local skies. I didn't know it then, but the push and pull between Jugo and Bora – the warm, humid breath of the south versus the cold, dry air of the north – would come to define my journey over the next few weeks, dominating my mental climate as much as the landscapes I walked through. In happy ignorance of that fact, I climbed on.

The summit was crowned by the dishes and spires of a tele-communications transmitter, painted space age red and white, next to which the meteorological station was engaged in its own silent readings. Disappointed in my fantasy of meeting a wise aeromancer who could reveal the secrets of the wind – everything here was automated – I crunched through crystalline snow to the path leading down the other side. It was a steep descent with iron chains bolted into the rock, and below the treeline something large and black – it looked like a huge shaggy goat – crashed through the woods and hurtled at terrific speed down the slope ahead, almost startling me off the path. But without further incident I reached the village I'd been aiming for, and a bedroom for the night.

It was my last night in Slovenia. My host plied me with home-made *rakija* – clear brandy flavoured with walnuts, blueberries, cumin and other ingredients I was soon incapable of remembering – and left me to rest my aching body by the heat of a clay stove. The next morning I walked eight miles east to the city of Postojna, where a train spirited me south, to the next stretch of my walk.

Razor-wire fences were going up on the Slovenian–Croatian border. It was the beginning of 2016; I was heading south as thousands of migrants were attempting to travel north, and I had been advised not to cross the border on foot. But there was little evidence of the refugee crisis over those forty miles, at least not from the train window; only scattered villages, densely forested hills and scores of storm-smashed pine trunks jagging in the direction of travel. Soon the smiling Slovenian conductor, bearded like a nineteenth-century philosopher, was replaced by the sterner faces of armed Croatian border guards, flipping through passports with studied suspicion. A battered sign welcomed me – as it clearly did not welcome asylum seekers – to Republika Hrvatska, emblazoned with a red and white checkerboard instead of Slovenia's gentler crest of river, stars and mountains.

Another small but significant change occurred on that guarded border: the Burja lost its 'j' – perhaps leaving it snagged on razor wire – to become the Bura, the third time in a week that the wind had changed its name.

The train eased into the grimy sidings of Rijeka, Croatia's biggest port; the second of the Bora's mouths between Trieste and Senj. Darkness had come and my first impression was of fast food restaurants, emergency sirens, casinos with garish flashing displays and white power graffiti daubed on sweating underpass walls, which made me long for the mountain again, and the silence of the Karst. The night was discomfitingly mild. Perhaps it was just my imagination but Croatian men seemed to stare me down, swivelling to watch me as I passed, in a manner I did not know whether or not to interpret as hostile. I had booked a bed in a cheap hostel on the other side of town, in what must have once been an elegant villa before being squeezed between flyovers and the floodlights of the industrial port, and I retired there early, feeling distinctly displaced.

During the night the dirty pall that I had glimpsed from the top of Nanos spread itself across the coast, catching up with me.

I awoke to a nicotine-yellow city, stained from sea to sky. The air was close, moistened by the warm action of the Jugo that laid claim to the atmosphere, squashing all beneath it; a weather condition, I soon learned, known as the *južina*. Rijeka was full of grubby ghosts wandering in twilight.

Despondently I walked down the Korzo, the grand pedestrian boulevard running through the centre of the old town, which was garlanded with harlequin carnival ribbons. Through the *južina*'s haze loomed the dubious features of the Morčić, a municipal mascot adorning banners across the city: a red-lipped, turbaned golliwog representing either a Moorish slave, or a defeated Moorish soldier in the service of the Ottomans. Its origins are entangled with the legend of a local hero who killed a Turkish commander with an arrow – God, meanwhile, rained down burning rocks on the invading army, knocking the turbans off their heads – or the device may simply have been borrowed from the Venetians, who were much enamoured of anything 'oriental'. I hadn't slept very well, and this caricature blackamoor became connected in my mind with the dark-skinned migrants being held back by fences at the country's borders, arrivals from Turkey and North Africa, feared – much like the Jugo – as an unhealthy influence from the south. There was more than coincidence there. It didn't come as a great surprise to hear pointed emphasis, from a waiter who served me coffee, to the Jugo as an 'African wind', an invasive force from the wrong side of the Mediterranean.

An old pseudoscientific belief, which has waxed and waned throughout European history, is that racial characteristics are determined by climate. According to Lucian Boia, Hippocrates compiled exhaustive lists of these climatic differences: 'mountain dwellers are tall, courageous and industrious; those who live in grassland valleys, where the hot winds blow, are short, stocky, far more timid and display little inclination for work.' To the Greeks and Romans, of course, the Mediterranean climate was the norm – barbarians both north and south owed their brutish characters to respective extremes of temperature – as it was to Arab scholars such as Ibn Khaldrun, who proposed that civilisation could only develop in one of three climates, while populations in the other four were doomed to savagery. But when cultural dominance swung to the north, perceptions of 'normal' did too: Enlightenment thinkers such as Robert Burton and John Arbuthnot, from the stormy British Isles, believed that cold acted as an intellectual stimulant. Arbuthnot formulated a view that the 'fibres' of the human body responded positively to changes in atmospheric pressure, which boosted energy and courage; in hot climates, where pressure was more stable, these fibres – in Boia's words – 'behaved in a more uniform fashion, making more uniform the dispositions of the mind. The resulting character was lazy and indolent and marked by a "disposition to slavery".' Hot southern airs, it was believed, were responsible for everything from fecklessness and lethargy to degenerate behaviour and uncontrollable passion.

I couldn't help thinking of those southern migrants, condemned by xenophobes as workshy scroungers, or else as terrorists and rapists. At the height of the refugee crisis, which was fuelling the resurgence of the far right across Europe, was a kind of climatic racism at work?

Rijeka was a fitting place for such thoughts, and not only because of the Morčić. Shortly after the First World War – when the city was still known by its Italian name, Fiume – an episode occurred here that helped birth Fascism. In 1919 an Italian poet and war hero called Gabriele D'Annunzio, outraged that the disputed territory was being ceded to the Slavs, led a contingent of nationalist troops to invade the city. When the Italian government refused to support the occupation, D'Annunzio declared

Fiume an independent state named the Italian Regency of Carnaro – with himself as Duce, or dictator – and proceeded to run it as a radical political experiment combining corporatism, syndicalism, nationalism and other confused strands of twentieth-century thought. Independence didn't last long; the troops were unruly, cocaine use endemic and within a year the breakaway state was under Italian naval bombardment. The rebels left, and D'Annunzio retired to a house on Lake Garda. Although the experiment had failed, his proto-fascist ideology and the symbols of his rebellion – the black-shirted legionnaires, the torchlit parades, the title Duce – went on to inspire Mussolini and his National Fascist Party, which seized power in Italy shortly afterwards. That spasm of nationalism, with its supremacist undertones, had implications that D'Annunzio surely never imagined. Two decades later concentration camps would be scattered down the coast, and the sinkholes of the Karst would be filling up with corpses.

It was getting on for afternoon. Attempting to gain a clearer perspective on the day's nebulousness, I climbed the 538 steps to the fortress of Trsat, but the murk had swallowed the view; the islands of the Kvarner Gulf were all but invisible, and a couple of hazy merchant ships lay becalmed in a static sea. I drifted back down to the harbour and stared into the glass-green water, riddled with tiny black fish, lulled by the peculiar melancholy of docks when no ship is landing. I lingered there for hours, my mind as blank as the horizon. My thoughts were dulled, my body slow. Darkness gave me the excuse to give up and collapse.

The forecasts showed Jugo winds for at least another week. Clearly I would have no luck in the second of the Bora's mouths. But the third lay a couple of days' walk south; I left Rijeka at first light and set my sights on Senj.

Croatia's coastline, packed with tourists from around the world in summertime, lay deep in hibernation. The industrial outlands of the city slowly gave way to barren hills with a texture like biscuit crumbs, headlands of stark grey rock, and shuttered villages in coves that looked all but forgotten. From the out-of-season resort of Crikvenica I followed the road past cypress trees and concrete jetties unlapped by waves, past villas standing white and empty, dead until summer returned. To my right the island of Krk lay like a grey shadow on the water, sometimes vanishing altogether. The stillness felt unreal. The *južina* did strange things to perspective, and buoys and fishing boats appeared suspended on a two-dimensional plane, devoid of depth or distance, less a seascape than an abstract painting. At a village called Selce the road ended at a cove like an empty mirror, and a walking trail plunged upward into jumbled trees. The only sound was a melancholy whistling, and the measured splash of oars as a solitary boat came into view, advancing with infinite slowness. I hurried on towards the woods, before the Styx ferryman claimed me.

The trail led along stunted cliffs through a forest of oak and hornbeam. Here and there appeared tumbledown walls, evidence of past terracing, long since abandoned and buried under weeds. Sometimes the trees opened up to allow glimpses of the limpid sea, with green pebbles trembling, but beyond that the elements merged into a milky whole. A cormorant performed an elegant dive, and every droplet was audible as it fell back upon the surface. I stood and watched the ripples spread, with nothing to distort their expansion, widening endlessly into the void of the sea.

Beyond the town of Novi Vinodolski – another seaside resort of white houses, frozen in limbo like the rest – there came a dramatic intervention. An enormity of rock thrust upward to my left, barrelling south-east in parallel with the coast: the foothills of the Velebit range, part of the Dinaric Alps that extend through Bosnia and Herzegovina, Montenegro, Serbia, Kosovo and Albania, where they meet the Pindus Mountains of northern Greece. In meteorological terms this vast natural wall, a vertical slab above the Adriatic, performs the same function as the Karst, bottling frigid air from the north until low pressure drags it seawards.

Senj was thirteen miles south, and I had been resigned to a wearying slog on the hard shoulder of the E65. The prospect of higher ground was appealing; I was sick of this dreaming coast. A path branched eastwards, away from the sea, connecting to a road that my map suggested would bring me to Senj through the foothills from behind. The start of the trail was marked by a boulder daubed with red and white paint, and soon I had scrambled up a scree slope into a different landscape.

It was grander and wilder than below, though every bit as barren: a desolate waste of rock barely broken by greenery, rust-coloured, bleached and grey, a land without lustre. For an hour, two hours, three, I climbed through unlovely scrub, past the occasional mean little pine tree clogged by dusty silken orbs – either cobwebs or enormous cocoons, I didn't want to look too close – and it became increasingly clear that I wouldn't reach Senj that evening. The trail was less a dedicated path than a vague insinuation. I lost my way completely for a while, and when, almost by accident, I stumbled on the route again, it brought me out at an old cemetery on a dusty hill. The light was faltering; the next painted marker was nowhere to be seen. I looked west, to where the *južina*'s murk was merging with the blackness of night, and realised that I would have to find a place to camp.

Finding level ground, however, proved almost impossible, and it was nearly dark by the time I located a grassy patch between two rubbly mounds, just bigger than tent-sized. It actually took me a while to realise that I had camped in a ruined fortress, a structure so utterly destroyed that it was hard to know where architecture ended and piles of natural rock began. There was no telling what it had once looked like, or in which distant war – involving Ottomans, Austrians, Venetians or other belligerents altogether – it had been so impressively demolished. An occasional vertical section hinted at a vanished wall, or a pit an exposed foundation, but mostly it looked as if heaps of stones had been dumped there and abandoned.

As I drifted to sleep I listened to a crowd of children playing. They were whooping on a nearby hillside, shrieking and giggling. The noise intensified into howls that mounted to hysterical wailing, before breaking down into weird chuckling laughter. I sat bolt upright in my sleeping bag. Those weren't children. I had heard that noise before, also from the flimsy shelter of a tent: European jackals, which have vastly increased their range over the past fifty years to colonise unfarmed land from Slovenia to Turkey. I heard them later in the night – first closer, then more distantly – making the stony hillsides ring with something between ecstasy and grief. In a ruined castle surrounded by jackals, I passed an uneasy night.

There was no sign of them by daylight; nor of much else either. The Jugo had firmly planted its flag, and an impenetrable mist covered everything from the mountains to the sea. The unconfident path frequently vanished as I clambered down the slope, necessitating long, frustrating searches until the next red blob appeared, but little by little I groped my way to the trailhead at Viniště, where I met an unsurfaced road striking out in the right direction.

All morning I swam through a stony twilight that flattened features, leached away colour and deadened every sound. The *južina* squatted over everything, suffocating the land.

Occasionally the road threaded through grey and silent villages whose cottages were half in ruins, half tenuously occupied – a battered motorbike here, a new plastic gutter there – but their inhabitants were in hiding from the breathlessness of the day. I thought of a passage from Janković: people exposed to sultry south winds, climatic determinists believed, 'suffered from bodily flabbiness, had humid heads, and irritable bowels unsupportive of wine; that women suffered from excessive menstruation, infants from asthma, and other adults from dysentery and haemorrhoids'. I imagined these tumbledown villages were full of sufferers of such symptoms, farting and menstruating inside gloomy little rooms, and felt thankful that my only complaint was nagging hunger.

Outside a ramshackle hamlet called Drinak I came upon a flock of sheep, bells clanging round their necks as they tugged on unyielding grass. A shepherd was flinging pebbles to keep them off the road, a squat, dark man with mournful eyes. I wished him *dobar dan*, 'good day', and was surprised when he replied in school-educated English. 'Be careful, please. There are ten dogs with me, up there on the hill. They will not be friendly to you. If you have any trouble call me.' And then, in puzzlement: 'What are you *doing* here?'

I told him I was looking for the Bora.

'Ah, Bura!' he said with a grin. 'In this part of Croatia we have a saying: "Beware the Lika Bura, and the girl with a moustache." Lika is the name of this region, very famous for the wind. Our Bura here is very strong. But we have Jugo now.'

'Does it bother your animals?'

'The sheep do not mind, because they have fat coats. The goats get cold, they do not like. The dogs – no, I do not think so. They are Lika dogs.'

'Does it bother you?'

'I am a Lika man,' he said, clapping his hand to his chest. 'I do not notice it. But when people come here from other places, they are in wonder.'

I continued to the next settlement, unappealingly named Bile, and Vrataruša after that, where the fog became so thick the air was almost solid. The sky was the colour of paintbrush water. The temperature suddenly dropped. As I walked I became aware of a huge, repetitive sound to my left: an unearthly whoosh and hum that occurred with mathematical precision somewhere high in the air, from two or three points at the same time. I couldn't imagine what it was; the mystery slightly scared me. I went off road to investigate, and found myself face to face with a woman feeding chickens in a farmyard; my apparition from the mist made her leap in shock. She recovered quickly, and when I explained I was bound for Senj she rummaged in a shed and gave me a stick to walk with. It was a good stick, whittled and polished, and I carried it like a charm. Using it to feel my way across the moor, towards the source of the noise, I made out a broad vertical axis that resolved itself into a steel tower, and then a wickedly curved blade descended out of the whiteness and vanished, descended out of the whiteness and vanished, and everything made sense. My quest felt even more quixotic; I was tilting at wind turbines.

Wind turbines! The significance of this didn't hit me until I was back on the road, where I noticed patches of snow to my left and right. The air was on the move again, flowing bitterly past my ears, rushing down towards the coast in an icy stream. It flowed over stunted pines permanently skewed south-west, some torsioned almost at right angles, and even the thick moorland grass was combed in the same direction. I thought of the Boreas myth recounted by Xan Fielding: 'When the nymph Pithys refused his advances he dashed her against a rock, and she turned into a pine, a tree that still sheds tears under the north wind's fury.' Rock, wind and weeping pines; I was on the right path now. This road cut directly through the gap in the mountain wall; I would be spat into Senj straight from the Bora's mouth.

But was this frigid current of air just *wind*, or the wind I wanted? 'Bura?' I asked the next people I met, a pair of impressively warty old ladies sitting beside a garden of beehives weighed with heavy rocks. Their answer, '*Ne*', was a disappointment, but then they consulted for a moment and pronounced: '*Nedjelja*,' Sunday. They seemed blithely confident in this prediction. I wondered how they knew. Further down the hill I met a third warty lady, presumably on her way to join the others; perhaps I had stumbled on a coven of weather-forecasting witches, something like Walter Scott's description of a wind-witch in the Orkney Islands:

We clomb, by steep and dirty lanes, an eminence rising above the town, and commanding a fine view. An old hag lives in a wretched cabin on this height, and subsists by selling winds. Each captain of a merchantman, between jest and earnest, gives the old woman sixpence, and she boils her kettle to procure a favourable gale.

A favourable gale was just what I needed. I should have crossed their palms with six Croatian kuna. But Sunday was in two days' time; with that hope, I reached Senj.

I liked the little town immediately. Beyond a muddle of branching lanes and high-walled, closely packed houses – built on an irregular pattern, it was said, to baffle the wind like a labyrinth – groups of amiable old sailors in rubber boots and captain's hats swapped fishing stories on the quay. Water slopped and seagulls screamed. Footsore from the stony road, I limped along the breakwater to look back at the grey foothills I had just descended from, and the cloud-blanketed wall of mountains above. The breakwater ended at a lighthouse that I recognised from photographs: famously in 2012, during the East European Cold Wave – when high pressure over Russia pushed unusually cold air into the Balkans – the temperature plunged to minus fourteen and the Bora created fantastical sculptures of ice in Senj's harbour. The lighthouse and the ornate iron lampposts were encrusted in bizarre crenellations, slender blade-like pillars of snow angled precisely north-east, and glittering seven-foot waves drove violently offshore.

The images were reproduced in media across the world, and locals were proud of that fame. During my few days in Senj I discovered that, as in Trieste, the Bora was a source of pride, celebrated as a part of the town's identity. Sang folk musician Krešimir Stanišić: '*Da ni bure, ne bi bilo ni Senja. Da ni Senja, ne bi bilo ni bure.*' 'If there was no Bura, there would be no Senj. If there was no Senj, there would be no Bura.'

'It blows for an odd number of days,' said Neven, the landlord of the guest-house I stayed in. 'One, three, five, seven. I do not know the science of this.' And there was another local saying, less memorable than the girl with the moustache, but perhaps more practical for a nation with 1,000 miles of coast: 'When Bura sails, you don't.'

Wandering Senj's streets by day I was struck by its resemblance to a Cornish fishing village: the bulging walls and narrow lanes, the cobbled alleys and secretive steps, and especially the same relish of a piratical history. On a hill above the town stood the squat fortress of Nehaj – its name means something like 'No care for danger' – once the stronghold of a warrior caste called the Uskoks. These fierce sea-marauders were descendants of refugees uprooted from Bosnia by sixteenth-century Ottoman invasions; filtering north they settled in Senj, promptly demolished the local churches to obtain stone for their castle, and were soon demanding taxes, plundering shipping lanes and generally terrorising. this part of the Adriatic. The Habsburgs who controlled the coast not only tolerated them but actively subsidised their activities, seeing them as a useful bulwark against further Islamic expansion. Bound by a strict code that promoted honour, revenge and bravado, they moved from preying on Turkish fleets to attacking the Venetian galleys that often escorted them, raiding the islands of Rab and Pag and slaughtering whole shiploads of men; 'May God preserve us from the hands of Senj', went a Venetian prayer. As their notoriety grew, attracting adventurers from across Europe, there were rumours that they ate human hearts and stirred their victims' blood into loaves of bread. By 1615 the Venetian Republic had finally had enough, declaring war on their Habsburg protectors; the resulting peace treaty called for the Uskoks to be disbanded, and two years later they migrated once again. The fortress of Nehaj stands as a testament to their reign. Like the Karst and the Debatable Lands, Senj was known for hundreds of years chiefly for winds and bandits.

In fact, in the case of the Uskoks, this link was possibly more than coincidence. Key to the buccaneers' success was their ability to navigate the treacherous waters of the channel between the mainland and the island of Krk, an area notorious for its extremes of weather. 'The Uskoks developed a technique of using this rough weather as a shield against their enemies, while they ran through it unperturbed,' writes Rebecca West in *Black Lamb and Grey Falcon*, her classic Balkan travelogue. 'Therefore they chased the Turkish ships up and down the Adriatic, stripped them and sunk them; and year by year they grew cleverer at the game.' I was soon to hear more about this: in an unprepossessing alleyway I stumbled on the town museum, and within a short space of time had been invited to a back room containing a stylish vampish lady – jet-black hair, heavy mascara and a black fur-trimmed coat – and a tough-looking man in a leather jacket. The woman was the museum's director Blaženka Ljubović, the man was a merchant sailor called Damir, and they welcomed me to the table and poured me a glass of *kuhano vino*, hot spiced wine. Damir was eloquent in English, and recounted a local legend that connected the Uskoks directly with the Bora.

'If the Venetians didn't pay tax, the Uskoks would go up in the mountains and light a fire in a secret cave. This would generate a terrible Bura, which they could use as a weapon to attack Venetian and Turkish ships. It sounds like bullshit, but actually there is a logic behind this. The region up in the mountains, Lika, is basically a huge pan. Cold air is sitting in this pan – all that is needed is temperature to get the air rolling downhill, and once it starts there is no stopping it. So the legend has a factual basis. And even if they didn't create the Bura, they knew how to take advantage of it – see, it blows offshore, so they used it as a propulsion system to fire their ships out into the sea before the Venetians knew what hit them . . .' He took a satisfied swig of wine, a professional sailor appreciating skilful technique.

Blaženka said something in Croatian, and he translated. 'She says tonight is Museum Night – this place stays open all night. There will be food, wine, *rakija*. You must join us later.' I was given a printed invitation, and another steaming glass.

When I came back around ten o'clock the museum was buzzing. Platters of *pršut* were doing the rounds, hibiscus-flavoured punch was simmering on a clay stove, and there was an atmosphere of tipsy neighbourliness as people greeted old friends and tousled each other's children's hair. Blaženka was delighted I'd returned and summoned various English-speaking people to escort me. There was a man called Mislav who was seeking funding for a Bora museum, along the lines of the one in Trieste – 'Why should the Italians get the fame? Our Bura is much stronger here' – and a retired economist who swore that the wind had lost its power: 'Twenty, thirty years ago it was every day in winter, it was like the Arctic here. Now it comes less and less. Look outside, it is January and already flowers grow. Climate change, that's what it is, that's why the wind has changed.' I asked if anyone thought it would come on Sunday, as had been predicted. 'No, no,' people insisted, 'next week at the earliest. Or maybe you will have to go south. It is not here now . . .'

An enthusiastic bespectacled man gave me a tour of the museum: amphorae from Greek and Roman ships wrecked on Krk during ancient storms, displays on the Uskoks – all red velvet cloaks and cummerbunds bristling with daggers – and the Croatian national revival, the nineteenth-century intellectual movement that laid the ground for independence. Then we reached the upper floor, where history suddenly stopped being history and turned, with shocking abruptness, into real life.

'This was the front line, just the other side of Velebit. The Chetniks, the Serbs, were only thirty kilometres from our town.' My guide was pointing to a map criss-crossed with coloured lines. With its contours and arrows it looked something like a weather map, but it showed a different sort of front. 'Our soldiers were up in the mountains, in the snow, holding them back. They never managed to surround Senj like they did in Dubrovnik. But many of us died up there.' He indicated a wall of photographs of locals who had lost their lives, grinning at the camera, their arms around one another, in combat fatigues and nineties haircuts. It looked less like a war memorial than a high school yearbook. 'That one I played with when we were children. That one was my neighbour. That one was in my class at school. It was a terrible war.'

Between 1991 and 1995 – the phase of Yugoslavia's break-up that Croatians call the Homeland War, or the Greater Serbian Aggression – between 11,000 and 16,000 of the republic's soldiers and civilians were declared dead or missing. The invading Yugoslav People's Army, dominated by Serbs and Montenegrins, used the country's mountainous topography with deadly effect: seizing high ground allowed them to surround the valleys below, devastating the cities with mortars and sniper fire. Atrocities were carried out on all sides – Croatian forces committed massacres, rapes and ethnic cleansing of their own in Bosnia and Herzegovina, notoriously destroying the ancient Ottoman bridge in Mostar – leading to reprisals as horrific as the killings they avenged. The chain reaction of these complex, interconnecting conflicts continued until NATO bombs rained down on Belgrade in 1999, forcing Serbian troops to end their genocidal campaign against ethnic Albanians in the province of Kosovo.

Kosovo is independent now, like Slovenia and Croatia, but many Serbs still see it as a spiritual homeland. As so often in the Balkans, memories run deep: it was on Kosovo Polje, 'the Field of Blackbirds', that an army of Serbs was annihilated by the Ottomans on St Vitus's Day 1389, ushering in centuries of occupation. The significance of that historical nadir threads through Serbian identity. Almost 500 years later that date was chosen by nationalists to declare war on the Ottoman Empire, beginning the independence struggle; on the same day in 1914 Gavrilo Princip assassinated Archduke Franz Ferdinand, the heir to the Habsburg throne, unwittingly plunging Europe into the First World War. And in 1989 Milošević used the occasion of the battle's 600th anniversary to deliver an infamous speech, which – with its reference to 'armed battles' which 'cannot be excluded' – was widely seen as foreshadowing the bloody wars to come.

The disputed region also gives its name to another wind: the Košava, or 'Kosovan'. It is caused by high pressure over Russia which squeezes cold air through the Iron Gates – the forbidding river gorge that separates Romania from the Balkans – and propels it at hurricane strength up the Danube, making it appear as if the river is travelling backward. Ironically for a wind whose name is so deeply meshed with Serbian nationhood, the Kosovan frequently blasts Belgrade, like a bitter reminder of land now lost; a connecting thread that links not only places, but 800 years of history.

But all that was far away from the portraits of smiling young men on the wall. I watched the museum's visitors filing in and out of the door, cupping their glasses of hot wine, examining a photograph here, a battered helmet or shell casing there, occasionally commenting on an image of someone they'd known. The clamour of the other floors was noticeably absent here. After some minutes my guide took my arm and ushered me back to the levels below; the struggles of Uskoks, Venetians and Turks, suitably softened by time, were gentler on the soul.

The next afternoon, with a spiced wine hangover, I turned my back on the sea and took the road to the mountains.

Sunday had come, and the Bora had not. The weather-predicting witches were wrong. The next stage of my journey led into the Velebit range, the chain of the Dinaric Alps that walls the wind behind its flank: a climb of about four hours to a hut called Zavižan, which – at over 5,000 feet – was the highest meteorological station in Croatia.

This, I reasoned, was a promising place to ask about wind. It was occupied, I'd been told in the dying throes of Museum Night – as the guests drunkenly trooped past cases of dog-eared taxidermied animals – by a resident meteorologist who lived there year-round, and maintained a mountain cabin for travellers to sleep in. From there I planned to walk south on the Premužićeva Trail that traces the top of the ridge, along the backbone of the range, hopefully stay another night in a second mountain cabin called Alan, and then descend back to the coast to take the boat to Rab. It would be a three-day walk, all being well.

From the village of Gornja Klada I followed red and white markers again, and it didn't take long to depart the lower world. A muffling of oak and pine enveloped the steadily climbing path and deer rattled among loose rocks, their antlers clicking on branches. Glimpses of Velebit flashed through openings in the trees; its bloated bulk rose above me like something gradually being inflated, grey with rock and black with trees, tousled with drifting vapours. After climbing for an hour I reached a layer of dense cloud, which brought about the sensation of entering a different realm. I waded upward through submarine light, condensation slapping on the wet forest floor like rain, with the muscular trunks of beech trees looming through saturated air. Deciduous trees gave way to pines. Here and there blobs of snow lay like stranded jellyfish.

And then, as if a switch had been flipped, I heard the wind.

It was huge, alarming in its size. The mountain roared like the sea. The tops of the trees were heaving, being threshed and churned about, their upper branches shrieking as they skinned each other's bark. The air was warm, sloshed with moisture from the damp forest layer, and it was coming not from the north but from above, behind, below, from every direction at the same time, driven by interlacing thermals and the topography of the slopes. Surrounded as I was by multidirectional registers of noise, it didn't seem too fanciful to imagine, as I had on Cross Fell, that the mountain was bellowing in a language of its own. Every pine tree I walked beneath had its particular inflection, its needles hissing in frequencies subtly different from the ones before – the dictionary term is 'psithurism', the noise of wind passing through leaves – an evergreen language that sounded like whispered words.

If the trees were telling me anything, it seemed to be: 'Don't go up.' The violence being inflicted on their upper bodies was immense, the trunks were writhing to the roots, and soon I would leave their protection and face the brunt myself. I paused, unnerved, below the treeline, and just as I was considering whether or not it was wise to go on I heard a very different sound: powerful respiration charging through the mist. My body tensed, half expecting the emergence of a wild boar, but through the trees hurtled instead a stocky, nut-brown man in his sixties chuffing at terrific speed, pounding the ground with his hiking poles and emitting regular snot-blasts from alternating nostrils. He whipped off a glove to shake my hand and introduced himself as Tomaš, also making for Zavižan. 'We will not be alone,' he said. 'Behind me is twenty people. Tonight will be a great feast, too much wine. They are crazy people, you will like them. There are no evil people on mountains.' From a flask he poured tea made from freshly picked mountain grass, tightened his rucksack and set off, gesturing for me to follow.

I did my best. His pace was relentless, and it was as much as I could do to keep his diminishing form in sight as we left the last of the trees and plunged into whiteness. Thick snow buried the path and suddenly I was ankle-deep, slipping and sliding in his wake, grateful for his bootprints to navigate by. A nameless gale was raging up here and visibility was appalling; a blinding white mist of ice covered everything from view. Shielding my eyes with mittened hands, I tracked his snow-bleached silhouette, and the mechanical blasts of his breath, up the final frozen slope until we reached the cabin.

It smelled of woodsmoke, soup and sweat. The walls were covered in nationalistic posters from the war against the Serbs, and a patchwork of alpinist stickers commemorating the conquest of various peaks. The moment we secured the door sleet splattered down outside, running in snotty trails down the windows; we had reached shelter just in time, and I realised that was the reason for his fearsome pace. 'The others will be cold and wet. You and me, we drink wine.' He pulled out a bottle of home-made red – it had an intensely nutty flavour, and was surprisingly delicious – cheese, and a loaf of caraway-seeded bread baked by his daughter. An ursine man in a lumberjack shirt poked his head into the room. This was the meteorologist, Ante Vukušić, whose job it was to monitor snow cover, temperature, atmospheric pressure, humidity, wind speed and other data to send every day to Zagreb for forecasting. I was keen to talk to him, but he gruffly replied he was busy; he had to prepare beds for the imminent arrival of the climbing party. We could talk later, he muttered, without enthusiasm.

After an hour the hut was transformed. Tomaš's friends had arrived at the same time as another large group – there must have been forty people in all – and the small wood-panelled room was crammed with boisterous shaven-headed men and uproarious women, swigging *rakija* like they meant it. The heat of bodies was intense. No nutritionally balanced ration packs for them: in the finest Balkan style they had scaled the mountain with bags of onions, sacks of potatoes and several chickens, and soon the smell of paprika-spiced stew had merged with the funk of steaming boots and clothes drying above the stove, until the air was so thick you could almost chew it. The tables were piled with sheep's cheese, pickles, *pršut*, cured meats, slabs of fat, and an alarming collection of home-made alcohol. I was not so much invited to join them as enveloped within their mass. I sat sandwiched between Tomaš and an enormous white-bearded man whom everyone called Santa Claus, but who acted more like a medieval warlord: between bellowing patriotic folksongs and sucking down chicken's feet, he was dancing triumphantly in the centre of the feasting hall, pounding his boots on the floor and emitting piercing whistles. The meteorologist sat by the door, looking distinctly dazed. Accustomed to spending four or five weeks alone in winter, the invasion of forty roaring drunks must have been quite a shock.

The conversation got louder, the *rakija* got stronger, and by midnight the survivors were singing nostalgic anthems from the former Yugoslavia, enthusing about how things were better under communism, when Croats, Serbs, Bosnians, Slovenes, Montenegrins and Macedonians were one. A cat-eyed man with prematurely white hair told me that all modern politicians – left and right, old and young – should be lined up against a wall and shot. 'Corruption, corruption and more corruption. That's what capitalism has brought.' Switching tack, he asked what I thought of the current refugee crisis, but didn't wait to hear my answer before delivering his verdict: 'Their war has been going on for years. Why have Syrians waited until now to come in such big numbers? Because Muslim leaders are sending them here, young men and young girls, to have babies. It is a plan to make Europe into a Muslim continent.' I attempted a rational argument – quite apart from anything else, the *logistics* of such a conspiracy seemed mind-bogglingly complicated – but of course rationality was not the issue. His ridiculous theory was easy to laugh off, but he followed it up with something I found harder to dismiss; and which brought me back, again, to Croatia's war-torn past. 'When the Serbs came to take *our* land, we did not run away. We did not leave our country. We stayed to fight, and we won. Young men in Syria should stay to fight Assad, stay to fight Isis, not run away. That is why I do not respect them coming here.'

Again I attempted to argue – argument becomes automatic after a certain amount of *rakija* – but found myself on less certain ground. This man had lived through a war himself, like most of the others in the room; having known only peace and stability, I was the misfit here. Unlike me, he viewed migration through the prism of invasion – an existential threat to a nation's integrity, which, in contrast to western Europe, was largely based on ethnicity – and while I might not have agreed with his views, I could understand that they were produced by fundamentally different circumstances. Like the other countries of the Balkans, Croatian identity is bound up with a folk memory of invasion stretching back hundreds of years, something I was reminded of when I asked about the T-shirt several people wore: the words *I ja sem Legenda*, 'I am Legend', above the image of a stylised rooster. 'When the Turks invaded, our village resisted, and they tried to starve us,' I was told. 'For months we got more and more hungry, eating all the food we had, until there was only one rooster left. But instead of eating it, someone had the idea of putting it in a cannon and firing it at the Turkish camp. When the Turks saw that, they gave up. "These people have so much food they are using it as ammunition!" So our village was saved, and our neighbours have called us Roosters from that time.'

Another round of drunken singing ended the conversation. War, migration and invasion vanished as people started dancing – or more accurately swaying, bear-hugging and bumping into one another – and when they settled down again the room's configuration had changed. I didn't see the cat-eyed man again, and found myself talking instead to a young sailor from the island of Vis, in the far south of the country, who had heard I was interested in stories of the wind. He told me how the Bora and Jugo, opposing powers from the north and south, played tug-of-war with the life of his island, dominating its psyche. 'In Jugo you feel like you have high fever, you can't work, breathe, move. People feel crazy. Their bodies hurt, their bones hurt. In Bura you are frozen to ice, but you feel alive. The fishing boats cannot sail. Women can predict which wind is coming because their hair changes direction.'

As the raucousness wound down, he recounted a mournful legend: that the Bora was caused by the grief-stricken sighs of a beautiful girl thrown into hell for her vanity. 'It is said you should never curse the wind, or you will finish up like her.' As a bedtime story, or a cautionary tale, it was an end to the night.

I woke up cramped on a wooden bench among the dregs of the party. Santa Claus was snoring in a nest of empty bottles. Stepping outside to clear my head, away from the stench of sleeping men, I came upon the meteorologist tending his garden of instruments – rain gauges, totalisers, evaporimeters, anemometers, weather vanes – collecting data like a beekeeper taking honey from his hives. Quiet and intense in his work, wrapped in his privacy, his diligence was a world away from the chaos of the night before. It didn't seem right to disturb him. After breakfast – gritty coffee and the remains of chicken stew – Tomaš attempted for the third or fourth time to encourage him to speak with me, but again he ducked away. It was hard to know whether he was shy, suspicious or obscurely hostile; whatever the reason, I resigned myself to his knowledge remaining hidden. As we prepared to leave Zavižan, it seemed ironic that the only person who didn't want to talk about the weather was the meteorologist.

Conditions had not improved overnight. In fact they were even worse. The top of the mountain was enveloped in a bellowing white cloud, with muscular blasts of wind driving horizontal sleet. The trail I'd planned to take led along the top of the ridge, directly into the blizzard, and Tomaš shook his head. 'You will never find the path. It is not a good place to be alone.' So with a blend of relief and reluctance I agreed to return with him to the lower world.

Halfway down the mountain, however, we came to a crossroads. Branching off was a smaller trail that appeared to lead along the mountain's flank, protected by thick forest, to arrive at Alan, the next hut, by a more sheltered route. 'I will walk with you for thirty minutes,' Tomaš said sceptically. 'If it looks possible you can go on. If not, we both turn back.' And then he charged down the trail even faster than before, forcing me to almost double my pace. We walked for much longer than thirty minutes; an hour, then two hours passed as I panted after him, crashing through beech trees thick with moss, up and down root-tangled slopes. Occasionally he paused to marvel at some wonder we came across: an area that had once been paddocks, with dew ponds and huge stone walls, evidence that these mountains had supported a sizeable population – 'People lived here to escape the Turks, the Venetians, the Austrians. Life was hard, but they were free' – and patches of recently upturned earth where wild boars had scavenged for roots. 'There are wolves here too, but you won't see them – and the bears are asleep until spring.' But he never allowed us to stop for long, and after two and a half hours, when he halted suddenly, I realised that we must be almost halfway to Alan.

'Do you have food? Water?'

'Yes.'

'Matches to make fire?'

'Yes.'

'Wine?'

'No . . .'

'You must have wine!' He handed me a battered plastic bottle. 'This is for the end of the day. The path is good. You will make it.'

We shook hands and he bounded away. Within seconds I was alone. It struck me belatedly that the ferocious pace he'd set had given me a terrific head start, and perhaps even been a test of endurance to make sure I was fit enough. His confidence in me felt like a blessing, and tempered my respectful fear at being on my own again, deep in the snowy forest, responsible once more for my own fate.

Twenty minutes later the trail vanished without a trace.

In increasing disbelief I searched for a smear of red paint, brushing snow away from rocks, and only ended up with aching frozen fingers. I trampled icy undergrowth for the faintest hint of a path, but there was nothing. It had simply disappeared. All I could find was an arrow with the word 'Rossi', which was the name of a smaller shelter midway between the others. It was already afternoon, cloud was descending thickly, and it was too cold to stand around for long. My confidence significantly rattled, I set off up the unknown trail as soupy whiteness poured downhill, reducing the trees to blurred stumps swimming past on either side. Soon I was deep in snow once more, winding up and down difficult slopes, dizzy at times from lack of breath, and my boots were sodden. In one steep pit between valley walls fallen trunks brought down by the wind had created an obstacle like a cage, the bars of which were too tight to squeeze through, forcing me to remove my rucksack and push it ahead of me while I crawled. In another place I waded through snowdrifts thigh- and sometimes waist-deep, continually pitching forward to plunge up to my elbows in snow, my mittens now as soaked as my boots. Miraculously the painted markers remained inches above the snowline – each flash of red was a small salvation – but I expected the trail to vanish at any moment.

Climbing higher, beyond the treeline that had protected me all day, conditions got bleaker. I was back on the outskirts of the gale, on the exposed ridge of the mountain exactly where I'd been warned not to be, and still there was no sign of the hut. 'It is not a good place to be alone,' Tomaš had said, and it wasn't. I advanced through a blizzard of boiling white dust, the wind driving furious veils of spindrift into my face and eyes, rushing me in flurried gusts from every direction at once. It started to feel impossible, but I couldn't go back; it wasn't long until dark and camping in those frozen woods, soaked, was not an option. All I could do was keep trudging on, angling one boot after the other, trusting blindly in the hut's existence. And just when exhaustion and despair were rising inside me in panicky waves, the hazy outline of a roof appeared, vanished and reappeared through the cloud. I actually pressed my hands together in prayer. There came one final moment of horror when I thought the iron door was locked, but this alchemised to joy when it swung to let me in.

It was a cleaner, more compact version of the bothy at Cross Fell. A table and benches of sturdy pine dominated the one small room, and a ladder led to a sleeping platform high in the rafters. There was a well choked with ice, half a dozen candles, some blankets and most importantly a stove and a pile of kindling. Once I'd got a fire blazing, removed my slush-sodden boots and clothes, it became quite cosy. I brewed coffee, ate spaghetti and cheese, and savoured the excellent nutty wine that was Tomaš's parting gift. My world shrank to the distance of four walls. Outside was crashing, sucking blackness; the wind head-butted the door and pounded the shutters like a brute, attacked the roof with hammer blows. Stepping out for a piss before bed was like being physically abused. It was a night that wanted to kill me. I lit a protective circle of candles and huddled in its light.

After draining the wine I fell asleep, wrapped in heavy blankets. The first thing I saw when I opened my eyes was the full moon goggling through mist, and then, when I opened them again later, shreds of a blue and orange sky. Overjoyed at the implications, I rushed outside to catch a glimpse of the plunging opposite slope, studded with rocks and pines. Within seconds the vision had vanished again, tauntingly snatched away by cloud, but it was enough to confirm, at least, that this mountain had visible slopes from which it was possible to descend, and that the mad white storm was finally boiling away. I swept out the cabin, lined my boots with plastic bags and set out through an amber haze, confidence restored.

I had hit the Premužićeva Trail, the metre-wide stone-paved track running the length of Velebit through the most beautiful part of the mountains, an entirely different species of path to yesterday's obstacle course. Though sections were buried under snow where it ran through hollows and lees, and slick with ice in some places, it was simple enough to follow. Along the bare line of the ridge it wound through an airy realm of pines and protruding contortions of rock – 'the hips of the mountain', someone back in Zavižan had called them – then plunged back into snowbound woods hopping with tiny birds. The sun burst out, turning the snow into a sparkling crystal field intercrossed by animal tracks – the cloven hoofs of deer and boar, the canine prints of wolves, perhaps – to which I destructively added my own, lurching and sinking. The beech trunks steamed in the light. When the view opened up the cloud was finally pouring away in thick, smoky tufts, like something being exorcised. The snow gave way to lank yellow grass, and to the west appeared islands scattered on a golden sea, across which ships scored tiny wakes. The expansion of vision was startling. The sky was dazzling blue.

Two hours later I reached Alan, my aborted goal of the previous day, made myself coffee and moved on, following the fall of the mountain. Now that I was on the descent it felt sad to leave the snowy woods, with their stippling of tracks; it was a starker, stonier world that lay beneath my feet. The trail plummeted into a region of towering pinnacles, turrets and whalebacks of bare rock, the limestone erupting from the earth as if staging one last uprising before dropping into the Adriatic. Presently I found myself in a mountain range below a mountain range, a dramatic upheaval of rock sluiced, gouged and carved by rain, the runnels leaving flint-sharp edges as if the stone had been knapped. The sun's heat funnelled through the ravines, and the air was so still that my ears rang with the silence. The bony, reptilian casts of the treeless islands below – steep-sided Rab, barren Pag and the smaller Goli Otok – loitered offshore like an alien fleet, streamlined and purposeful. The ground was so densely littered with rocks it looked like the sky had rained meteorites. Reaching sea level again I turned to look back at Velebit – that vast, intimidating barricade rising in two separate tiers – and then resigned myself to the coast. It was a smaller world.

That night I found another bed in Croatia's lowest mountain hut, a rather mournful tin-roofed house with lemon trees growing in its garden, overlooking the soporific harbour of Jablanac. The tiny village was populated only by the elderly, and a pair of ragged white dogs that set up a slow, booming bark every time they caught sight of me, even from great distances. A very old sailor took half an hour to shuffle from one side of the harbour to the other, and that was the most exciting event of the evening. I fell asleep in a mousy bunk bed to the sound of lapping waves, and followed a rocky path the next morning to the port of Stinica, arriving just as the Rab ferry nudged alongside the quay.

I was entering my journey's last stage. Having walked the Karst and the coast, climbed the mountains to the highest weather station in the land, and poked my head into one after another of the Bora's mouths, I was still no closer to finding my desired wind. I had heard only whispers, rumours. Rab and Pag lay on my route as two more landmarks of the trail, but also because, quite honestly, I didn't know where else to go. The trail had gone . . . well, warm. The wind was simply blowing the wrong way, and there was no sign of it changing.

My flattened mood was oddly suited to the crossing of that sea. The receding hump of Velebit was veiled in a gauze of cloud, giving it the two-dimensional look of a film backdrop. The sea and the sky were engaged in their best impressions of one another, each limply reflecting its opposite, as if neither wanted to stick out. The other passengers on the ferry conversed in muted tones, their faces wooden. The waves offered no resistance. It took less time to cross the channel than it had taken the ancient sailor to cross the harbour the night before, but leaving the mountains for the islands felt like exile.

For many this journey had meant not merely exile but death. The Italian Fascists used Rab as a concentration camp in the war, interning Slovenes, Croats and Jews from the newly captured territories, and thousands died of disease and starvation; in 1943 the Germans took over, transporting the remaining Jews to the gas chambers of Auschwitz. After the war the camp was closed, but the communist authorities of Tito's Yugoslavia continued from where their wartime enemies had left off: in 1949 a prison and labour camp was constructed on nearby Goli Otok – the name means 'Naked Island' – and over the next forty years a total of 16,000 political prisoners were incarcerated there. Conditions were brutal, with a regime of forced labour and frequent beatings; exposure to the freezing Bora added to the misery. Hundreds died, many of them murdered by other inmates. This was the dark underside of Titoism, belying its carefully fostered image as a kinder, gentler version of communism than the regime exemplified by the gulags of Soviet Russia.

At first glance Rab looked as bleak as its past. The eastern portion of the island resembled a bleached yellow moonscape, its horizons interrupted by pylons and incongruous billboards advertising holiday resorts. Attuned by now to such clues, I recognised the Bora's handiwork, and wasn't surprised to learn that the island had once been dense with trees (its ancient name, Arba, meant 'Black', from the forests that covered it), before they were felled for timber used in Venetian galleys. That cover stripped, the bitter wind – as well as rapacious flocks of sheep – ensured that its surface remained as naked as Goli Otok. But during my haul along the coast I discovered that Rab was an island of two halves, bisected between yellow and green. While the eastern, Bora-facing side was arid, the western side, sheltered by hills, was verdant with cypresses, olives, palms and stubby forests of holm oak, with villages tucked along the coast. It gave the impression that every life form, whether plant, animal or human, was cowering out of the Bora's reach, trying desperately not to be noticed.

The main town was also called Rab. I reached it at the close of day, feet stinging from the long road: a tightly packed peninsula settlement built on a honeycombed sandstone shelf, surrounded by massive sea-fronting walls. Every shop was shuttered and closed. The alleyways were possessed by cats and little girls having bicycle races down deserted lanes. I wandered through a muddle of ochre streets, past Romanesque churches and profusions of leathery maguey cactus, resting under the giant holm oak in Trg Slobode, Freedom Square. The pink and white striped cathedral nearby was said to contain the crowned skull of Christophorus, the island's patron saint, who saved the town from invading Normans during a battle in 1075 by turning their arrows back at them in the air. The story sounded suspiciously like events at the Frigid River, and I spent some time investigating: the Norman ships would have come from the south, the only possible approach to the town, so a Bora blasting from the north would have done the saint's job for him. But when I enquired about ferry times in the ticket office on the quay, I was abruptly reminded of *the other wind*, whose name I was sick of hearing. 'The forecast says Jugo tomorrow, it might last a couple of days. The catamaran will not sail. If you want to get to Pag you must take the boat this evening.' Once again cursing all things southern, I took the woman's advice.

The catamaran came in on time, sliding sleekly on the water. I was the only passenger boarding, walking the gangway against the flow of disembarking families loaded with supplies from Rijeka. The boat leapt away with the last of the light and the slender blade of Pag slid past, starker and stonier even than Rab, a knife in the gathering darkness. Four winters previously, during the East European Cold Wave that had frozen the harbour at Senj, that shoreline had seen a Bora so fierce that fish were hurled from the sea and littered dead upon the beaches like a sign of apocalypse. The bridge that tethers the island's south to the mainland regularly records wind speeds of over 100 miles per hour, and another bridge nearby, spanning the Maslenica Strait, holds the local record of 154. On an evening as still as this, it seemed the stuff of legends. Wind warning signs were scattered the length of the road from Novalja, where the catamaran docked, to the main settlement of Pag town; I arrived long after dark to the glimmer of lights around water. Desperately hungry, I tramped up and down the deserted streets in search of food, but takeaway after takeaway was in out-of-season hibernation. Dinner was miso soup, which I heated on my camping stove crouched on my guest-house balcony, keeping the flame low so the landlady didn't hear it.

I expected to hear the south wind in the night, but the pressures must have changed. Even the anticipated Jugo had failed to arrive. I woke with a heavy head and a sense of despair. Pag achieved the difficult task of looking even more desolate by daylight than it did in darkness; awaiting me when I opened my eyes was a hard-edged, monotonal town squeezed between a shallow bay and a brackish plain of saltpans, hemmed by devastated hills that offered no shade or shelter. It was a sloped stone desert, scoured of life. Still hungry from the night before I bought a lump of *Paški sir*, the intensely salty local cheese that gains its flavour from herbs and grasses artisanally sea-salted by the Bora – another food, like Karst *pršut*, dependent on wind for its quality – and gnawed it disconsolately as I wandered towards the harbour. The cheese, admittedly, was very good, but Pag was dismal. Its harbourside was dominated by a hulking salt warehouse – salt production and salty cheese being the main industries here – and roads and turbines blighted the hills, as if they weren't scarred enough already.

The quayside was deserted – no boats, no birds – and my body drifted listlessly to a standstill by the water. The winds had left me, north and south. I was in the doldrums.

The doldrums is a windless limbo where the spirits languish. The word comes from the Old English *dol*, meaning 'dull' or 'stupid', but it refers to an actual place as well as a state of mind. The meteorological name for this region is the Intertropical Convergence Zone: an area of low pressure wallowing along the Equator, created by air expanding and rising in the heat. Its location isn't fixed but depends on the passage of the sun, shifts in ocean temperature and the way that air masses in the northern and southern hemispheres converge and interact; it has been dubbed a wandering 'equator of the winds'. Low pressure means stagnant air, with hardly a breeze to disturb it; sailing ships can find themselves becalmed for days or even weeks. The diary of one J.T. Morris gives an account of being stuck in the doldrums on an emigrant ship called the *Strathallan*, en route to New Zealand in 1859:

> Becalmed all day. Starling came on board, and a hawk. Several whales about the ship . . . Dead calm still. A woman died this

morning. Funeral at half-past 4 . . . Fine morning. Becalmed, looking out for the Trades . . . Wet. Buckley and Tobin fought. Becalmed all day . . . Becalmed. A large ship in sight all day and yesterday . . . Becalmed still. Ship still in sight. Very hot. Sharks' fins in sight . . . Shark for breakfast fried in butter. Shark for tea stewed in vinegar. Very light winds all day. Ship still in sight . . . Pickles sent to prison for 12 hours. The 30th day since we saw land . . . Mrs Kohn's child died this morning. Funeral at half-past 4 . . . Becalmed all day, the sea as smooth as a sheet of glass . . .

In a curious spiritual text entitled *The Doldrums, Christ and the Plantanism*, philosopher Rogelio Garcia Barcala describes his own experience: 'The heat, of course, is very intense, the waters so quiet, almost no wind, and your body experiences a strange feeling, a very rare sensation . . . Everybody is conscious that something unusual pushes you down. It is not the heat from the Sun, it is something else, a kind of vacuum . . .' After experiencing this, he says, 'you are not the same person, but somebody else'. But the most famous description of the madness induced by windlessness comes from Coleridge; cursed for killing an albatross, the doldrums is the punishment inflicted on his Ancient Mariner:

> Day after day, day after day,
> We stuck, nor breath nor motion;
> As idle as a painted ship
> Upon a painted ocean.
>
> Water, water, everywhere,
> And all the boards did shrink.
> Water, water, everywhere,
> Nor any drop to drink.

The very deep did rot: O Christ!
That ever this should be!
Yea, slimy things did crawl with legs
Upon the slimy sea.

The doldrums, though, are not the only breathless region of the sea; the Intertropical Convergence Zone is bordered to the north and south by subtropical highs known as the 'horse latitudes'. These areas of high pressure, generated when the air that has soared upward from the Equator cools and plunges earthwards again, stretch in two long bands around the globe, creating the world's major deserts – the Sahara, Arabian, Kalahari, Mojave, Sonora, Atacama and Australian – as well as corresponding deadly calms over the oceans. The name may derive from Spanish crews, becalmed when crossing the Atlantic, throwing their horses overboard when water supplies ran low. The image of dead and dying horses bobbing in a millpond sea just about encapsulated what I thought of Pag.

I waited on a bench by the harbour, wondering where to go from here. My mouth was parched with cheese. My journey had come to a windless lull. There was no path ahead.

Then I checked my emails for the first time in five days.

'Hello Nick. How are you? Tomorrow could be Bura here.' It was a message from Damir, the leather-jacketed sailor from Senj. I checked the date; it was sent yesterday. I fell upon the forecasts.

Damir was half right. The readings for Senj showed wild fluctuations between strong northerlies, which were good, and strong southerlies, which were not; a classic, bipolar struggle between Bora and Jugo. But as I checked further down the coast – scanning isotachs and isobars, counting the notches on wind barbs, manically thumbing the screen of my phone – I became increasingly excited: Zadar and Šibenik were more promising, Split was even better. Strong, cold, consistent winds were predicted from the north-east at forty, fifty, sixty, then seventy miles per hour, with hurricane-strength gusts of up to eighty. By morning a Yellow Warning ('Be Aware') would be in place, with the potential for promotion to the more threatening Orange ('Be Prepared'). It looked like the Bora was coming to Split. But Split was a hundred miles south. I stopped checking weather forecasts, and switched to bus timetables.

Fleeing the salty desolation of Pag, I reached Split four hours later. The long line of the Dinaric Mountains shadowed my journey along the coast, culminating in the crumpled, hazy peaks of the Mosor range; suburbs and industrial zones spilled across the narrow plain between the foothills and the sea, while the city's more ancient portion abutted the Adriatic. One of this coastline's oldest cities – and Croatia's second biggest today – Split was settled by Greeks and Romans, sacked by invading Avars and Slavs, and served its time respectively in the tussling empires of Byzantines, Venetians, Austrians, Napoleonic French and Italians. This sense of historical gravity lends a certain weight today; there was a feeling of grit and purpose that I liked, after the slumbering islands. The bus deposited me near the harbour, lined with oily fishing trawlers and ferries built for serious sea travel, not just pottering down the coast. The waterfront promenade had suffered some grand renovation – with its millennial street furniture, palm trees and anglepoise streetlights it looked like an architect's diagram – but was reassuringly grounded by the locals smoking and walking their dogs, the groups of gossiping old men, the purple faces of the drunks arguing on benches.

Turning inwards from the sea, I passed between the high walls and narrow alleys of the old town, under arches and pigeon-fouled buttresses, enjoyably lost in a warren of streets spreading from the cannibalised remains of Diocletian's Palace. Still remarkably intact after seventeen centuries, this sprawling complex of villas, temples, courtyards, barracks and perimeter walls was built as a retirement home for the former emperor – scourge of Persians and Sarmatians, persecutor of Christians, cabbage farmer in his old age – but has long since been absorbed into the city that surrounds it. Among the pitted limestone lanes it was hard to tell where the palace ended and where it began; later aeons of construction clung like a parasitic growth. Outside the city walls an old man, with superstitious compulsion, was rubbing the great bronze toe on the statue of Gregory of Nin – a medieval bishop who championed the Croatian language over Latin – a custom performed so many times that it was burnished gold.

This ritual is thought to bring luck. Perhaps we were going to need it. Above the mountains disturbed clouds rolled in ominous masses of grey, vaster than the city, vaster than the sea. I went wandering again and found myself back at the same spot. The man was still rubbing away. The wind was rising.

I located a cosy, sheltered room at the base of Marjan Hill, the forested peninsula at the city's western point. Shutters banged and windowpanes rattled like teeth as I fell asleep. Something big was in the air. The walls knew it was coming.

You wait three weeks for a Bora, then two come along at once.

The first one woke me at five in the morning, and it was Black. There was a bellowing in the streets, and gobs of rain smacked down like ripe fruit; a few plucky passers-by staggered beneath umbrellas. 'Bora?' I called to the nearest one, who ploughed onwards without response, but the next raised his head. '*Crna Bura!*' he yelled. 'Black Bora!' This was the rarer variety, which I had not expected to meet – caused by a centre of low pressure in the southern Adriatic known as a Genoa Low, bringing dark skies instead of clarity – but whatever its colour its strength was enough to heave me backward in the street. Half asleep, wrapped in waterproofs, I waded through the air. The city was newly populated by sounds that had moved in overnight – the rolling and scraping of displaced objects, the jangle of masts from the marina, water surging everywhere – and cars crawled down the road with wipers blindly thrashing. The wind came in short, aggressive gusts, rushing thuggishly through the streets; stepping around certain corners was like being shoved by invisible assailants. Dodging shrapnel, I climbed the steps, rapidly turning to waterfalls, that led to the top of Marjan Hill, conscious only of wanting to be exposed beneath the sky. At the summit a concrete plateau rose above flailing pines. The Croatian flag on its pole roared like an uncontrolled fire, convulsed by violent ripples. Scaling a wall to see the sea, I was at once thrown off again. It was too strong to stand against; too strong even to look at. My lips and eyebrows were numb with cold. I was stupidly happy.

Then the Black Bora departed, and the White Bora took its place.

The first thing I knew of this transition was the change in the light. The dark clouds suddenly fled, leaving clarity in their wake. Villages that were invisible before leapt into focus on distant coastlines, every detail picked out cleanly, and the horizon went from a smudge of crayon to a sharp pencil line. The sea was lucent, silver-flecked, the waves driven offshore like animal fur smoothed the wrong way; giant cat's-paws ruffled the surface, spreading fanwise to the south. Turning inland I saw, with shock, a monstrous snow-covered mountain that hadn't been there before. It appeared to swell as I looked, growing brighter and bolder in all dimensions, as the ranked apartment blocks shrank before its size. It might have been Hyperborea – the mythical land that the ancient Greeks believed lay 'beyond Boreas' somewhere in the far north, a place of perfection and purity – but as the vision consolidated I realised it was Mosor. Yesterday it had been brown; now it was blinding white.

At the bottom of the hill the citizens of Split were inspecting the damage, walking their dogs, scurrying from shop to shop clutching supplies to their chests. Workers were out with rush brooms, sweeping away the debris. Pigeons rattled in disturbed flocks, keeping close against the walls. Everything had been disarranged, the very air unsettled. I bumped into my landlady, who was in an exuberant mood. 'That was Black Bura, now we have White. You should climb Mosor this afternoon – when Bura blows, you can see Italy. Take a bus to Gornje Sitno and keep going up . . .'

The following day, in dazzling sunshine, I would see crowds surge through these streets for the start of carnival. Children in fancy dress – superheroes, devils, pirates, witches, soldiers, punks, princesses – would process through the crumbling lanes, and bands of masked and antlered mummers, with cowbells clanging from their waists, would perform a slow and sinister dance to the drone of goatskin bagpipes. These pagan Zvončari, whose task it was to hasten spring and drive away evil spirits – invading Moors and Turks included – were the shaggy monster-men of the mountainous hinterland, stamping and snorting their way down upon the civilised coast. I would see the city transformed, the well-behaved giving way to the wild, stirred to passion as much by the wind as the Resurrection.

But for now I was heading to Mosor, and my appointment with the Bora. I took a bus through the outlying suburbs and into the Dinaric Alps, where streams tumbled under bridges and vineyards terraced the slopes. It was a new white world up here. Gornje Sitno was the highest village, the end of the road. Six inches of powder snow squeaked under my boots as I climbed, snowballing at the tips of the laces, making lion's tails. The snow had favoured the windward side of every leaf and blade of grass, while tree trunks and telephone poles were vertically scored with a furred white line angled precisely north-east, as if magnetised to a new pole. The world had been perfectly bisected, divided between spring and winter.

Sheltered by the slope at first, I could only hear it. But then I reached the top, and the Bora was upon me.

It was on my skin, freezing my face, blizzarding into my eyes. My eyelashes were frosted, my beard stiff with ice. I made the mistake of removing my mittens and my fingers throbbed so much it felt as if they'd been slammed in a door. The chill of it pushed me back, forced me to proceed in a crouch, as if advancing under fire. Or as if I was bowing.

It was in my ears, but it wasn't blowing; nor was it moaning, whistling, howling, or any of the other words usually used to capture wind. It was less a sound than a sensation, a nameless energetic *thing* that erased the line between hearing and feeling; for the first time in my life, I understood sound as a physical force. It was in my lungs, under my skin. Like a religious maniac, I roared my appreciation.

The Bora roared right back at me, and the mountainside ignited. An eighty-mile-per-hour blast lifted veils of powder snow, frozen spindrift that swirled like smoke, spinning itself into ice tornadoes that leapt from slope to slope before blowing apart again in mists of agitated dust. It happened again and again as I watched, each white eruption spreading and merging to create gyrating clouds that travelled as fast as a forest fire, hurtling down the mountain. The Bora's face was visible in each fleeting pattern of snow, each convolution and curlicue, each vortex, twist and coil. I saw the invisible appear, the formless given form.

What did the Bora say to me, on that frozen mountainside? I could not read its words. Its language was too large.

FOEHN

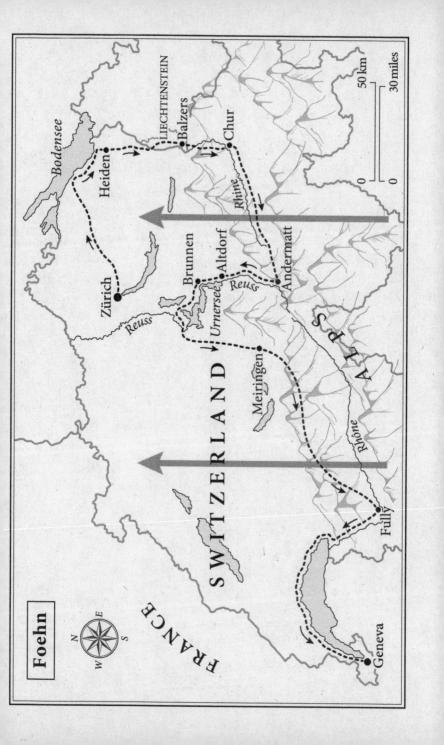

If one is a native of the mountains, one can study
philosophy or natural history for years and do away
with the God of old, and yet as one feels the *Föhn*
approach once more or hears an avalanche break
through the thicket, your heart throbs in your breast
and your thoughts turn to God and to death.

Hermann Hesse

As I crossed Place de la République a man was doling out free
hugs next to the memorial to the Bataclan massacre. I submitted
and was enveloped in his chubby, patchouli-scented warmth,
before hurrying on to catch my train from the Gare de Lyon.
Paris looked bleak, with grey-faced people frowning down graffitied streets. The only people wearing smiles seemed to be the
Gypsies.

On the fold-out table of the TGV I attempted, for the sixth
or seventh time, to plan the route of my next walk on a 1:300,000
scale map of Switzerland. Riven with valleys, intricately wrin-
kled, its fractals of purple mountain chains branching and
subdividing, the topographical complexity confounded me once
again; it resembled less a potential journey than the lobes and
hemispheres of a brain, sprawling and shapeless. I'd been studying it for weeks, and still it made no sense to me. My train was
bound for Zürich – a city picked more or less randomly as a

gateway to the Alps – but beyond that my journey's trajectory was uncertain.

My third wind was the Foehn (Föhn in its native German spelling), which dominates the Alpine valleys as winter turns to spring. It is a warm, dry katabatic wind – meaning it blows downslope as opposed to anabatic, upslope – that lends its name to a genera: other 'foehn-type' winds include the Chinook of the Rocky Mountains, the Santa Ana of California, Poland's Halny, South Africa's Bergwind and even the Helm of Cross Fell, a diminutive English cousin. But the Foehn of the Alps is the original, and the most notorious. I'd mentioned it to a friend from Hamburg and her immediate response had been: 'Ah yes, Foehn, that's why everyone in Bavaria is crazy.' Associated with causing migraines, anxiety, depression and even suicides, and a contributing factor to the raging wildfires that sweep the resinous forests of the Alps, it is also linked to clear skies, warmth and the end of winter.

This turning point between the seasons is described in Hermann Hesse's *Peter Camenzind*, a *Bildungsroman* about a young man from a fictional Alpine village. Introverted and melancholic, the protagonist breaks free from the conservatism and narrow-mindedness of his provincial home, and throws himself into the world on a quest for experience and knowledge. His intellectual and spiritual pursuits, and doomed love affairs, lead him to Italy, a world away from the austerity of his native land, and the roaring of the Foehn is a soundtrack to this journey:

> In childhood days, I was afraid of the *Föhn*; I even hated it. But with the dawn of my adolescent wildness, I grew to love this rebel, this perennially young, insolent fighter; the herald of Spring. It was glorious to see it embark on its mad career, full of life, exuberance and hope, raging, laughing, moaning,

howling down the gulleys, whipping the snow from the mountains, bending the tough old pines in its strong hands, wresting great sighs from them . . . It is the South hurling itself with all its heat and violence against the breast of the poorer, inflexible North, announcing the news to the snow-covered Alpine villages that primroses, narcissi and almond trees are once again in flower by the shores of the not too far distant purple lakes of Italy.

My journey began in late March, just as the snow was beginning to thaw, and I hoped to catch it at the right time; I just didn't quite know where. Folding away the map I lost myself in Hesse's words, hoping the route would fall into place with my first few steps of walking.

It was night by the time I arrived. Zürich's station was a palette of dark silvers and greys above an expanse of polished floor, booming with echoes. Two uniformed conscripts with 1940s haircuts sat smoking at a station bar while a third ran for his train, hoiking an automatic weapon like an awkward piece of luggage; despite its famous neutrality, Switzerland, which enforces military service for all able-bodied men, is paradoxically one of the most heavily armed countries in Europe. I crossed the river to the old town, stopping at a beerhall with a meat-heavy menu of *schnitzel*, *bratwurst* and the horribly named *rindfleisch*, the clientele as lumpen as the food they shovelled down. When my meal came I thought there had been a mistake: the burger I'd ordered was smothered by an egg and drenched in sauce the colour of boot polish, and what I'd expected to be chips was a mound of potato hash sizzling with cheese. The cuisine alone was a certain sign that this was the German quarter of Switzerland, a culinary world away from the French or Italian regions. After chomping through this stodge I located a hostel down the road, but it was a restless night; the dormitory was

haunted by a squat golem plagued by chronic breathing prob-
lems, who spent hours gulping and gasping, and in some
moments practically choking, in the bunk below. I left in the
grey light of dawn, having slept almost as badly as him.

Zürich came to life mildly, its streets full of sensible cyclists
and fresh-faced businesspeople who undoubtedly spent their
weekends skiing and snowboarding. My impression was of a
functional city of jutting, angular spires, gilt clock faces like
giant Rolexes and a distinctly Germanic predilection for heraldic flair: a bronze stork here, an iron stag's head there, rampant
lions clutching swords and quills, and someone had even painted
eyes on the mooring posts along the river, turning them into
exhibits from a bestiary too. But these streets were too far from
the mountains to feel the fierce effects of the Foehn. I retraced
my steps to the station and took the first train east.

A plan had emerged earlier, as I breakfasted on pretzels. A
helpful contact at MeteoSwiss – Switzerland's federal meteorological institute, which has kept meticulous weather records
since 1863 – had suggested I start my hunt in the Rheintal Valley
to the east, indicating a possible Foehn in the coming week. If I
followed the valley south, slicing deeply into the Alps, I could
cross the mountains westwards at the Oberalp Pass and follow a
second Foehn valley – the Reuss – north again to Lake Lucerne,
or Vierwaldstättersee. Continuing with this strategy, tracing
valleys south, north and south, would allow me to zigzag my
way across the country without risking the high peaks, which,
at this time of year, were perilous with snow. A pattern was
beginning to form in the map's complexity, and three major
rivers stood out as conduits to carry me west: the Rhine, the
Reuss and the Rhône, a pleasing alliteration.

Villages of conformist houses and the flat, featureless fields of
Switzerland's uninspiring lowlands swept past for half an hour
as the train rushed towards Bodensee, known in English as

Lake Constance. This vast body of water, which forms part of Switzerland's border with Germany and Austria, is really a bloated expansion of the Rhine, which empties into the plains from its Alpine headwaters as if pausing to gather strength before its 500-mile journey to the North Sea. When I disembarked at Romanshorn the lake was enveloped in white mist, the villages of Baden-Württemberg oblique on the German shore. The plastic wind mobiles were still. Flags drooped like dishcloths. Once again – it was becoming a theme – my journey had begun on an utterly windless day.

I walked east along the shore, following the friendly yellow signs of a *Wanderweg*, or walking path – as frequent in Switzerland as cycle paths in the Netherlands – through neighbourhoods of bungalows, allotments and static caravan parks. It was a prim, suburban start, the neatly bordered gardens peopled by gnomes, woodland animals, porcelain cherubs and stone Buddha heads, kitscher descendants of Zürich's heraldic devices. By midday I was eating potato salad in the ancient town of Arbon – a motley clutter of timber-framed houses four or five storeys high, painted in greens, blues and reds, with heavy Gothic lettering and shutters loudly striped – and by late afternoon was approaching Rorschach, my first hint of higher ground.

The foothills above the town were patched with snow, white on black, like reversed ink-blot tests. Even though I'd been waiting keenly for a glimpse of mountains all day, that intimation of what lay beyond produced a small thump of fright. Those snowy slopes announced the beginning of the Appenzell Hills, which lay between me and the Rheintal Valley.

Half an hour's climb above Rorschach I simultaneously reached first snow, first sun and first sweat. The trail twisted through mossy woods to emerge into untrodden white fields, pastures where flocks of sheep clanged their bells in a satisfyingly Alpine way. Wood-shingled farmhouses now appeared on the slopes, spreading smoke and the comforting stench of live-stock and manure. Looking back I saw the cloud that had smothered the lake all day being rolled away in a thick white wave, exposing fragments of Germany lying in disorder beyond, like something waiting to be put back together. After two hours of rising and falling on the meanders of the trail I crested the final hill to see the village of Heiden, my destination for that night, a cluster of wooden houses lit by pale sunlight.

I had called ahead to book a room, and found my way to a tumbledown chalet with Harley-Davidson signs on the walls and an uproar of dogs within. No one was home, but a voice on the phone guided me to a hidden key, and through a series of corridors – 'Ahead of you is the door to the kitchen. You can use the kitchen. Beyond that is the door to the dogs. Do not go to the dogs' – to a cosy pine-panelled room with heavy blankets on the bed and a complimentary Toblerone, which I ate at once. Exhausted from those fifteen miles, I stretched out and closed my eyes. When I opened them night had come, and the moon was almost full. I stuck out my head to feel the air. There was still not a breath of wind.

In Switzerland there are two types of Foehn, and the division is emblematic of the divided country itself; that unlikely confederation of twenty-six autonomous cantons, containing over 2,500 communes, each operating largely in isolation from its neighbours. But the biggest division is topographical: Europe's greatest mountain range erupts through the middle of the land, heaving its two halves apart, separating not only languages and cultures but weather too. The Nordföhn, North Foehn, blows from the north down the southern slopes of the Alps into Italian-speaking Ticino, while the Südföhn, South Foehn, blows from the south down the northern slopes into the German-speaking regions that comprise most of the country, the isolated Romansh-speaking valleys of Graubünden, and the canton of Valais, split between French and German. That massive barrier of rock creates a stark weather divide – if it is clear in Graubünden, say, it will be raining in Ticino – and the Foehn can be predicted, in the same way as the Helm, by a corona of smooth white cloud suspended above the summits. The wind is formed by what is termed, poetically, a rain shadow: the lee of a mountain wall that remains perfectly dry while cloud piles up on the other side, dumping its moisture. Because its condensation has fallen as rain as it ascends one slope, the air as it rushes down the other is not only dry but warm, causing temperatures to soar, which gives the Foehn its marvellous nickname *Schneefresser*, 'Snow-eater'. But this blast of warm, dry air can also cause calamity, which is why I had strained my legs through the hills to Heiden. Famously, in 1838, the combination of Foehn and fire had almost wiped this village off the map.

'It looks like a nice day, doesn't it? But look, see the smoke.' The museum had opened especially for me, after my confused early morning appeals in phrasebook German in the town hall, where kindly receptionists had taken pity. The English-speaker they had summoned turned out, serendipitously, to be a historian called Andres Stehli, who led me to a framed illustration on the wall.

At first glance it depicted a bucolic rural scene, showing the village with its steepled church and neatly laid-out cottages. But on closer inspection the omens were as stark as a cautionary tale: a woman's blue dress billowing in the same direction as smoke from a smithy, which, looking even closer, had sparks flying from its roof. This was Heiden's Pudding Lane; the South Foehn carried the fire north, engulfing the buildings in its path, and within a matter of minutes 129 houses were blazing away. A second illustration showed the scene several hours afterwards: a wasteground of charred earth, the church in ruins, the woman in blue replaced by two girls fleeing, clutching their possessions above their heads. The conflagration was so fierce that the glow could be seen ten miles away on the far shore of Bodensee; the museum housed a battered helmet left by the German firemen who had crossed the lake to help, though it was far too late.

'That's all that's left,' said Herr Stehli, pointing through the window at a house much older than its neighbours. 'The mayor ordered the people to save it at all costs, even if everything else burned down. It was his house, of course.'

Amazingly, within two years the village had been completely rebuilt, but its appearance was altered beyond recognition. Designed by a single architect so that every house looked the same, it was an anomaly, totally unlike its neighbours not only in its architecture but in its outlook. The new houses were constructed in the Biedermeier style, a Mitteleuropean aesthetic synonymous with bourgeois values and the emerging middle class, representing a clean break from the rural, superstition-bound past; a conscious attempt to forge a link with the new, enlightened Europe. Reborn as a fashionable resort, no longer a village of God-fearing farmers but of hoteliers and restaurateurs, Heiden plunged with gay abandon into the Belle Époque; the tiny railway, which today only rattles to Rorschach and back, once brought the continent's elegant classes all the way from Berlin. I leafed through faded photographs of ladies in enormous hats and gentlemen in bowlers and spats taking their tea on shaded lawns. 'All this was because of the fire, because of the Foehn. It allowed new ideas, new ways of thinking. If we had not had this fire, Heiden would never have achieved such fame in the nineteenth century.'

And hadn't there been a second fire, I asked, in the twentieth? I had read about it somewhere. 'Ah yes, that was very unfortunate

– it was 1936, on the celebration of our National Day. The church burned to the ground again, along with all the archives of the commune. But it was not the Foehn that time. They were cooking *raclette* in the church, and it got out of control.'

'*Raclette?*'

'It is like fondue . . .'

Leaving the village, I couldn't help feeling delighted that its disasters had been so absurdly Swiss: the first from the mountain wind, the second from the patriotic melting of cheese. What I was only to realise later was that Heiden's inferno was far from unique; I lost count of how many towns and villages, built almost entirely from pine, had been immolated over the years. Every story started the same way: 'The Foehn was blowing that day . . .'

After clearing the outskirts of Heiden, past sawmills and light manufacturing plants, the walking trail threaded south into the rising, plunging hills of Appenzellerland. Comprising two of the country's smallest and most traditional cantons, this deeply conservative region is famously hidebound in its ways – in Appenzell Innerrhoden decisions are made by a show of hands in an annual citizens' assembly called the *Landsgemeinde*, a form of direct democracy dating back to the Middle Ages; less democratically, women were only granted the vote in 1991 – and it gave me a glimpse of what the fire had allowed Heiden to break away from. The openness and suburbanity of the flatlands were gone; these steep slopes, deceptive valleys and cosily tucked-away villages were an entirely different world, and the landscape had an enclosed, hidden feel, as if concealing secrets. Farmhouses and cattle barns whose eaves almost touched the ground were shingled in wood like flaky scales, with log piles stacked compulsively and snowmelt gurgling in gutters. Shaggy goats with clonking bells grazed on sunlit grass. A pattern began to emerge: the south-facing hillsides were free from snow, exposed not only to the sun but to the temperate breath of the Foehn, while the northern slopes lay blanketed. I made my ascents in black and white and my descents in technicolour, the brilliant green of melted meadows bordered by violets and primroses, passing from winter to spring every time I reached a summit.

The topography made distance deceptive. What looked like a short stroll on the map was elongated by the contours of the hills, the miles compressed like information encoded on a circuit board, and when, hours later, I looked back to see how far I had walked, I was dismayed to see Heiden's church standing clear on its hill just a few miles behind me. But by mid-afternoon the view ahead dipped and opened up again: the blue haze of the Rheintal Valley, which would be my corridor into the mountains proper.

Leaving Appenzellerland for the larger canton of St Gallen plunged me back into functional modernity once more. The valley was broad and perfectly flat, neatly arranged on a north–south axis, its motorways, railway lines and pylons paralleling the Rhine; after the maze of hills the sudden transition to linearity was oddly disconcerting. I followed a straight country road through Altstätten, an industrial belt ringed by pungent dairy farms, until I reached Oberriet, where I'd arranged to stay with a generous host I'd only contacted the evening before. Nomi was a trainee carpenter who shared a house with her father on the outskirts of the village, and over a meal of salmon and rice, washed down with crisp white wine from Valais, they took it in turns to tell me stories of the wind.

'We moved here from a village nearby, but high in the mountains where there is no Foehn. Our neighbours used to say that the wind makes valley people weird. Now we live in the valley, maybe we get weird too.'

'They say it blows for three, six, nine or twelve days. So if it's been blowing for three and is still blowing on the morning of the fourth, you know you've got three more, at least.'

'The pressure is really, really bad. The air is so dry my nose sometimes starts bleeding. At night it can get extremely warm, twenty, twenty-five degrees, so you are sweating in your bed.'

'People who have always lived here, maybe they don't mind it so much. But for us it's difficult, it's something we have to get used to. On the other hand, where we lived before is still deep in snow this time of year. Down here the grass is already green, and the flowers have come . . .'

As I set out the following morning they shared a final piece of wisdom: 'The local people call the Foehn the Oldest Man of the Rhine. He has been in this valley longer than anyone.' It was a fitting start to the day, for after a fifteen-minute walk I was on the Rheindamm, the Rhine's broad embankment, where I became aware of a curious confluence of names. In Germany, western Europe's second-longest river is affectionately called Old Father Rhine, so if the Foehn is the Oldest Man then the coming together of river and wind is a meeting between two venerable, ancient and respected beings; a harking back, it seemed to me, to a time when both were gods. The name Föhn has two possible roots. One is the Gothic *fōn*, 'fire' – the fate of Heiden explains that connection – and the other is the Old High German *Fönno*, which derives from Favonius, the Roman god of the west wind (the link is clearer in Italian-speaking Ticino, where the Foehn is still called the Favonio). This divine lineage was puzzling, however. Favonius was the Romanised version of the gentle Greek god Zephyrus; how did a westerly wind known for its mildness lend its name to northerly and southerly blasts notorious for causing headaches, nosebleeds and devastating fires? Perhaps the clue was in its warmth – zephyrs are associated with the coming of spring – but somewhere in the mists of history the name must have slipped its compass direction, attaching itself to the winds of the Alps like a lost spirit finding a new host. It was pleasing to think that the old god had found his way over the mountains to inhabit modern speech, in however confused a form. There was no sign of him today, however – again not a whisper stirred the trees – so I had to be content with one Old Man, not two.

Already a wide and confident river, skirted with gravelly beaches and lit by a soft pinkish light, the Rhine looked muscular and mysterious despite the roads that zoomed alongside. Austria lay on the eastern bank, and for a change of nationality I crossed the bridge and strolled through it for a while, following the waterway's broad bends beside densely mistletoed forest. It was not a lengthy visit, and I met no one at all. After just a couple of miles I came upon a simple stone engraved with the letters FL, planted unobtrusively on top of the embankment. This marker, so easy to miss, told me that I had already left Austria, and was now in the Fürstentum, or Principality, of Liechtenstein.

Until a few weeks previously, I would have had trouble finding Liechtenstein on a map. Tucked between Austria and Switzerland, the world's sixth-smallest country occupies about sixty square miles of the Rhine's eastern bank and a slice of the overshadowing Alps, and is ruled by the absurdly named His Serene Highness Prince Hans-Adam II von und zu Liechtenstein. The only thing I knew about the place – apart from its location in the brunt of the Foehn – was its reputation as a tax haven notorious for its system of anonymous numbered accounts, attracting corrupt politicians, oligarchs, criminal organisations and anyone else with an interest in concealing large amounts of wealth. Dimly I had expected to find something like Monaco or Andorra, an international playground of hotels, casinos and luxury cars, with bejewelled and mink-clad tax evaders hiding around every corner. I was both relieved and disappointed to find that nothing much had changed: the Rhine flowed on, the highway hummed, crows flustered in the trees, and distant tractors did the rounds of dull green fields. Ruggell, the first village I reached, was a dreary suburban place without a crooked accountant in sight, though the towering mountains behind formed a striking backdrop. After several hours of plodding upriver through a landscape of smudged greens and browns, I arrived, with blunted expectations, at the capital city Vaduz.

Again, the scenery was spectacular – a rising mass of forested rock, snowcapped and streaming with clouds – but the city itself was resolutely unimpressive, an unlikely capital for an unlikely country. Its extravagant football stadium was fringed by goat farms and muddy fields, and the residence of His Serene Highness, perched on a rocky bluff of the mountain wall abutting the city, was a moderately large *schloss* rather than a palace. Nonplussed Chinese tourists wandered the pedestrianised main street as if unsure exactly what they were meant to be photographing, browsing shops selling selfie-sticks, Swiss Army knives, cuckoo clocks and postcards of the royal family, who all looked a bit like bankers. The blue and red banner of Liechtenstein drooped alongside the red flag of the People's Republic of China outside stores selling Rolex and Patek Philippe. Further down the road the modern art museum – a vast, matt-finish cube of black concrete – wouldn't have looked out of place in Los Angeles or Abu Dhabi, apart from the fact that a mud-splattered tractor was parked outside. A girl on a dappled horse rode by without once looking up, her face bathed in the white glow of her smartphone.

That night I slept on a sofa in a house of graduate students from Romania and Nigeria, who were studying information systems at the university. They all seemed a little lost – the Nigerians, particularly, were treated poorly by the locals, and rarely appeared to leave the house – and they hadn't lived there long enough to distinguish the Foehn from any other wind. In the morning, as the first coachloads of soon-to-be-disappointed tourists filtered into the main square, I stepped into the tourist office to enquire about it there.

'I get very bad headaches,' said the buxom lady behind the desk in flawless English. 'They start a day before each Foehn. You can feel the pressure in the air. Oh God, I cannot stand it.' And then, switching back to her role, she handed me a brochure called 'Liechtenstein in Figures', containing statistics about the principality's annual revenue and expenditure, clearly a PR campaign to make its accounts look transparent. On the wall, two enormous screens depicted idealised national scenes – beaming farmers in folk costumes, aerial footage of Alpine peaks – which had the effect of a high-budget propaganda broadcast. Back on the Rheindamm, as I left Vaduz, the country's identity crisis increased: a battered horse and trap clopped past, next to the warehouse headquarters of Swarovski crystals, next to a ploughed field reeking of manure. It produced a distinctly bipolar impression. This was clearly a nation of farmers on which the burden of mega-wealth had been imposed rather uncomfortably – with twice as many international companies registered as there are actual people – and everywhere I could see the joins where the two did not fit together.

As I walked I became aware of two more contradictory forces: the back of my neck was being chilled while my face was growing warmer. I stopped, confused at finding myself between two opposing currents: a frigid northerly breeze from behind and a warm southerly from ahead, the latter streaming incongruously from distant snowcapped mountains. Was this an advance breath of the Foehn? I had been warned that sometimes its coming is preceded by its opposite, a provocation that demands a response. The mugginess increased by the mile, and the air became heavy with pressure. As the mountains drew ever closer, tightening around the valley, I had the impression of progressing into a warm, sticky gullet.

The town of Balzers was announced by the angular castle of Gutenberg, rising from the valley floor on a green, breast-shaped hill. Behind it soared a fantasy backdrop of tumbling pine-forested slopes, sheer rock walls and jagged peaks, and as the sun broke through the clouds the vision sprang into focus with the unexpected intensity of a dream. I asked directions from a man with a deeply lined and weathered face, unmistakably a coun-tryman – though his image was reflected in a gleaming Mercedes purring past as he spoke – and made my way to the Alte Pfarrhof, the old vicarage. The windsock flapping in place of a flag told me that I had reached the right place. The exhibition inside was devoted to the Foehn.

'We say that Foehn is the Oldest Man of Liechtenstein. In Balzers it blows stronger than anywhere else in the country.' Curators Ruth Allgäuer and Markus Burgmeier were expecting my arrival, and welcomed me warmly as a fellow wind devotee. They took my coat, stowed my rucksack, pressed coffee into my hands and launched into the tour, an experience reminiscent of Trieste's Museo della Bora but conducted with typically central European efficiency. With hundreds of wind-related artefacts ranging across three floors, it was a journey from love to hate, revealing the kindly face of the Foehn in addition to the cruel. A grape-press and a corn-shucking machine reflected two lovely honorifics: *Traubenkocher* and *Maisvergolder*, 'Grape-cooker' and 'Corn-goldener', which joined *Schneefresser*, 'Snow-eater', in my lexicon of deific names. There was a bizarre costume made for a carnival parade – cushiony blue and white clouds billowing on the wearer's front, a blazing yellow sun on the back ('Good weather comes behind Foehn') – which turned out to be just a few years old, an object of modern ritual. Other artefacts demonstrated how the wind has entered popular culture: a classic Foen brand hairdryer – the name is used generically in German-speaking countries in the same way that Hoover has come to mean 'vacuum cleaner' in English – and a bottle of Föhn Sturm whisky, slanted for effect. My favourite was a newspaper clipping about a Vaduz hairdresser who invented a Foehn-proof hairstyle in the 1970s. Unsurprisingly for the era, it involved large amounts of hairspray.

But then came the Snow-eater's darker and more vengeful side, manifesting in *Föhnkrankheit*, the notorious Foehn-sickness. A 1942 magazine advised that if a Foehn-sick person was swiftly removed from the area they would recover quickly, 'just as a seasick person recovers quickly away from the sea'; more recent testimonials complained of *Kopfschmerzen*, 'headaches', *Reizbarkeit*, 'fretfulness', and a host of other ailments including depression, anxiety and suicidal despair. A seventeenth-century German map portrayed the Foehn as a leering face puffing out not a blast of air, as is customary with winds, but a shower of skulls. Gothic script condemned its effects as *warm, schädlich und ungesund*, 'warm, harmful and unhealthy', while another map depicted it simply as a grim death's head.

All these artefacts, however, were really a preamble to the top floor, which marked the thirtieth anniversary of Balzers's great Foehn fire. The disaster came in 1986, when the Swiss Army was engaged in a shooting exercise south of the town while an extremely powerful Foehn was roaring down the valley. The commanding officer ignored warnings about using live ammunition, a spark ignited the undergrowth and the wind quickly bore the flames north, through the tinder-dry pine forest; photographs show the mountainside immediately above the town as a wall of orange flame. The inferno raged to within fifty metres of the nearest houses, incinerated hectares of forest, and took days to extinguish. 'This is our town hero,' said Ruth, pointing to a photograph of a young man grinning from a heli-copter. A local lad, David Vogt was the only pilot with the experience to navigate in the ferocious wind, and did repeated bucket-drops while his Swiss counterparts refused to fly. 'He is still a great celebrity here. He never has to buy himself a drink. This one, however' – she pointed to an image of the officer responsible, emblazoned across the front pages of the local news-papers – 'this one is the villain. He did not admit his mistake, would not apologise for a long time. Historically we have had good relations with the Swiss, but this caused enormous anger. The arguments lasted for years.'

We left the exhibition together, and Ruth and Markus accompanied me up the hill to the castle of Gutenberg. The charred forest had long since regrown, concealing all trace of the disaster, and the mountain slopes that walled the fields to the east shone green. Looking south, where the valley rose towards Switzerland, they pointed out how the land described a long, descending funnel squeezed between the mountainsides and a smaller peak called Fläscherberg, which had the effect of mould-ing the wind into a tight conduit, intensifying its flow like water channelled through a hose. I could almost see it pouring down, gathering speed and temperature, breaking like a tidal wave on the unprotected houses. But the promising breath I'd felt on the Rhine had sadly dissipated, and the windsock drooped limp outside the Alte Pfarrhof. There would be no showers of skulls over the town today.

We turned the other way, to the north, the direction from which I'd come. Sunshine washed the valley and Liechtenstein was suddenly lovely: the fuzziness in the air had gone, the grass was luminescent green and the slopes on every side glowed like rucked velvet. We could see clear to Vaduz five miles back along the Rhine, where the *schloss* of Hans-Adam II squatted on its bluff. 'From here you can see almost our whole country,' said

Markus with odd pride. Rooks chattered on Gutenberg's turrets as we descended the hill again, past terraced vineyards awaiting the coming of the *Traubenkocher*.

My new friends waved goodbye as I took the path towards Fläscherberg. It was a blue-skied, green-leafed day and the forest was heady with wild garlic, the first lizards flickering nervously over the rocks. I crossed the border without noticing, passed the wooded defile where the Swiss Army had accidentally declared warfare on its tiny neighbour, and soon reached the top of the rise where a gatehouse and barracks eclipsed Liechtenstein, a country that had taken me seven hours to walk through.

Far ahead, so intangibly distant they looked like paintings on the sky, rose the highest and whitest Alps I had seen so far. Like a surge of hope the wind heaved from the south, trembling the snowdrops, and a brown horse excitedly performed a small dance in its field. Farmers say that animals grow nervous and fretful during the Foehn, as teachers attest that schoolchildren become uncontrollable – I'd heard reports of schools even cancelling classes altogether – and I allowed my excitement to mount; but once again the wind's strength stumbled, staggered, died. It was another false alarm, but the horse's thrill stayed with me. The meadows through which I descended were an acoustic lake of cowbells, providing a gently jangling music on every side, and I stopped to close my eyes and listen to its tintinnabula-tions. The absence of this lovely sound, so quintessentially Swiss, was once believed to cause anguish among mercenary troops campaigning abroad, a form of aural homesickness specific to these mountains. It reminded me of a line from Hesse – 'Whoever has once heard it in childhood, hears it for the rest of his life, sweet, strong, fearful, and never escapes its spell' – but he was writing not of bells but the Foehn, 'that hollow roar which the alpine dweller hears with trembling and horror and yet increasingly longs for when he is away from home.'

It would be growing dark before long. Rather than dropping back into the valley, where towns and highways sprawled in a dim suburban maze along the Rhine, I kept to the altitude of the hills and followed the trail through forest. I couldn't have asked for a more pronounced reintroduction to Switzerland: an hour's walk carried me into the heart of Heidiland. This region of high pastures and picturesque villages is marketed as the setting for Johanna Spyri's classic *Heidi*, published in 1881 – still hugely popular, and brought to a global audience by a Japanese animation series – a calculated repackaging of Switzerland at its cutest. With its eye on the yuan and the yen, the nearby village of Oberrofels had rebranded itself 'Heididorf', and signs scattered along the road pointed to the Heidihof, the original Home of Heidi. Hunger forced me reluctantly into the Heidihof Hotel, an impressively ugly building glowering over an empty car park, where I drank chicken soup to a soundtrack of Céline Dion surrounded by Heidi souvenirs and an atmosphere of sterile tourist-fleecing. The tablecloth invited me to 'Cast off the grey monotony of daily life and discover the multicoloured splendour of Heidi's World'.

I did my best, though Heidi's World was growing dimmer by the minute. Searching for a place to camp I paid my respects to the Heidihof – an unremarkable log cabin with an excavator parked outside, closed for renovation – and made my way through steep forest towards the Heidi Alp. The ascent was marked at intervals by signs purporting to show the place where Peter the Goatherd watered his goats, where Alm-Uncle collected firewood, where Heidi herself marvelled at one multicoloured splendour or another, as if the Catholic tendency could not resist imitating the Stations of the Cross. At the end of a day's walk, it felt just as gruelling. Finally, in crepuscular light, I stepped off the pilgrimage trail and reached open pastureland, locating a camping spot on a knoll between two Scots pines. The trees blackened, the grass grew grey, the Rheintal Valley collapsed into vagueness, and white-rumped deer bounced through the woods as if they had been planted by the local tourist board.

The Heidi branding was absurd, but when I read the book itself I was delighted to find the Foehn twisting through its pages. As much a paean to nature as a childhood adventure story, the novel describes the young girl's summers and winters on the *Alm*, the seasonal mountain pastures high above the town of Maienfeld, where she is sent to live with her aged grandfather. Falling head over heels in love with the beauty and wildness of the mountains, she is carried into ecstasy by the sound of fir trees on windy days: 'She would stand underneath them and look up, unable to tear herself away, looking and listening while they bowed and swayed and roared as the mighty wind rushed through them.' The sun-drenched meadows and blue Alpine skies – the picture-perfect Switzerland that tourists seek so ardently – are a function of the 'stormy south wind' that rattles her grandfather's hut, threatening to blow it away, yet fills Heidi's heart 'so full of gladness that she skipped and danced round the old trees, as if some unheard of joy had come to her'. Although it is never mentioned by name this south wind is unmistakably the Foehn, rushing down from the mountaintops with its gifts of sunshine, life and flowers, and its presence in the book is that of a benevolent god:

> Now she stood still to listen to the deep, mysterious voice of the wind, as it blew down to her from the mountain summits, coming nearer and nearer and gathering strength as it came, till it broke with force against the fir trees, bending and

shaking them, and seeming to shout for joy, so that she too, though blown about like a feather, felt she must join in the chorus of exulting sounds.

It made me think of the horse's dance, and my own exhilaration.

The dawn light woke me, aching but rested, and I continued south. Church bells rang as I reached Jenins, a village of weathered wooden barns sonorous with grunting pigs and water running in slender canals; viniculture was much in evidence, with murals of scrolling vines and peasants bearing purple grapes, giving the impression of a Foehn-warmed cornucopia. The road continued past slopes of vineyards stretching to the valley floor – a glimpse of rectilinear fields and railway tracks along the Rhine – to Malans, another wine-making village, with a profusion of gold-tipped ironwork twisting from its walls. An elderly couple wished me *Gueti Reis*, 'good journey', and I attempted conversation, trying to get my tongue around the knots of *Schweizerdeutsch*. Swiss German, incomprehensible to speakers of Germany's standard *Hochdeutsch*, was an ever-evolving enigma, shifting its dialect with each day's walk; the *Grüezi*, 'hello', of Bodensee was already pronounced differently to the greeting used in Rheintal. I told them I was looking for the Foehn, and the old gentleman scowled so deeply that his wrinkles doubled in number. Tapping out his pipe on his trouser-leg, he uttered one word: '*schlecht*', 'bad'. Then his smile re-emerged as he waved me on my way.

Switzerland, I was discovering, is a land deeply sympathetic to walkers – a cultural heritage going back at least two centuries, when waves of Romantics tramped its peaks in search of beauty and the sublime – and almost everyone I met gave a friendly greeting. A rucksack, battered walking boots and an unshaved countenance felt like a badge of acceptance. With the network of yellow-signed paths that branched like arteries through the landscape, connecting towns and villages with glaciers and mountain summits, walking sometimes felt almost too easy, as if being guided so clearly was a form of cheating. That day's trail led me fifteen miles practically without meeting a car, through primrose- and gentian-sprinkled woods, artfully skirting the smokestacks of industrial Landquart below, before making its final descent into the sprawl of Chur.

The capital of Graubünden canton – Grisons in French, Grigioni in Italian, Grischun in Romansh – and, by some accounts, the oldest city in Switzerland, Chur lies at the elbow-bend where the Rheintal Valley cuts south-west, deeper into the mountains where Old Father Rhine has his source. It marked the end of the north–south stretch in which I had hoped to encounter the Foehn, and I wandered its streets with a feeling of despondence. The bright skies of Heidi's World had given way to clouds and rain, pattering insistently on the darkly reflective pavements. Every shop, café and bar was pulling down its shutters. Luckily I had been offered a bed not far from the centre of town, and made my way there drippingly to find a pretty wooden house inhabited by Urs and Daniel, two hungover forty-somethings 'reliving some sort of hippy communal life' after the termination of respective jobs and marriages. Effortlessly welcoming, they offered me a hot shower and uncorked a bottle of wine from Urs's family vineyard, which sparked enthusiastic talk about the Grape-cooker. 'I love the Foehn,' said Urs, chain-smoking as he stirred the stew. 'Wine-makers use the *Oechslegrad* scale, the measurement for sugar in wine, and one day of Foehn equals one degree – you can measure it exactly. If we have a lousy summer a week of Foehn dries the grapes, stops them getting mould, so we don't need pesticides. There have been vineyards here since the Romans, when the rest of Switzerland was only goats and shepherds. You could say the Foehn has brought this valley civilisation.'

They were entertaining hosts. The night involved much wine-sampling – Urs insisted my research required several vintages – and ended with Polish vodka and uproarious laughter. My happiness was increased when I checked my emails later, and found messages from not one but two of the excellent Swiss meteorologists whom I had badgered for information – Patrick Hächler and Daniel Gerstgrasser, both sympathetic to my cause – with tip-offs about an imminent 'Foehn event' in the next few days. The latest charts from MeteoSwiss suggested that a positive pressure gradient between Zürich and Lugano, which determines airflow over the Alps, might produce suitable conditions in the Reuss Valley sixty miles west, between the town of Erstfeld and Lake Uri. This necessitated a journey by train. Now that I had walked *up* the Rhine, probing into the heart of the Alps, I couldn't go anywhere without crossing extremely high mountains, the passes of which lay deep in snow. The road through the Oberalp Pass, connecting Graubünden to Uri canton, was closed for another two months, the hiking trails buried in ice; the mountain railway was the only lifeline between the two.

The next morning I awoke to a different city. The cloud was streaming away from the mountains, revealing one peak after another like a magician tweaking away a white sheet. The houses appeared freshly painted, and the golden domes of the churches burned with outrageous brightness. Chur had blossomed in the light: a flourishing of market stalls selling cured meats, fresh ravioli and waxy rounds of cheese; noisy throngs of shoppers in the squares; the cathedral garlanded in leaves and yellow and white ribbons. Amid the guttural burr of Swiss German I strained my ears for a word of Romansh, which my hosts from last night had said could sometimes be caught in these streets. One of Switzerland's official languages alongside German, French and Italian, Romansh is descended from the spoken Latin of the Roman Empire; a peculiar blend of Italian and German, it counts tens of thousands of speakers, mostly in the isolated valleys in Graubünden's south. They call the Foehn the Favuogn, but that was the only word I knew. Rather than Romansh I was immersed in the bubbling of Hindi, passing an Indian wedding party whose saris and gold jewellery flashed too bright to look at.

From the station, compacted hours of walking rushed past with every shudder of the train. The track ran through the narrowing valley along the bank of the Vorderrhein, one of the two sources that feed into the Rhine proper, between sheer rock walls and out again into farmland, where slatted barns and grey cattle were dotted up the slopes. Suddenly the mountainscape was streaked with snow. At the village of Disentis/Mustér (the latter name a quick flash of Romansh) I changed and boarded a different train that hauled itself up the drastic gradient towards the Oberalp Pass. It plunged into a long tunnel, and when it emerged there was an almost panicked fumbling for sunglasses; the glare was painfully bright, a vista of pure, blinding snow that felt as startling as being shocked from sleep.

The next stop brought a clumping of ski boots and a clatter of poles as the carriage filled with helmeted and begoggled men and women. At Oberalp they disembarked, and I was carried with them. The platform was hard-packed snow. I staggered in the white, feeling as exposed as a deep-sea diver without a tank. Emergence into this new realm, 6,700 feet above sea level, was completely extraordinary, and with the intensity of the light – I've never liked sunglasses, and had nothing to shield my eyes – it took me a while to understand what was going on. When I could partially see again I made out brave, tiny specks plummeting down alarming slopes, ski lifts swinging people into an immense blue sky. Tramping with difficulty uphill I found two restaurants roofed in snow, an *après-ski* atmosphere, with woolly-hatted sunbathers arranged on striped deckchairs. Children barely old enough to walk swept past on skis no longer than my arms, miniature versions of their parents in identical costumes. Everything was bewildering; I had never seen a ski resort before. Sinking up to my knees with each step I clambered up a virgin slope to an isolated stone cross protruding from higher ground. Opening my eyes to the view, I almost had to close them again. This was my first real vision of the Alps.

Europe's greatest mountain range stretches for over 700 miles, connecting, or perhaps dividing, Slovenia, Austria, Germany, Liechtenstein, Switzerland, Italy, Monaco and France. The backbone of the continent, the dividing line between north and south, these mountains have a profound effect on weather and climate for hundreds of miles, forcing warm air upward into the higher atmosphere where it cools and dumps its moisture – rain, sleet, hail, snow – into the glaciers and streams that form the headwaters of Europe's greatest rivers: the Rhine, the Rhône, the Danube and scores of tributaries. Like the Foehn with its foehn-type cousins, the Alps have given their name to a wider category: 'alpine' is used to describe mountain climates from the Andes to the Himalayas, from Africa to Australia. The Dinaric Alps I'd climbed in Croatia were a distant derivation. From this lofty vantage point I could pinpoint the two halves of Switzerland, and the two halves of the wind: the zigzagging demarcation line between the Südföhn in the north and the Nordföhn in the south, creating the crucial interplay between parcels of shifting pressure. This vast upheaval of rock – veined with glaciers, bright with snow – was the source, and the cause, of the Foehn's existence.

It also formed a midway point in the journeys I was taking. Away to the north skulked the Helm, far over land and sea. To the east the Bora, to the west the Mistral, and in the valleys north and south the Foehn still waited to be born; this Alpine ridge on a clear day was the calm spot in between. But being on the meridian between two of Europe's hemispheres brought to mind a different wind: the Tramontana. I had chosen not to follow its path because variations of it appear almost everywhere, travelling from north to south in the Iberian Peninsula, France, Italy, Corsica, Sardinia, Sicily and across the Balkans, flowing from continental Europe to the Mediterranean. Its evocative name, however, comes from the Latin *transmontanus*, which means 'from across the mountains'; the mountains in question were the ones that lay beneath my boots. In ancient times the Alps marked the boundary not only of the Roman world but of civilisation itself; anything coming from beyond these peaks was foreign and barbarous. In the minds of urbanised toga-wearers, with their literacy and rule of law, the cold blast of the north was associated with the wild Germanic, Celtic and Scythian tribes who wore different clothes, worshipped different gods, and ultimately would be the cause of Rome's destruction.

It is certainly barbarous in its effects, even into modern times, blamed, in the manner of the Foehn, for driving people insane. Gabriel García Márquez titled a short story after it, describing a family taking refuge from the 'harsh, tenacious land wind that carries in it the seeds of madness' and blows 'without pause, without relief, with an intensity and cruelty that seemed super-natural'. The story ends with one character hanging himself and another leaping to his death into a ravine. 'The wind coming from over the mountain will drive me mad', runs the refrain of

Victor Hugo's poem 'Gastibelza', which the French singer Georges Brassens later turned into a song. And in 1859 the poet Elizabeth Barrett Browning wrote in a letter from Italy, in the throes of an independence war: 'we spend the winter in Rome, because the great guns of the revolution (and even the small daggers) will be safer to encounter than any sort of tramontana.'

If it has one saving grace the Tramontana, as a force from the north – marking the cardinal direction as reliably as a compass – is connected not only with madness, but with navigation. The wind makes you lose your mind but also helps you find your way, and this strange dichotomy has filtered into language too: an old French expression, used by Molière, is to 'lose your tramontana', or become disoriented. Brassens's lyrics reflect this too: '*J'ai perdu la tramontane en perdant Margot*,' he sings in another song. 'I lost my tramontana when I lost Margot.'

Until I found the Foehn, I had lost my Tramontana. But at least I had mapped the terrain: west to the village of Andermatt, and north down the Reuss Valley. Before continuing the journey I lingered by that stone cross, trying to comprehend the enormity of the rumpled whiteness stretching as far as I could see, and failing absolutely. Every time I shifted my view it astounded me once again; staring at the immensity as if from behind a protective screen I knew that I could not take it in, that I could look at it for ever and still not come close to understanding. Some things are too large for words; this was one of them. Being humbled in this way felt fitting, in the home of gods.

Reluctantly I took the train onwards, but only as far as the next halt; a glimpse of a yellow *Wanderweg* sign flashed up the possibility of walking. With the slopes still frozen, the hiking trail had become a cross-country ski run, and on the descent to Andermatt I found myself constantly overtaken by a traffic of gliding figures. On quieter slopes it was easier to clasp my rucksack with both arms, lie on my back and join them, hurtling downhill on a toboggan consisting of myself. After an hour of walking and sliding, and a descent of 2,000 feet, I was beneath snowbound roofs and back on solid ground.

Stepping on to tarmac again was like coming off an escalator, my body lurching forward unaccustomed to the firmness. The ancient village lies at the crossroads of several important trading routes – connecting passes through the Alps from north to south, and east to west – forming a natural transit point from one side of the mountains to the other. Gangs of heavily armoured skiers lumbered through its streets like an occupying army, and I took another train away from these lurid crowds, dropping down to the beginning of the Reuss Valley.

At Göschenen I disembarked for the final time. I was beneath the snowline now and a thawed path opened up all the way to Lake Uri, tucked out of sight for now behind the valley's folds. At Schöllenen Gorge the trail descended past the famous Teufelsbrücke, the Devil's Bridge above the Reuss, said to be constructed by Satan in exchange for the first soul who dared to cross. When the mountain people tricked him by sending a goat instead of a human, the devil was so furious he seized a boulder to smash the bridge, but the intervention of a holy man forced him to drop it near Göschenen, where it lies today; albeit in a different location, having been moved, by public demand, to escape destruction during the building of the motorway to Ticino. Now this motorway shares the valley with roads, railway lines and the tumbling river far below. These conduits seemed to perform a sinuous dance around one another as they descended the narrow cleft, plunging into tunnels here and soaring on high viaducts there, while my walking trail threaded tenuously around them. Under my feet, though I couldn't see them, burrowed yet more thoroughfares: the Gotthard Rail Tunnel and the Gotthard Road Tunnel riddled their way through the rock, and work was nearing completion on a third, which, at thirty-five miles, would be the longest in the world. These routes connect Switzerland's north and south, its German with its Italian cantons, replacing precarious mountain passes once traversed by horse and mule with high-tech, high-speed infrastructure for the modern age. Perhaps in distant times to come, people will look at those holes through the mountain and say that the devil built them.

By the time I reached the village of Wassen the gorge was deep in shadow. The remaining snow on the mountaintops had an unhealthy waxiness, with glistening patches here and there like grease-spots on a tablecloth, where the Snow-eater, and the spring, were performing their warming work. Gradually the valley flattened out. Tumbledown farmsteads appeared on the slopes, many abandoned, their dark boards rotting, roofs slipping after too many winters. The villages had a small, serious look, respectable bourgeois outposts standing up, with pompous defiance, to the hugeness of what surrounded them. The Reuss broadened and slowed its pace, rattling on its pebbly bed, and tracing its bank in fading light I arrived in the village of Erstfeld.

I'd called ahead to book a bed, and retired to it early. From my window the white mountains glowed like pearls in the dark, as if generating their own light, and stars emerged in the blue-black night to shine brilliantly over the peaks. In the morning the first thing I saw was the flag of Uri canton – a stylised black bull's head with lolling crimson tongue on a mustard-yellow field – streaming northwards. Half asleep, it took me a moment to understand the implications.

The house was full of peculiar pressures; a bulging feeling to the air. When I stepped outside the wind was flowing from the mountains in irregular flutters, soft yet insistent. The air was warm but strangely cool; my skin felt disturbed. Dry leaves clattered down the streets like the claws of running dogs.

It was Easter Sunday, and bells were ringing in the church by the river. An old man with heavy brows was making his way towards it, and I pointed into the wind and called out, 'Foehn?'

'*Jo, jo,*' he said cheerfully, then switched to English. 'It comes down, down, down, pfffft!', with a dramatic sweep of his arm. 'But this is only a baby, it will not stay long.'

I started to walk, but the man was right. Just as I was growing accustomed to the tepid current from the south, the north wind staged a counterattack: a sustained blast of cooler air that neutralised the Foehn's advance, driving it back into the crotch of the upper valley. Vanquished, it did not return. A lone lenticularis cloud was soon the only clue to its coming, and I battled against a bitter headwind for the rest of the morning, my disappointment undercut by exhilaration. It had been brief, but that opening breath confirmed that I was in the right place, and suddenly the pressure gradient charts and automated station forecasts were theoretical abstractions no longer, but indicators of something I had felt upon my skin. However fleetingly, it had established proof of the Foehn's existence.

Now all I needed was a base to wait for its return. A much stronger, longer happening was forecast in four days' time, but the expense of accommodation was eating into my finances, and all I could find that afternoon was a campsite on Lake Uri. It was a six-mile walk downriver, and I kept a wary eye on the sky; the Foehn's visitation had provoked the inevitable counterreaction and as I reached the outskirts of Altdorf – up the eastern slope of the valley away from the grumbling N2 – the northerly wind had dampened the air, muting the day's clarity. Rainclouds bunched over the lake; the mountains swelled purple like fruits about to burst. I went quickly through the town, past churches and down cobbled lanes, following a winding trail under railway lines, over canals, weaving between gardens and allotments, anxious to pitch my tent before the clouds dumped their rain.

I didn't make it. The lake when I reached it was drizzle-specked, grey-green, the clouds hanging open like paper bags with their bottoms torn out. Lake Uri, or Urnersee, is really a long, appendix-like extension of the much larger Lake Lucerne – Vierwaldstättersee in German – the point where the narrow walls of the Alps spring apart and flood with space, and the openness felt liberating. I stood on the quayside in the rain, watching the colourful cantonal flags – bearing the heraldic symbols of bulls, bears, rams, keys, crosiers, pilgrims, eagles, stars – rippling in the wet breeze. They pointed southwards now, not north. The village of Flüelen, not much more than a lakeside suburb of Altdorf above, consisted of a few hotels, a marina full of rattling masts and two rival churches displaying different times, both wrong, on their clock faces. The campsite lay along the shore. They let me pitch up in the rain, not questioning why I would want to, and as I struggled with pegs and poles a man strolled out of the shower block and hooted with laughter at the sight, before retiring to his luxury mobile home. I lay in the narrow tube of my tent as the downpour intensified, unable to move without touching the sides, directing evil thoughts at him. This was the beginning of four days of waiting.

The night was chilly and long. The rain kept up till morning. Then I stood on the shingle beach and watched the steeply dropping cliffs on the far shore of the lake, the dark-pined mountains, the seams of snow, the vaporous white cloud. Everything was muted, dulled. The Foehn seemed another season away, a dream of warmth and clarity that had vanished the morning before, and retracing my steps into Flüelen I struggled to maintain the faith that it would come again. Every type of weather imposes itself with totalitarian absoluteness; it's always impossible to imagine it being any other way.

Certain subtle signs, however, appeared like beacons. Passing some moored boats I saw, with a jolt of recognition, that the rusted sculpture on the quay – a woman's profile stooped to the south with her hair flying raggedly to the north – was a representation of the Foehn, its motion fixed in metal. And in the café at the railway station, where I went to cheer myself up with pastries, a social-realist mural entitled *Föhnwacht*, 'Foehn Watch', depicted two firemen equipped with a brass warning horn, whose job it was to patrol the streets when the Foehn was blowing. Historically the Watch had the power to enter homes to extinguish fires, and the smoking of cigarettes was punishable by a fine; the mural suggested calamity might strike at any time. But the greatest discovery of the morning came in Altdorf, Uri's capital: somewhere in the liminal space between history and myth, the Foehn had led, indirectly, to the birth of Switzerland.

Outside a painted tower in the cobbled heart of town I came across a statue of the national hero. In stockinged feet he struck a noble pose, broad, muscular and curly-bearded, his trademark crossbow over his shoulder and a protective hand around a child, whom I guessed to be his son. I had heard his name, of course, but I knew almost nothing about the story; in truth, I'd barely even known that it was Swiss. I certainly hadn't been aware that his exploits represent Switzerland's foundational myth, or that the Foehn had roared its way into the national legend.

The story dates from the early fourteenth century, when much of the country now called Switzerland was a collection of peasant cantons under the thumb of Habsburg Austria, the imperial superpower of the age. Uri was of high strategic importance – the Reuss Valley formed a gateway to the newly opened Gotthard Pass and the Italian states beyond – but had historically enjoyed a large degree of autonomy; its people were stubborn, independent-minded, like the scowling bull on their flag. A tyrannical official named Gessler, attempting to assert control over the honest folk of Altdorf, stuck his hat on a pole near the town linden tree and demanded that people bow to it as they crossed the square. A passer-by named Wilhelm Tell – in some accounts just a local farmer, in some an anti-Habsburg conspirator – patriotically refused, and was arrested. Gessler, having heard of Tell's skill with a crossbow, wanted to make an example of him with a cruel and unusual punishment: he ordered him to shoot an apple off his son Walter's head from a hundred paces away.

Tell took two crossbow bolts from his quiver, and plugged the apple with the first; when asked what the second bolt was for, he replied that it was for Gessler's heart if the first had missed. For this treasonous statement he was sentenced to life imprisonment. But during his transport across the lake a terrible storm blew up, raising enormous waves that threatened to sink the boat; Tell convinced his terrified guards to remove his manacles so he could steer, then staged a dramatic escape by leaping on to the shore. Lying in wait in a forested region inland, where he knew Gessler would come, he ambushed and assassinated the hated official as he rode by, sparking a full-scale peasant revolt which, after spreading to neighbouring cantons, eventually succeeded in driving the Austrians out. After this victory Tell went on to fight in other righteous battles, but perished in the Schächenbach River, in an attempt – what else? – to save a drowning child.

The legend is almost certainly untrue, bearing a close resemblance to an older Scandinavian tale featuring the Danish hero Palnatoki, also forced to shoot an apple off his son's head. Similar folk stories, in fact, appear all over Europe. But that doesn't stop the village of Bürglen – a pretty place of timber-framed houses a short distance up the valley – proclaiming itself as Tell's birthplace. I followed a trail of reverent signboards that narrated the story blow by blow – again, unmistakably similar to the Stations of the Cross – and arrived at another statue of the hero and his son, this time decked out in the yellow and black colours of Uri. A fresco of Tell adorned Bürglen's church alongside the motto *Gott und Freiheit*, 'God and Freedom', and nearby lay a *Tellskapelle*, a dedicated Tell Chapel, displaying a sequence of murals with the essentials of the plot: the hat on the pole, the apple-shot, the escape from the boat, the assassination. Appropriately enough its resident saint was Sebastian, pin-cushioned with arrows, which is presumably what would have happened to Walter if his father had missed.

More than anything I was struck by the story's religiosity. This was no mere children's tale: despite what amounted to the cold-blooded murder of his foe – presumably a fellow Catholic – Tell was practically revered as Switzerland's patron saint. But whether or not such a figure existed, this region *was* the epicentre of an uprising against Habsburg rule which began the independence struggle, and it is here that the legend segues into history. Twelve miles north of where I stood, on Urnersee's western shore, lies a grassy plateau called the Rütli Meadow, venerated as the site of the fabled Rütlischwur. This fourteenth-century oath of allegiance pledged between three cantons – Uri, Schwyz and Unterwalden – formed the confederate nucleus of the modern Swiss state. The anti-Habsburg alliance quickly expanded to include cities such as Lucerne, Zürich and Bern, and in 1386 an army comprised mostly of peasants audaciously crushed imperial troops when they tried to reassert control, beginning Switzerland's fiercely guarded tradition of independence. Adopting the name of the Eidgenossenschaft, or 'Fellowship of the Oath', the confederates went on to defeat the Burgundians and Swabians, launched an invasion over the Alps to seize Italian-speaking Ticino from the Dukes of Milan, and over the next few centuries became so renowned as mercenaries – fighting on just about every side in the bloody Thirty Years War and the religious conflicts following the Reformation – that they were hired as papal bodyguards in the Vatican, a tradition that continues today. From Urnersee to the Holy See, it was all a long way from an uprising of farmers.

With such a history it was easy to see why Tell became mythologised as an emblem of plucky resistance, a scourge of tyranny. Centuries after the Rütlischwur, the three original oath-takers – Walter Fürst, Werner Stauffacher and Arnold of Melchtal – were reinvented as the Three Tells, a cross-pollination of myths, and the name was later adopted by peasant revolutionaries rising against the new oppressors of the land-owning class. The story was kept alive by the *Tellenlied*, 'Song of Tell', and retold in traditional village plays called *Tellspiels*, which have been performed annually since the Middle Ages. In the eighteenth and nineteenth centuries, as nationalism spread across Europe, the legend was reappropriated; the Romantic writer Friedrich Schiller wrote his drama *Wilhelm Tell* in 1804, which – despite the fact that he was German – did more than anything else to popularise Switzerland's myth. His fictional version of the Rütlischwur, written five centuries after it happened, is the most widely known today:

> We will become a single band of brothers,
> nor shall we part in danger and distress.
> We shall be free, just as our fathers were,
> and sooner die than live in slavery.
> We shall trust in the highest God
> and we shall never fear the power of men.

Schiller went on to inspire Rossini, who based an opera on the story, and a certain overture became one of the most widely recognised pieces of music in the world. Later attempts to question the myth were met with nationalistic fury; in Altdorf books were publicly burned, and one historian was torched in effigy on the Rütli Meadow. It was no coincidence that the outrage bordered on what we might now call religious extremism; after half an hour in Bürglen I realised I was looking at a pilgrimage site. The statues, murals and *Tellskapelles* were the devotional objects of a Tell-worshipping cult.

But what of the Foehn? That twist to the story wasn't revealed until the next day, when, after another night camped uncomfortably in the rain, I walked the path along the lake to a place called Tellsplatte. The prefix gave it away: this was Tell's Plate, or Plateau. Here I found another example of quasi-religious veneration that mixed the sublime with the ridiculous: beside the lake was a *Tellskapelle* with a slender tiled steeple, its interior adorned with romantic frescos that related the story once again, while a giant glockenspiel nearby chimed the William Tell Overture with the mechanical jauntiness of an ice-cream van. The chapel was built to mark the spot where the hero leapt ashore; he persuaded his guards to give him the tiller, because, as a local lad – like the helicopter pilot of Balzers – he was the only one who knew how to navigate the wind. That wind, of course, was the Foehn: a deus ex machina from the Alps that intervened decisively in the cause of Swiss independence.

On the steps of the chapel, above the water, I pulled up an email from Hans Richner, an atmospheric physicist who has studied the Foehn for over forty years. 'There is an amazing satellite picture of a foehn storm on Lake Uri, which shows that the winds are minimal at exactly the place where he escaped.' There was no storm that day but I could see the northerly wind in the pattern that textured the lake, combing it into a rough grain; the area around Tellsplatte, however, perfectly reflected grey clouds rolling across a white sky. The discovery made me very happy; no matter how overblown or distorted, the legend was based on natural truth. Switzerland's creation myth rests not only on archery, but on accurate local knowledge of the national wind.

To celebrate this I packed my tent and left the miserable campsite behind. With two days still to wait I was sick of damp and cold, and a hurried internet search had found a guest-house I could afford; the only catch was its location, several thousand feet up the mountainside directly above Altdorf. The only way there was by cable car up the valley's eastern wall, and soon I was rising at dizzying speed above pine forest, over pastures of white goats, as the rooftops and the roads shrank to specks on the valley floor. There was something endearingly normal about that ride through the sky: I shared my car with a bored schoolgirl so unimpressed by the commute that she never glanced out of the window, while I had my nose pressed to the glass and my heart in my mouth. My ears popped halfway up, the girl disembarked and cycled off towards a distant cottage and then my ears popped again and I was flying over whiteness. With one final alarming lurch the car cleared the gantry to the hamlet of Eggberge. Reeling from the altitude, I stepped on to snow.

My lodgings were in a perfect log cabin, with red and white checkered curtains and a roaring stove. I was greeted by two dogs the size of gerbils and the landlord, Leonhard, who spoke only *Schweizerdeutsch*; he brought me chicken and barley soup, directed me a friendly scowl, then gave me the key to an attic room with twelve unoccupied mattresses and rolls of army surplus blankets. In this eyrie I waited for the wind to blow.

The mountains of the Schwyzer Alps greeted me the following day: the snouted peaks of Rossstock, Hagelstock, Diepen and Schön Chulm. The trampled snow around Eggberge had the consistency of wet sugar, still too cold to melt but too warm to hold itself together, and walking was comically difficult; but once past the village it lay like flour, so dry it hissed with each footstep. I spent the day wandering in a pre-Foehn wonderland. There was a path that led through pines, with snowdrifts around the boles of trees and icicles encaging the streams, where I saw no one but a skier who passed so swiftly and silently she was like a spirit crossing from another realm. Beyond the trees was a rising, falling ocean of white summits, multiple sunlit and shadowed faces catching or deflecting the light; far below in a sculpted bowl lay tiny chalets, buried in drifts that smothered them like felt. I waded up a steep hill topped by a wooden Christ whose suffering face was turned from the wind, a sacrifice hung to dry, then dropped into the valley, deeper into snow. I followed interspecies trails – the tracks of foxes, deer, birds, skis, the splayed claws of snowshoe walkers – crashing, sinking, lurching, collapsing, until I had achieved a state of euphoric exhaustion. The snow imposed its terms on the land so absolutely it seemed impossible that all of it would soon be gone – that flowers and grazing animals would return to these evacuated slopes – but the wind was rising as I approached Eggberge, bulldozing the clouds from the sky and leaving behind a luminous brightness as clear as a tropical sea.

The cable car operator was drinking schnapps with Leonhard. 'You don't want to get down any time soon, eh? Tomorrow will be a very great Foehn. If it comes, the car will not run. Afraid you must have to walk.' His words were already coming true: outside the window the pines thrashed with a sound like shredding newspaper, and the grimacing bull on Uri's flag shuddered as if it were having a fit.

I went to bed early, exhausted, with an anxious Christmassy feeling. My sleep was partial and uneasy, despite the tiredness in my bones. 'When the *Föhn* is on its way,' writes Hesse, 'its presence can be detected several hours beforehand by men and women, mountains, bird and beast . . . Nothing could be stranger or more precious than the gentle *Föhn* fever that overcomes the mountain-dwellers, especially their womenfolk, robbing them of their sleep, bewitching all their senses.' So it was with me; the Foehn fever had begun. All night I listened to the attic walls thump and groan, the timbers shifting with the strain, an intermittent percussion of sighs that I either felt or heard. The tiny dogs yapped downstairs, and I imagined Leonhard lying with schnapps-breath scowling into the dark. The restless mountain heaved, twitching with insomnia. I woke shortly after dawn to a hollow boom and headache-inducing light. The wait had not been in vain. The Snow-eater had returned.

Stepping outside was like being plunged into a warm, stormy sea. Channelled, diverted and rebuffed by the complexities of the slopes, the Foehn's northwards flow was confused, broken into conflicting currents that rushed nervously against one another, so that one moment I was standing still and the next propelled alarmingly forward at speeds I could hardly control. The cable car was grounded, its gantry and trembling wires caught in one unending scream; the only alternative route to the lake was the three-hour trail down the mountain. The forest was a static roar, and the pines bent like rubber with the impact of each gust. When the world emerged below, it looked as if layers had been removed to reveal it for the first time.

The surrounding mountains had jumped closer, dabbed with Tippex-white snow, each crease and ripple illuminated to a hyperreal degree. The rooftops of Altdorf were so defined it was like looking through a telescope: every chimney, turret and tile had been tuned to perfect focus, giving everything an oddly computer-generated quality. Descending to the windswept town was like turning a dial and zooming in, the picture growing more precise with each step. Once again I had to stop and dig Hesse from my bag, for his words so closely described what I was looking at now:

> [T]he whole landscape shrinks in terror. It is then possible to count the rocky spurs on mountain peaks which shortly before were brooding in the remote distance, and in villages which previously looked like brown flecks, one can distinguish the roofs, gables and windows of the houses. Everything appears to close in – mountains, meadows, houses – like a panic-stricken herd of cattle.

Loud with sunshine, bright with wind, Altdorf was a different town from the rain-streaked place I had left. The temperature had leapt ten degrees and warm air coursed the streets, flapping the shirtsleeves of gossiping elders, hurling the water from orderly fountains and driving tornadoes of leaves through the lanes. The keys, crowns and pretzels of ironwork shop-signs swung madly over doorways, and woodcock feathers vibrated in the brims of Alpine hats.

Now that I had found the wind, I had to follow it. There was only one direction: blossom, leaves, litter, dust and plastic bags all chased north, and the clothes on washing lines had turned to weather vanes. I joined this flurried migration back to Flüelen and the lake, where the water had turned an unreal blue, flecked with magnesium flares. A steady procession of white horses roared offshore in repetitive ranks, divisions of cavalry on the move; on the quayside an elderly man sat watching the waves, wind-bathing.

The energy overwhelmed my senses, made me drunk with it. With the Foehn's encouraging hand at my back I fairly flew along the trail, under the Ober Axen cliffs, through a tunnel in the rock where the air was funnelled so intensely it forced me into a clumsy jog, and soon I was back beside the lakeside chapel at Tellsplatte. The foaming waves that covered the lake were entirely absent in that spot: again the legend was correct, for the water was as smooth as glass. I stayed a few minutes there, the point at which the crossbowman had leapt from captivity and into seven centuries of patriotic storytelling; I ate an apple from my bag, and gave its core to the lake. Soon after that the black bull of Uri was replaced by a white cross on red: I had entered the canton of Schwyz, which gave Switzerland – Schwyzerland – its flag, and its name.

At the village of Sisikon the path turned steeply uphill. Clambering high above the lake I had a last glimpse of the Reuss Valley; over the Alps to the south clouds were heaped like snow-drifts, dumping their cargo of rain over the piazzas of Ticino. A dirt road led beneath rubble-strewn hillsides where signs in Swiss German and French warned of the dangers of tumbling rocks – *Nicht Stehen bleiben! Ne pas s'arrêter!* – and I took their advice and did not stop, imagining that a gale-force Foehn was a perfect time for landslides. On the wall of a barn another sign cautioned against lighting fires: *Kein Feuer bei Föhnwind! Pas de feu en cas de Fœhn!* These urgent exclamation marks felt like appropriate punctuation. Melodrama was everywhere – in the lake, the trees, the grass, the birds, the mountains, the sky, the light – and the intensity became exhausting. By the time I reached my destination I was worn ragged from the struggle and desiccated by the warmth, my skin wind-blasted and raw, my lips cracking.

Brunnen, 'Fountain', was an old resort town situated at the right-angled bend where the two lakes meet: long, narrow Urnersee flowing into the tentacle sprawl of vaster Vierwaldstättersee, the fourth largest in the country. I descended through fields of soft grey cows stoically turning their rumps to the gale, and found myself among grand hotels with the look of a nineteenth-century spa: balconies, classical façades and even a line of thrashing palm trees testified to the famously mild Foehn-warmed microclimate, beloved of everyone from William Turner to Mad King Ludwig II of Bavaria. Was it a coincidence that these two men – the famous painter of weather and the depressive-romantic monarch who almost bankrupted his kingdom in a castle-building spree – both spent time on this shore? Turner painted several landscapes here in the 1840s, and Ludwig allegedly enjoyed being rowed across the lake while musicians serenaded him with giant alpenhorns. At the harbour I arrived to a serenade of my own: floating scum-islands of sodden leaves, broken branches and plastic waste were slopping rhythmically on the quay, and the percussion of flagpoles, the manic para-diddles of masts and discordant metallic moans all combined to produce an infuriating music. In a lull between gusts came a scale of softer notes: the open necks of scaffolding poles were being played like panpipes.

At the end of a wide canal was a specially designed *Föhnhafen*, 'Foehn harbour', that sheltered a fleet of trembling boats. An assortment of waterfowl had also sought asylum there, hiding their faces in their wings, their feathers back-combed. Waves slammed with brutal persistence, drenching the harbourside in foam. The Foehn had brought a holiday atmosphere: families ran screaming from the spray or advanced determinedly into it, wheeling their babies backward in prams to shield them from the brunt. A leather-jacketed biker gang unleashed their long hair and let it fly, before being drenched by a freak wave that forced a general retreat; strangers laughed together like children at the soaking they received. I was surrounded by kindred spirits sharing in the same delight, but kept myself apart from them. I had walked a long way, and wanted this moment alone.

Vertical bands of spindrift waltzed far out over the lake, roaring walls of spume that savaged the water's surface. Occasionally one would form into a whirling cylinder that galloped from shore to shore before shedding itself in veils, carving shallow runes that erased themselves as they formed. I had seen this wind-writing before, in the snow of a Croatian mountainside, and stood for a long time reading new meanings in its script: that wild calligraphy described my happiness better than my own words ever could. When I finally turned inland, my face ached from smiling.

That night I found a camping spot a mile or so outside town, pitching my tent in the path of the Foehn on a plateau above the lake. I drove the pegs deep into the earth, and though the walls shuddered like jelly it remained intact throughout the night. In the morning the air was dim, birds singing as if reassuring themselves. The lake was still, and the words had vanished from its surface.

A limp, exhausted atmosphere hung over Brunnen when I returned. People spoke in hushed tones; the colours had lost their vigour. There was a climate of convalescence, almost of embarrassment, as if everything was in recovery after great exertion. This was the hangover after the wild night.

After the thrill of the previous day, when the world had felt breathtakingly new, I was taken aback by the disappointment of the comedown. One taste was not enough; like an addict, I wanted more. According to the latest forecasts and my allies at MeteoSwiss, conditions were shifting west: having blown itself out on Urnersee, the Foehn appeared to be regrouping in Haslital, another north–south valley slicing through the central Alps.

From the window of a train I watched the landscape pull away, fleeing Schwyz for the Bernese Oberland, keeping one eye on the view – lakes, mountains, steepled towns – and the other on my smartphone screen, where the rising, plunging graph-lines of atmospheric pressure charts resembled the peaks, troughs and plateaus of abstract mountain ranges. It was a symptom of obsession: those imaginary summits of pressure felt more real than the world flashing past outside.

Obsession, addiction, exhilaration: pursuing the wind across Switzerland put me in the same category as the breed of weather fanatics known as 'storm chasers'. A typically North American – and typically male – activity, storm chasing is enabled by wide open spaces and cheap gasoline; a high-octane, motorised version of my own wind-walks. Its adherents drive thousands of miles in pursuit of hurricanes and tornadoes, often filming their adventures with vehicle-mounted cameras; one practice, known as 'core punching', involves deliberately driving into the wildest part of the storm and out the other side.

The phenomenon started in the 1950s, when a high-school graduate called David Hoadley – the 'father of storm chasers' – became obsessed with extreme weather after seeing the damage inflicted by wind on his home town in North Dakota. He took to the road for several seasons, chasing thunderstorms across neighbouring states, keeping records of what he observed and teaching himself meteorology. Over the next half-century Hoadley experienced more than 200 twisters, travelling an estimated three-quarters of a million miles up and down Tornado Alley – the vast expanse of plains and prairies that stretches from Texas to Canada – and founded a magazine to inspire his fellow chasers. One acolyte, Tim Marshall, survived seventeen hurricanes, including Katrina in 2005 and Ike in 2008; other pioneers were not so lucky. On a fatal day in 2013 a veteran chaser called Tim Samaras died when the El Reno tornado – the widest in recorded history – unexpectedly changed direction, picked up the car he was travelling in and hurled it half a mile down the road, also killing his son Paul and his colleague Carl Young. When the police located the vehicle it was a battered cube of metal, only identifiable by a single hubcap.

Marshall and Samaras also claimed their fascination stemmed from childhood storms, as if the early exhilaration were imprinted on their brains. Marshall was hooked by the Oak Lawn tornado outbreak of 1967, which killed fifty-eight people across three counties in Illinois, including classmates at his school; Samaras was influenced by the tornado scene in *The Wizard of Oz*, which he watched when he was six. 'I've a feeling we're not in Kansas any more,' says Dorothy after the twister has carried her off to a magical land, and soon she's away down the yellow brick road. Perhaps my own formative storm, when my body was lifted by the wind, had touched me in a similar way; from the snowcapped mountains outside, I wasn't in Kansas either.

That evening I reached Meiringen, the heart of the Haslital Valley, and made my way to a guest-house across the River Aare. It might as well have been Munchkinland: a cuckoo clock of a house built in dark gleaming wood, with boxes of flowers on the balconies and a stout landlady who sat me down with a tankard of beer and a plate of roast lamb. Her husband, disconcertingly, was vomiting loudly in the next room; he emerged with shaking hands and green cheeks, and after she had sent him to bed she gave me his portion too.

'Tomorrow Foehn will come,' she said, looking distinctly unhappy about it. 'It will be a bad one, I think. When it comes I try to concentrate on doing things inside the house, but my head doesn't work. I can't think straight, I am worried all the time, and it is horrible trying to sleep. There is always something making noise, something banging on the walls, like it is trying to come in . . .' And then – following the theme of disruptive forces blowing through the valley – she swung the conversation around, so deftly I didn't see it coming, to refugees from the Middle East. 'It frightens me. We should not let them in. Our culture is not right for them. Even the ones who are not refugees. If I get a request for a booking and the name sounds Arab, I tell them we are full.' She must have seen me tensing up, and attempted to backtrack slightly. 'I don't do it rudely, I am always polite. But they might upset the normal guests. I know there is a war and I feel sorry for them, but they shouldn't come here. Why don't they stay where they are from?'

Suddenly I felt extremely weary. It was a sadly familiar sensation: the moment of realisation that someone who has treated you kindly, and welcomed you warmly into their home, possesses views that are ignorant, uncharitable and callous. It reminded me of the Croatian climber who'd believed that the refugee crisis was a conspiracy to Islamise Europe, but on this occasion I didn't have the shield of drunkenness. I tried to give my opinion, but there wasn't much point. She grew upset, alternating justification of her views with attempts to retract everything she'd said, and the meal descended into an awkward exchange of platitudes. I went to bed depressed, wishing the conversation hadn't happened. This was the insular face of Fortress Switzerland.

As ever, intolerant tendencies are harboured in the prettiest places: the view from my balcony in the morning was like a Romantic engraving, the valley walled by blue-shadowed mountains and a waterfall thundering down a rock face in a mist of spray. The sun was bright, the air was rich with cowbells and wildflowers shivered in the breeze. Breakfast occurred in a spirit of truce, with both of us carefully avoiding the topics of the night before, and she stood on the veranda waving for a long time as I walked away. In a few hours her picture-perfect home would be under violent siege; I imagined her fretting inside, her husband still lying queasy in bed, as the windows rattled in their panes and the flowers were torn from their boxes.

The invading force from the south wasn't forecast until afternoon, so I took my time in Meiringen before continuing up the valley. The town is famous for two things: being the birthplace of the meringue and the deathplace of Sherlock Holmes, who plunges to his fate with the fiendish Moriarty over the nearby Reichenbach Falls at the end of Arthur Conan Doyle's 'The Final Problem'. Meiringen makes huge capital out of this fictional reckoning, and soon I had seen the Sherlock Holmes Hotel, the Sherlock Club, the Sherlock Lounge, the Sherlock Holmes Museum and the bronze statue of Sherlock Holmes – an honorary citizen – sitting pensively on a rock with pipe and deerstalker. In the grand old-style hotels there still lingered a fading trace of the English literary gentlemen who had wintered here in times past, seeking inspiration in nature, with the promise of a roaring fire and a glass of schnapps when the day was done. With my dirty countenance, I felt like a down-at-heel version. I bought the requisite meringue and consumed it as I walked through the older part of town whose houses had been spared the Foehn conflagrations of 1879 and 1891; with the frequency of these fires, it seemed amazing there were any wooden structures left in the country at all. Meiringen's third claim to fame is being the last town in Switzerland to abolish its *Föhnwacht*, who patrolled the streets dousing fires and confiscating cigarettes. Here the Watch had persevered into the 1990s, when its authority was transferred to the regular fire department. Passing the station, I saw the firemen stretched out like sleepy cats in the sunshine, perhaps in anticipation of a long day's work.

Brushing meringue dust from my beard, I followed a trail through mixed woodland up the valley's eastern side, past churning streams and waterfalls frothing at the mouth, tracing the path of the Aare as it coursed from higher ground. It was almost noon when I became aware of increasing warmth. I had to stop to remove my coat, and soon afterwards stopped again to change into a lighter shirt; the air felt suddenly closer, denser, harder to draw breath with. At last I crested the final bluff to see the view yawn ahead – the distant village of Innertkirchen under grey, ice-veined peaks – and at that exact moment, the trees around me buckled. There was a warning creak from all sides. My body braced instinctively, but before my feet could root themselves a throbbing blast from the mountains heaved me backward several steps, lifting the skirts of leaves to reveal naked trunks below, making branches thrash in distress. It was thick and muscular, like something you could touch. When it came again I was ready, pitching forward into it and wallowing down the hill, as if through coursing liquid. It was unmistakable, changing the terms of everything: right on schedule the Foehn had come, with Swiss punctuality, and the Oldest Man of Haslital already felt more powerful than the Oldest Man of Altdorf.

Innertkirchen – a functional place of scattered farms and half-built chalets sprinkled untidily along the banks of the Aare – felt like the end of the line, which is exactly what it was: the terminus of the single-track railway that connects it to the north, enclosed on the other three sides by vertical walls of rock and the gradients of the Alps staggering into the distance. A day's walk south lay the Grimsel Pass leading to Francophone Valais, but that was blocked by snow for at least another month. It was a natural cul-de-sac, and the finality of this destination – not to mention the physical difficulty of actually travelling in these conditions – brought me to a standstill. The Foehn was no longer coming in blasts but streaming in a continuous roar, a ceaseless bellow of white noise, thundering from the narrow cleft between the slopes ahead. Channelled by the valley's topography, it coursed like dry liquid; walking against that current felt more like swimming. In this confusion of elements I struggled to a campsite by the river and hammered on the nearest door.

'Are you sure you want to do this?' shouted the lady who ran the site when I announced my intention to camp. 'It is a bit . . . a bit *windy*.' But she seemed pleased when I insisted – I got the impression that I conformed to the stereotype of an English eccentric – and pointed to a tormented peach tree thrashing in a field. 'You can put your tent up there. If it falls over in the night, take shelter in the picnic cabin.'

'The tent or the tree?'

'Both, perhaps!' Retreating to a safe distance she watched as I attempted, vaingloriously, to wrestle the billowing flysheet into submission. Every time I got one side down the other leapt violently away, flapping like a distressed manta ray, but peg by peg I restricted its movement until it was pitched firmly. The Foehn slammed into its facing side, trying to batter it from the earth. I left it to take its chances.

'It is very strong today, yes,' the lady said once we had withdrawn to the lee of the house. 'Maybe stronger in Urbachtal.' She indicated to the west, where a side valley branched from this one.

'How do I get there?'

'Just follow the road. But do not leave the path. The mountain will be unstable.'

I followed the switchbacking road up the slope, bracing myself in the off-gusts, taking breaths from a cupped hand. This Foehn felt altogether different from the one I had met two days before: sticky, heavy on the lungs, it was as warm as a car exhaust and created a kind of vacuum effect, forcing me to turn my head to one side to draw breath. Taking amphibian gulps of air, running with sweat beneath my clothes, I felt clumsy and light-headed by the time I reached Urbachtal's mouth.

Ahead, the valley wriggled its way between unforgiving rock walls towards the point where ice and snow closed it like a trap. In the hamlet of Unterstock a man in a stocking cap was shearing the hooves of a trussed-up cow with what looked like a circular saw, paying the Foehn no heed; a pair of dogs rushed from a gate to snarl at my heels; and thick-necked farmers in camouflage jackets turned their backs at my approach. There was a sense of inwardness, even of resentment at my presence; the tourist kitsch of Meiringen felt far away. This was a tougher, grittier side of Switzerland than I'd seen before, where the quaint rusticity stemmed from peasant practicality rather than any consideration of aesthetics. The valley itself was much the same: the beauty of the rock faces and the stark, serrated peaks came from the violence that had sculpted them, the glaciers that had brutally thrust the walls apart. The waterfalls slicing down the cliffs – I counted over a dozen, lying on the rock like long white hairs, unthreading themselves into mist as they fell – were the products of snowmelt and the shift towards the spring. And the Foehn gagging me was an action of the mountains, a corollary of pressure changes between north and south.

An increasingly ominous sensation accompanied me from this point, as I struggled deeper into the dead-end of the valley. The farmsteads scattered along the road were secretive, sober dwellings devoid of superfluous detail; in fact they looked entirely deserted, each lying apart from its neighbours in mutual guardedness, sharing the broad valley floor with enormous glacial rocks deposited in the dying days of an older, colder age. Now that my eyes were attuned I saw waterfalls everywhere, slithering like snakes down the rock, making the walls appear writhing and alive. Nearing the snowline, each cascade poured itself out on the blunted tip of a dirty pyramid of ice the size of a two-storey house, ghostly replicas of the barns they overshadowed. The road ended and snow began; I followed the bootprints of previous walkers, winding up towards nowhere.

A shelf of wind slammed into me and passed on its way. There was a second's lull and then an altogether different noise: a muffled thud from high above, which I felt as much as heard. My eyes leapt hundreds of feet up the rock face to pinpoint a white, tumbling plume, a waterfall in slow motion, foaming from ledge to ledge and widening as it fell. There came a deep, explosive crunch and then another, larger cascade that plummeted at the same time as my mind formed the word 'avalanche'; but even as I registered this it subsided with a hiss, leaving a trail like spilled flour down the dark rock.

That hair-trigger ice cascade was the Snow-eater's work, a symptom of disturbance. Wind plays a deadly role in the Alps, scouring snow from ridges and escarpments and heaping it in broad drifts known as 'wind slabs'; these slabs can form rapidly, top-loading the slope with precarious weight, and all it takes is a slight vibration – a stronger gust, a misplaced footstep or, apocryphally, a sneeze – to send the entire mass plummeting downhill. As the snowpack collapses and the slide exponentially gathers more snow, a slab avalanche can catalyse a far more devastating powder snow avalanche, a billowing cloud weighing millions of tonnes and moving as fast as a bullet train, levelling hectares of forest and burying all in its way. Dozens of people die every year, and occasionally this average is spiked by even greater disasters: in 1999 thirty-one were killed in the Austrian village of Galtür, and between 1950 and 1951 – in what became known as the Winter of Terror – a record 649 separate avalanche events took the death toll into the hundreds, and destroyed thousands of buildings. Andermatt suffered six in a single hour. Between collapsing snow and the Foehn – which, at its most intense, has the power to bring down cable cars and derail mountain trains – springtime can be deadly.

The Romantics, of course, loved avalanches; Turner's famous painting, *Snow Storm*, depicts one crashing down on Hannibal's army as he crossed the Alps with his elephants, probably not far away from where I was now. Having made the decision not to walk on, I settled instead for a bottle of beer, some bread and a hunk of Gruyère cheese, and spent a dreamlike afternoon, in fine Romantic style, watching avalanche after avalanche crack, boom and thunder down the vast arena of mountainsides that filled my entire field of view, sometimes setting off chain reactions as the wind hurled man-sized chunks of snow to explode on virgin slopes of ice, as if furiously attempting to erase all trace of winter. It was entertainment fit for gods, and by the time I finally left – the Foehn at my back, steering me homewards like a supernatural boon – I felt many worlds away from meringues and the Sherlock Holmes Hotel.

Against all odds my tent was still standing, but rest was impossible that night. The bellow was deafening, and every few seconds the groundsheet bucked as if trying to throw me off. At midnight I awoke from a nightmare that a circle of maniacs was kicking and stamping the flimsy walls; after hours of fitful semi-consciousness, drenched in sweat, I accepted defeat and fled for shelter to the picnic cabin. Even there I could not escape, for my assailants surrounded that too, shaking the nails loose in the joints for what remained of darkness.

At dawn the Foehn was still in full flow, making chaos of the trees. Its roar never faltered, never diminished: an elongated train crash. A store of limitless energy appeared to have been unleashed, a reaction that had no end. Some time in the last twelve hours a switch had flipped in my brain: I was not enjoying this any more. I had come a long way to find the wind, but now for the first time – sticky-skinned and sleep-deprived as I was – I had the strong sensation of wanting it to stop.

I wanted it to stop as I rolled up my tent, struggling for breath. I wanted it to stop as it shoved, hindered and abused me at every step, turning everything into an effort that I was too weary to make. I even wanted it to stop as I saw, upon leaving the village, a waterfall being blown in reverse, travelling vertically up the cliff, because the sight was simply *wrong*. My feet dragged, my muscles ached, my thoughts came thick and slow. It was only a few miles back to Meiringen – a distance I had strolled almost without noticing the day before – but now it felt like a terrible trial, and climbing the steep wooded rise I had to rest a dozen times, breathing hard and wrestling down an unaccustomed sense of despair.

'I felt myself shaking in the wind like a mast. Hollowed out by my surroundings, eyes burning, lips cracked, my flesh became so dry that it was no longer mine,' wrote Albert Camus of exposure to another warm, dry wind. '[B]uffeted so long by the wind, washed by it for more than an hour, dazed out of resistance, I lost consciousness of the pattern traced by my body. I was polished by the wind, worn down to the soul . . . never have I felt so strongly both my detachment from myself and my presence in the world.' He was writing of Algeria rather than the Alps – and probably of the Chili, the local variant of the Sirocco – but existentially I felt the same: wind-polished, soul-worn. The Foehn seemed to flow not around my body but underneath my skin, an effect that was both invasive and depersonalising. My plan was to travel by train over the mountains to Valais, where another Foehn valley, the Rhône, would form the last stretch of my walk, but when I reached Meiringen I just wanted to lie down and sleep.

Boarding the train did not help; nor did the hours of high-speed travel that engulfed the rest of the day, from Meiringen to Interlaken, Interlaken to Grindelwald – where I detoured to see the triple peaks of the Eiger, Mönch and Jungfrau but found the experience ruined by souvenir cowbells, watch boutiques and menus in English, Japanese and Korean – Grindelwald to Spiez, Spiez to Visp, Visp to Martigny. The Foehn was general over Switzerland: on every platform flowed the same warm, willowy gusts from the south, viscous currents I could practically wrap my fingers around and squeeze. After the slow certainty of walk-ing, transport was disorientating; my only concept of direction came from that bath-water wind. The journey felt like someone cranking the handle of an old-fashioned funfair ride, the scenery wheeling by in a whirl of cut-out images: cardboard mountains, painted lakes, chalets made of matchsticks. I was increasingly fearful of change. For some reason the thought of leaving the folksy German-speaking cantons of the east, and entering the Francophone world of the west, made me intensely anxious.

This anxiety grew and grew. Tracing the Rhône Valley west the language barrier suddenly flipped – place-names like Gampel-Steg, Turtmann and Salgesch gave way to Sierre, Chalais and Ardon – and by the time I disembarked at the tiny station of Charrat-Fully, I was well on my way to becoming a nervous wreck.

The landscape was jarringly different here. Gone were the cool, resinous forests and meadows dotted with wildflowers; Valais is Switzerland's driest region and around me mounted arid hillsides, stark vineyards and stone-speckled fields, a palette of desiccated browns. The houses were no longer shingled barns whose sloped roofs almost touched the ground, but squared apartment blocks painted in anaemic yellow shades. Everything was bleached and bright. There was French signage, a glaring sun, a field of dusty donkeys. Stumbling up the road towards Fully, where I'd been offered a bed that night, I was struck by the ugliness of vineyards – row upon row of agonised trunks pollarded into brutal contortions – and longed for the sound of cowbells. I crossed the greasy Rhône, so tired I could hardly walk. The Foehn still thundered down the valley, and I felt miserable.

Some refuge was afforded me by that night's accommodation: I stayed with a paraplegic Buddhist lady in a saffron-draped apartment with mandalas on the walls, gently glowing golden shrines and a Labrador specially trained to bark for help if she fell. Her whole family lived in the vicinity, working the vineyards on those dry slopes, and when I said I'd been travelling through Graubünden, Uri and Bern she frowned: 'I don't know those parts. Here we don't have much to do with the German-speaking places.' Those words reinforced the feeling that this was a different Switzerland. Landscape, culture and people had changed, and only the Foehn remained constant.

Despite her hospitality my mood did not improve. After she went to bed I collapsed in the living room. A nameless apprehension gnawed at me, a feeling that somehow, something had gone extremely wrong. I thought of the journey still to come, and felt only exhaustion. The rucksack-pain in my shoulders and the boot-pain in my feet: I simply wanted them to stop. I was sick of this restless travelling, of endlessly meeting and parting from people. I was sick of the mountains, the valleys, the light; I was sick of wind. But mostly I was sick of myself. What the hell was wrong with me? I had come all this way to meet the Foehn, and now that I had found what I wanted – or it had found me – I felt completely wretched.

And then the lightbulb came on in my head. This was how I was *meant* to feel.

Anxiety, irritability, depression, lethargy, fatigue. All the symptoms of *Föhnkrankheit*. It was glaringly obvious. For the past three weeks I'd been told anecdote after anecdote of agitated animals and uncontrollable schoolchildren, as well as darker mutterings of madness and psychosis. I'd heard innumerable complaints about headaches and sleeplessness; I'd seen the antique German map with the face exhaling showers of skulls. Yet I'd never considered the possibility that I might be affected.

Both the classic Foehn of the Alps and the other foehn-type winds that occur around the world are associated with similar psychological disturbance. In her essay 'Los Angeles Notebook', Joan Didion describes the effects of the Santa Ana, or Devil Wind – a Californian cousin to the Foehn – which blows down the Sierra Nevada on to the Pacific coast:

> There is something uneasy in the Los Angeles air this after-noon, some unnatural stillness, some tension. What it means is that tonight a Santa Ana will begin to blow, a hot wind from the northeast whining down through the Cajon and San Gorgonio Passes, blowing up sand storms out along Route 66, drying the hills and the nerves to flash point. For a few days now we will see smoke back in the canyons, and hear sirens in the night . . . To live with the Santa Ana is to accept, consciously or unconsciously, a deeply mechanistic view of human behavior.
>
> I recall being told, when I first moved to Los Angeles and was living on an isolated beach, that the Indians would throw themselves into the sea when the bad wind blew. I could see why.

As with fires, suicides and other violent incidents, it is popularly believed that the murder rate spikes when the Devil Wind blows. 'On nights like that,' writes Raymond Chandler, 'every booze party ends in a fight. Meek little wives feel the edge of the carving knife and study their husbands' necks. Anything can happen.'

Such stories abound with the Foehn, and many of the people I'd met had numbers to prove their theories. The statistics changed with every teller, as with fishermen's tales: in some regions I'd been told that violent crime and traffic accidents rise by half, or a third; in others that medical treatment is required 20 per cent more often, or 30 per cent, or 50 per cent, during Foehn conditions. These varying figures were repeated in tones of bar-room confidence, but no one seemed to know where they came from; one frequently quoted study by a Munich university, which claimed that the suicide rate increases by 10 per cent, proved impossible to track down. Another popular assertion was that in certain cantons the Foehn was historically considered a mitigating factor in crime cases; that if a defendant successfully argued that 'the wind made me do it' – that its effects were sufficiently maddening to cause temporary insanity – they stood a chance of receiving clemency in court. I heard this so many times I lost count, from one side of the country to the other, but again supporting evidence was always strangely lacking. Markus Burgmeier, whose exhibition I had visited in Liechtenstein, found one transcript from 2007 recording the case of a foreigner whose aggression towards his wife was attributed to the Foehn: 'The defendant . . . never felt at home in Liechtenstein and always expressed disparagement over the country and the people. In the course of the marriage the appli-cant felt more and more abused by the defendant . . . for example, when the latter got headaches because of the foehn weather.' But that excuse wasn't enough to reduce his sentence. Perhaps this judicial anecdote was little more than popular myth; as with all myths, of course, the truth it contains is real.

But what's the scientific connection between wind and mind? Biometeorology – the study of how atmospheric conditions affect living things – is even more of a minefield than statistics, and proving such claims is notoriously tricky. Human beings are complex systems, and it is impossible to isolate one factor from another; correlation is easy to find, but seldom causation. There are many theories, though, ranging from increased ozone levels – too much ozone makes it hard to breathe, inducing sensations of suffocation and panic – to pressure fluctuations and sferics, which are electromagnetic effects caused by atmospheric phenomena, associated with dry winds as well as lightning strikes. Lyall Watson suggests that wind-stress produces a classic alarm reaction, pumping adrenalin through the body:

> Metabolism speeds up, blood vessels of the heart and muscles dilate, skin vessels contract, the pupils widen and the hair shows a disturbing tendency to stand on end, producing prickles of apprehension. This is a fine and useful response to an emergency, a good prelude to instant action; but when it is provoked by an alarm that goes on ringing, by a wind that blows for hours or even days on end, it puts a lot of strain on the system.

Another theory finds disruption on the atomic level. In the 1950s and 1960s Israeli scientists studying the Sharav, or Khamsin in Arabic – another desiccating wind which reportedly affects one in three people – found increased levels of serotonin in sufferers deemed 'weather-sensitive'. While serotonin is generally associated with happiness, too much of it can be a bad thing: young people experienced migraines, nausea and irritability, and older people became tired and depressed. Overproduction of this hormone was itself attributed to increased concentrations of positive ions.

Ions are atoms that carry a positive or negative electrical charge. An atom becomes a positive ion when it loses an electron, and a negative ion when it gains an extra one; electrons can be knocked off by the friction of air molecules rubbing against one another during periods of atmospheric disturbance. Rather confusingly negative ions are associated with positive moods, and positive with negative; the former occur around rain and running water – part of the reason, perhaps, that people feel happy by waterfalls and rivers – while the latter are generated by electrical equipment, radio and television transmitters, power lines, air conditioners and strong, dry winds. As Didion's essay concludes: 'In any case the positive ions are there, and what an excess of positive ions does, in the simplest terms, is make people unhappy. One cannot get much more mechanistic than that.'

Whether evil atoms were to blame, or breathlessness, or simply sensation – whatever channel of disturbance the Corn-goldener entered me through – I felt profoundly relieved that my mood might have a cause. I'd committed the classic error of assuming I could remain unaffected by what I had come to observe, and the realisation was humbling. I drifted to sleep in the golden glow of the shrine in the corner of the room, imagining the malevolently buzzing ions – sub-microscopic versions of those baleful German skulls – might be counteracted by the Buddha's loving-kindness. In the morning the sky was a gentle blue, fluffed with white clouds. My hostess was feeding her rabbit granola. When I stepped outside my mind was clear, and the hillsides suddenly didn't look so desolate after all.

The Foehn had disappeared overnight, and my *Föhnkrankheit* had gone with it. I'd felt an unreasoning antipathy towards my surroundings the evening before; now I found unexpected delight in the Frenchness all around me. I strolled past the Hôtel de Ville, bought a croissant from a *patisserie* – speaking more French in thirty seconds than I'd managed in Swiss German in three weeks – and set out along the footpath on the right bank of the Rhône. Poplars spurted along the river. The vineyards had lost their ghastliness. Valais seemed a fresh beginning, full of possibility.

This was the last phase of my Swiss journey, my final Foehn-swept valley. I had entered the country up the Rhine, so it felt appropriate to leave it down the Rhône, another of Europe's great rivers, emptying into Lake Geneva before continuing its course through France to the open sea. That river led to my final wind – I would follow it all the way to Provence on the trail of the Mistral, the final chapter of this book – and Valais was my zone of transition, a perfect Venn diagram between Switzerland and France, a palimpsest of two cultures. As the waterway swung north-west, past the distant château of Martigny, I also crossed another frontier that I had not expected yet: a sudden frosty blast barrelling down the valley from the north, cutting through the Foehn-warmed air like a shot of schnapps through fat.

'*Quel vent?*', 'What wind?' I asked a jogger. I was used to asking such questions by now. '*C'est le Bise,*' she called back, as if it were perfectly normal. The Bise! I'd heard its name before. Merciless and freezing cold – the name ironically means 'the kiss' – it has been commented on for centuries by travellers to Geneva, but I had no idea it probed this far east. A windsock sign on the river bend warned of these opposing forces, the icy north and the sultry south, like a flag on a battleground. I didn't know it at the time, but that was the moment I said goodbye to the Foehn and its positive ions.

Pleasantly chilled for the first time in days, I followed the path downriver. The valley narrowed as it tapered north-west, the river pulling tighter as if drawstrings had been tugged around it. Once away from the starkly cut vines, the descending slopes of the hillsides were covered in blossoming trees, explosions of white like avalanches of flowers rather than snow. I passed stone farmhouses whose roofs were a craze of irregular slate; wind turbines and power lines; dozing brown and white cows with thick-veined udders full to bursting. My energy had returned and I practically sailed through the villages of Vernayaz, Dorénaz and Collonges – its name onomatopoeic with the bells tolling for midday – and then up a track through forest under over-hanging rock, leaving the emerald river churning far below. Dandelions and wild rape flickered like flames along the path. Beyond the trees lay meadows bright with daisies and forget-me-nots, goats munching slyly on clover outside shuttered cottages. Then I was back on tarmac again, descending with many twists and turns into Saint-Maurice.

In this ancient abbey town I had to keep reminding myself that I was not yet in France. Café tables lined the cobbled Grande Rue, the buildings were plastered in yellows and greens, and ornate wrought-iron lamps cast branching shadows. I stopped to demolish a falafel wrap – food prices were still Swiss, and the ever present Turkish takeaway had been my mainstay during this journey – then continued up the road to visit the famous abbey. Founded in 515, one of the oldest pilgrimage sites north of the Alps, its basilica is an important stop on the Via Francigena which winds from Canterbury to Rome, and several people glanced approvingly at my walking boots. Inside loomed pillars as tall as trees, and red light filtered through stained-glass wounds in scenes of cartoonish violence on the windows: depictions of death by axe and sword, dripping heads held aloft, bodies hacked and trampled under the flailing hooves of horses. I did the rounds dutifully, pausing at gold-mantled saints and sacred hearts in gouts of flame, but emerged feeling like an impostor. I was following different gods.

Downriver, on the wall of a barn – along an especially idyllic meander fringed with silver birch – I came across a political poster: '*Oui au renvoi effectif des étrangers criminels*', 'Yes to the effective removal of foreign criminals'. It was illustrated with a cartoon so racist I almost did a double-take: a white sheep kicking a black sheep out of the picture. Once again the prettiest places harboured the ugliest undercurrents, the fear of the dark-skinned that had become a perennial theme. And yet, in Valais and Vaud – the canton past Saint-Maurice – I saw more brown faces than I ever had in the east; neither migrants nor foreign criminals, but Swiss citizens. In contrast to the riddled valleys of Graubünden and Bern, with their isolating mountain walls, there was a sense of openness here that had much to do with the Rhône, a clear pathway to cosmopolitan Geneva, France, western Europe, the Mediterranean and beyond.

In the psychology of the wind, there was a difference too. The Foehn begins in the impenetrable mountainous heart of Switzerland, pushing outward through the valleys as if to drive intruders away; the Bise, on the other hand, burrows its way in. I felt its chill inside my nostrils as I walked my final miles through terraced yards of Pinot Noir grapes, tramping in dust-dry soil, until I saw the glow of the distant lake.

That night I pitched my tent beyond Aigle, a town of cooing doves and magnolia trees. Vineyards were planted between the houses, and lavender between the vines. Its Romanesque church was a world away from the drastic steeples of the Germanic world, sanded smooth at every corner by time and weather. The massive Château d'Aigle stood guard above concentric ranks of vines resembling a puppet army of hooked, contorted limbs. The sun collapsed in the west. I celebrated the end of my journey with a glass of crisp local wine, deliciously cold and clear.

By noon the following day I was on the shores of Lake Geneva.

The body of water was dulled by mist. Swans floated in silver vagueness. Its serenity reminded me of Bodensee, where I had begun this walk on a similarly windless day, a pleasing circularity.

I had followed the Rhine, the Reuss and the Rhône from one great lake to another, from the Germanic to the Gallic, north-east to south-west. The still space between two winds was a moment to draw breath.

And what of the Bise? I never felt it again, though its presence haunted Geneva as much as the ghost of Jean Calvin or the wars of the Reformation. I spent the next three days in that city and clues of it were everywhere, lurking inside alleyways, squares and conversations. It was in the parallel streets between the waterside and the old town, where houses were termed *Côté Bise* or *Côté Vents* – Bise-facing or other-winds-facing – depending on the angle of their walls, leaving its psycho-geographical mark as surely as the fire-and-brimstone zeal of the Rue du Purgatoire or Rue de la Croix d'Or. It was in the ironwork and the stone, and the writer Nicolas Bouvier conflates its chill with the strict Protestantism for which the city is still renowned: 'No doubt the Calvinist experience, along with the *bise noir* (Geneva's icy north wind), has given a darker cast to the Genevan charac-ter and endowed it with strength and endurance. No doubt it shaped a moralistic and puritan society . . . a city of pedagogues, scientists, and introverts.'

But the Bise, famous as it may be, is far from the only wind to whistle on Switzerland's greatest lake. I stayed with an erudite Canadian named Michael, a friend of a friend, who had lived there for twenty-five years – with his horn-rimmed glasses and Trotsky beard he resembled an old-time Russian émigré – in an elegantly shabby apartment of books and creaking parquet floors. Over cigarettes and good red wine he produced a wind map of Lake Geneva, so criss-crossed and bisected by lines it looked like a butcher's chart. 'The Bise, the Bornan, the Jaman, the Joran, the Séchard, the Môlan, the Vaudaire, the Rebat, the Maurabia, the Vent Blanc . . . there are something like twenty-eight winds on the lake. The old sailors can predict them down to the minute, pretty much. In the old days cargo came up the Rhône on these flat-bottomed sailing barques, and from here it's only a short distance through the mountains to the start of the Rhine – so Geneva lay at the connecting point between the Mediterranean and the Baltic. Knowledge of the winds was crucial for trading from one sea to another.' Beyond the Foehn's sphere of influence, then, it seemed to be a free-for-all; I had the image of competing forces tussling for control of the lake like rival claimants to the throne in a power vacuum.

Such a confluence of winds suited Geneva's cosmopolitan soul. It went with the easy intermingling of European languages, the United Nations headquarters, the Sécurité Diplomatique limousines waiting at red lights. It suited the plaque I stumbled across to L.L. Zamenhof, creator of Esperanto – written, of course, in Esperanto – and the dreadlocked free spirits in the Parc des Bastions, drumming and tightrope-walking under the disapproving statues of Calvin and other stony-faced fathers of the Reformation. Both unmistakably Swiss and so international that at times I forgot which country I was in, Geneva was an appropriate hinge between two parts of my journey.

The city also possessed its own anemometer of sorts. The iconic Jet d'Eau is a fountain that spurts water 500 feet into the air – originally a device to release excess hydraulic pressure, and moved to its location in the harbour purely for aesthetic appeal – operated by retired Genevois tram conductors. The direction of its spray indicates which wind is blowing as surely as a weather forecast; during the Bise it is disabled to prevent it soaking a wide area, or even sinking pleasure boats moored along the quay. This is Geneva's Tower of the Winds, its liquid weather vane, a continual reminder of the forces acting on the city.

'There are two types of Bise, black and white,' said Michael. 'The Bise Blanc blows frequently, and the Bise Noir is the rare storm wind. I've experienced it only once. I was on a paddle steamer on a hot August day, it was absolutely calm. And then, I've never seen the like of it – a black wall of cloud, you could see it coming. It knocked me flat. I'd left a king-sized bottle of Coke on the rail, and it was blown with such force that with a single bounce off the deck it flew seven or eight metres through a glass window. The boat almost keeled over. We were lucky. Another boat sank that day, people were killed.'

I spent my final afternoon in a café in the old town, plotting the route of the Mistral through the south of France. That night Michael taught me the mysterious art of making soufflé, right down to the chemical science of emulsifying the roux. It was a nice touch for the road; 'souffle' is another word for spirit, breath, or wind.

MISTRAL

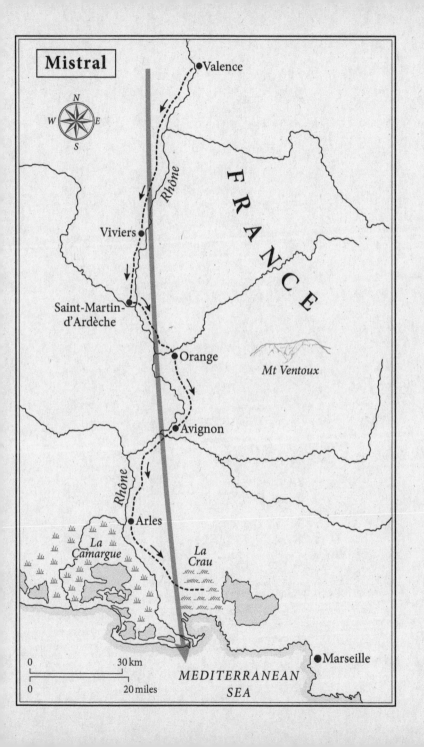

I have sometimes worked excessively fast. Is it a fault? I can't help it. For instance, I painted a size 30 canvas, the 'Summer Evening' at a single sitting. Take it up again? – impossible; destroy it? – why should·I! You see, I went out to do it expressly while the mistral was raging. Aren't we seeking intensity of thought rather than tranquillity of touch?

Vincent Van Gogh

The railway followed the Rhône from Geneva through steep wooded ravines, past swaying beds of pale reeds, the foothills of the Alps loping past and diminishing behind. The train was poured from the valley walls into the spreading plains of France like liquid from a flask, and soon the mountains were as insubstantial as the clouds. There was an amber uniformity to the villages flashing past, and long avenues of trees strobed along straight country roads, a sight as indelibly French as hedgerow lanes are English. I changed platforms at Lyon – the coffee was better than in Switzerland, and men kissed on both cheeks – then took a local train for the last few miles, due south.

The Mistral didn't take long to find. As soon as I stepped out at Valence, it hit me in the north side of the face.

'*À Valence le Midi commence*,' a popular expression goes, 'At Valence the Midi starts.' The Midi is an old term for the region of the south of France from the Alps to the Pyrenees, Languedoc to Corsica – the word means simply 'middle day', as the sun is in the south at noon – but '*À Valence le Mistral commence*' would be just as true. France's most famous wind is said to begin in this city – or more specifically, according to some, in the Pilat massif a little way back up the track – created when cold air is forced from high pressure areas inland to low pressure areas over the Gulf of Lion, channelled by the Rhône Valley and gathering in ferocity as it rushes down the river to the sea. It takes its name from the Latin *magistralis*, which means 'dominant' or 'masterly', similar to the Maestro wind in parts of the Adriatic. It is also called *mange-fange*, 'mud-eater', for its desiccating effect; other dubious honorifics include 'the wind of madness' and 'the idiot wind', the reasons for which would become apparent over the next two weeks.

As I'd discovered researching this walk, the Mistral, like the Bora, is something of a celebrity, almost a household name among people who have never heard of other winds. Travel forums for Provence are full of worried holidaymakers hoping it won't spoil their vacations, and cyclists carefully avoid travelling north. The name had also been in the news recently for other reasons: the French government was dithering over whether or not to sell two deadly Mistral-class assault ships to Russia, under embargo for its actions in Ukraine and Crimea. There was something telling in this choice of name: while the Germans affectionately nickname their hairdryers after the Foehn, the French use the Mistral to describe a state-of-the-art warship.

Already I could see why: it was like being under attack. I crossed the street in defensive posture, shielding my eyes with a chilled hand, heading for the nearest park – grandly called the Champ de Mars – where the fountains on either side of the bandstand were emptying in flailing arcs. The tricolours on municipal buildings were doing their best to tear away from their flagpoles, and people walked at forty-five-degree stoops, their hairstyles heading south. '*C'est le Mistral?*' I asked a passer-by to be certain. '*Oui,*' he replied, 'the famous wind. This is the place with the most wind in France. Here when there is no wind, soon there will be wind.'

Slightly shocked to have found it so soon, exactly where it was meant to be, I wandered the provincial streets. True to its name, the Masterly dominated every aspect of the city, lurking ominously in alleyways and magnificently erupting across the expanses of civic squares, harrying pedestrians and knocking birds off their flight paths. It rattled the weather vane on the roof of the Hôtel de Ville – a building in grand Gallic style with *Liberté Égalité Fraternité* above three separate doors, as if applicants must decide which to choose – and battered at the awnings of café-bars and kebab shops. A plastic chair skidded across the pavement, colliding with a woman's legs. Car alarms were wailing. This wild overture was a welcome not only to a different country but to a different world of weather; I threw myself into both.

The shape of the journey ahead contrasted starkly with the topographical meanders of my walk through Switzerland, reflecting the simplicity of the wind's direction. There were no mountains to cross, and only one valley – the Rhône – the course of which I would follow south with scarcely a deviation, through the *départements* of Ardèche, Gard, Vaucluse and Bouches-du-Rhône, until I reached the Mediterranean and could go no further. It was a walk of a hundred miles, and my first steps took me across the bridge that spanned the river to the west; I stopped halfway, suspended in the wind, a bitter current that flowed as constant as the water.

The bridge, as it happened, was called Mistral, but not after the wind. It owed its name to Frédéric Mistral, the flamboyant nationalist poet who won the Nobel Prize for Literature in 1904. Portraits and statues of him are scattered throughout the Midi and Provence – with his wide-brimmed felt hat, twirled moustaches and natty beard, he bears the distinguished rebel appearance of a gentleman from the Deep South – as if in competition for fame with his namesake wind. His epic pastoral poems are odes to the beauty of his native land, its landscapes, culture and particularly its speech: not French but Provençal, a dialect of Occitan, which he termed the 'first literary language of civilised Europe'.

Occitan, or *lenga d'òc*, was the original language of Occitania, a historical region extending from Italy through the south of France and into parts of Spain. It was spoken by the troubadours, who wandered the land composing songs of chivalry and courtly love, inspiring much of the literature of medieval Europe. The poets' decline coincided with conquest by the French in the fourteenth century, and attempts to eradicate Occitan as a spoken language. This linguistic genocide, continued in one form or another by the French state for hundreds of years – a series of repressive policies now condemned as *la vergonha*, 'the shame' – was what Frédéric Mistral was still fighting five centuries later. His ambition to restore Occitan to its former exalted status saw him compile a dictionary, found a literary association, build an ethnographic museum and transcribe the troubadours' songs, but he is most famous for 'Mirèio', an epic poem about a Provençal maiden: '*Vole qu'en glòri fugue aussado/Coume uno rèino, e carresado/Pèr nosto lengo mespresado*', 'I'll build her up a throne out of my song/And hail her queen in our despisèd tongue.' Due at least in part to his efforts, Provençal is still spoken by several hundred thousand people today, and street signs are bilingual across a broad swathe of the south.

I continued over the bridge. Beneath my feet was graffitied in thick black letters: LES FLOTS M'EMPORTENT JE ME

PERDS DANS LA NUIT LE VENT SOUFLE ET ME LAISSE QU'UN SENTIMENT AMER. 'The waves carry me away/I lose myself in the night/The wind blows/And leaves me bitter.' Mistral on Mistral, I presumed, but there was no one around to ask.

Across the Rhône lay stubby forest and yellow cliffs striped with trees. On top of a limestone massif the sunset gleamed through the broken walls of the ruined Château de Crussol, which had once defended the river. It looked like badlands, ambush country; coarser and wilder terrain from the France I thought I knew. I had entered the Land of Middle Day, the culture and temperament of which were resolutely different from the mentality of the north that Frédéric Mistral scorned. 'He who has seen Paris and not Cassis has seen nothing,' he wrote with provincial defiance. Also: 'Wherever the Mistral rules, you are in Provence.'

That night I slept in Saint-Péray, a dozy wine-making village built in the same pale stone as the cliffs. The Mistral whipped and whistled through the tall bamboo outside my window, a noise that sounded, in my dreams, like knives being sharpened. In the morning divisions of clouds had assembled to the east and west, rolling southwards in two fat bands perfectly aligned with the river, while the wind swept a clear corridor of blue directly overhead. I set out down this centre line, and on a lamppost near the church spotted the clue I was looking for: a small blue sticker emblazoned with a yellow *coquille* – the scallop shell symbol of St James, which more closely resembles a comet or star – indicating straight ahead. The main valley of the Rhône was clogged with towns and motorways, and I had discovered a gentler way: I would be a pilgrim.

Before leaving home I had learned of the existence of the Chemin de Saint-Jacques, an ancient pilgrims' path that winds down the river's west bank, one of the many feeder routes to

Spain's over-walked Camino de Santiago. I had sent a stamped addressed envelope, and received an eccentric photocopied booklet that described a trail all the way from Valence to Arles, at the mouth of the Rhône, accompanied by hand-drawn maps that were almost impossible to interpret. As it turned out, however, I hardly needed to refer to them; once my eyes were attuned I spotted the symbols everywhere – on lampposts, fenceposts, road signs, rocks – dashes of yellow on blue that guided me through the streets, over a small bridge and up a dusty track between farmhouses into dense, shaded forest, a regular breadcrumb trail through the dark woods.

I emerged into arid light on the crest of Crussol, near the ruined château. The pathway threaded through shattered rocks and parched foliage, and down the far side of the ridge into the vineyards and forested dales of the Ardèche. It was a green and gentle land, far removed from what I had glimpsed of wider, more populated Drôme – the Rhône and the Mistral form the border between them – and I spent the rest of the morning following empty country roads, happier with every step that the wind had brought me here.

The flow of the air was so precise I could almost do without the *coquilles*, navigating by its chill – if it was on the back of my neck the road was striking due south, if it was on my right cheek the road was bending to the west – or else by the spreading waves that fanned across the meadows. I passed a farmer scything grass in long, rhythmic sweeps, and stopped to watch a fretting horse, her coat metallic with light, whose body was moved into manic ripples at every fresh upheaval. The Mistral seemed to be inside the land, not merely passing over it. Somewhere above a skylark sang, holding position against the flow like a trout in a powerful current.

Near a village called Toulaud I saw my first *mas* houses. The *mas* is the basic model of farmhouse in the Midi: stocky, well-defended dwellings hunkering behind strong walls, built in solid local stone, as resolute and independent as the culture that made them. Each resembles a miniature fortress, and their guarded self-sufficiency reminded me of houses I had seen on the Slovenian Karst, or even of pele towers in the borderlands of Cumbria, but – even more than in those wild places – the architecture of these buildings is shaped by the wind. Over hundreds of years they have evolved to protect against the Mistral, like shellfish accumulating layers in colder waters. Their shallow terracotta roofs are streamlined, offering the least resistance, their orchards protected by palisades of closely planted cypress trees that form living windbreaks from east to west. Most strikingly their northern walls are practically windowless, giving me a reliable means of orientating myself in this land; if I could see a blank wall, I was facing south. Approaching a *mas* from the north is to approach its blind side – was it my imagination, or did dogs bark louder when I came that way? – and a backward glance over my shoulder revealed south-facing windows and doors, tableaux of normal family life that I never quite expected. It rendered me oddly invisible, entering each village unseen; I imagined all they glimpsed of me was a rucksack and a sunburned neck as I receded from view.

People have been building their walls to the north for a very long time. Excavations of prehistoric settlements near Nice, at the site of Terra Amata – now on the slopes of a mountain but once an ancient beach – show remains of hearths constructed with north-west-facing walls to shield fires from the prevailing Mistral. Four hundred thousand years old, these firepits are among the earliest evidence for domestication of fire in Europe; the butchered bones uncovered nearby are not only from deer and boar but from straight-tusked elephant, auroch and rhinoceros, and the wall-builders themselves – while human, in the wider sense – were not *Homo sapiens* but *Homo erectus*. In later times it seems the site was occupied by Neanderthals, our long-lost evolutionary cousins, with whom our species shared the continent for thousands of years. I imagined the changing generations squinting into the same Mistral, stoically piling stone on stone until they formed those blank *mas* walls. Dwelling on that incomprehensibly vast expanse of time, and the parade of human species that has come and gone in these lands, the wind became a continuous thread running through the millennia; linking the experience of Paleolithic hunting groups with Provençal lavender farmers, or straight-tusked elephants with the horse in the field behind me.

In the meantime, everywhere I walked lay evidence of the centuries in between: the ruined tower outside Soyons that looked like giant teeth had taken a bite out of it; and above Saint-Georges-les-Bains an abandoned medieval town, overgrown and almost entirely recolonised by forest. In late afternoon, however, I was snapped jarringly back into the industrial age: rejoining the Rhône at Beauchastel, I ended the day's walk beside a hydroelectric dam. Powerlines crackled overhead, and the wind, still blowing strong, screamed in high wire fences. My guidebook for the Chemin de Saint-Jacques indicated a campsite nearby, on the long, tapering island to which the dam provides access, and ten minutes later I found myself at a scrappy plot of caravans and mobile homes on the island's eastern shore. The site was run by a possible descendant of the Neanderthals: a soft-faced ogre with the bloodshot eyes and pitted skin of a lifelong boozer, whose hands were either shaky with drink or the lack of it. Gruffly he showed me where to pitch my tent, in a clearing surrounded by silver birches, and, with unexpected kindness, only charged me half the rate. The grass was rich with clover and daisies, and blossom from cherry trees scattered thickly in the wind. It was not a bad place to be, despite the hum of power from the dam nearby.

The village of Beauchastel itself was a pleasant, tumbledown place of wisteria and sun-warmed stone. I followed the Mistral's current through the deserted streets, past the helmeted First World War soldier standing vigil over the names of the dead – *Morts Pour La France* – and stepped into a shady bar, the only place that was open. Thirty seconds was enough to dispel any illusions I held that the French are classy drinkers; the smallest and drunkest man I've ever met was staggering in circles inside, to the jaded amusement of a group of house-painters doing their best to catch him up. Instantly he latched on to me, as drunks often seem to do, and when he heard where I was staying embarked on a ridiculous quest to phone the owner – that other drunk – to convince him to let me camp for free. No amount of insistence could dissuade him from this mission, but he kept forgetting what he was doing, getting into fights with other customers and tripping over the furniture, at one point almost falling through a plate-glass window. Eventually he managed to phone, but returned disappointed: the Neanderthal was asleep, presumably drunk as well. Between bouts of his pestering I managed to have a conversation with one of his more sober companions, who had plenty to say about the Mistral. It made people crazy, he said; angry, stressed, irrational. It didn't have this effect on the locals, who were 'born with it in their ears', but outsiders were badly affected. I should be careful, he warned.

'What about him?' I asked, pointing to the tiny drunk, who was now involved in a comically inept slap-fight with someone he'd insulted. 'Is he crazy because of the wind?'

'No, he is from this village. All of us, we are used to it. That one is crazy not from the *vent*, but the *vin*.'

Under the Mistral's chilly breath, that night camping in the south of France was colder than the Alps. For a second the following morning I even thought that it had snowed: thick white blossom covered the ground, gathering in troughs and dimples, ringing the puddles like a heavy frost. It was migration season: a V-formation of returning geese flew high above the Rhône, and a long line of cyclists mirrored them below. The sky was clear, but the Mistral had blown itself out for now. It is commonly believed to last for three, six or nine days – broadly similar to the supposed length of the Bora and the Foehn – and I wondered whether this was connected with some superstition about odd numbers, which, like left-handed people, have always been associated with the sinister or unlucky. However long this particular one had lasted, it was gone today. The only thing stirring in Beauchastel was the *boulangerie* – I stuffed my bag with croissants for the road – and once I was past La Voulte-sur-Rhône the country emptied again. On one occasion I surprised a man urinating prodigiously, whose wife, mortified by my approach, covered for him by yelling '*Beau!*' and pointing wildly at the sky, but apart from this awkward encounter I met no one. The pilgrim signs led away from the river, through the commune of Saint-Julien-en-Saint-Alban and up a steep winding trail to the crest of another massif.

For hours I walked in a reverie, my mind at peace. In the vacuum of the wind's departure my thoughts slowed to the pace of my steps, perfectly balanced and content, with no prevailing force to stir them to urgency. Hardly a sound disturbed the air other than the background drone of bees, the occasional clatter from a distant kitchen window, and faraway Sunday bells. From slumbering village to slumbering village I made my way unseen, past one sightless wall after another, then up another steep track into dense acacia forest.

Five hours later, I had not emerged. The hills went on and on. On the rocky, winding pathways of the Massif de Barre, sweating in the hot sun, I drank the last of my water and became silly with thirst. This interminable scrub was my least favourite type of forest: a purgatory of tangled trees that had the effect of trapping heat rather than providing shade, buzzing with tiny flies and clogged by yellow dust. Hunger struck around noon, but all that remained of my supplies was croissant crumbs. Somewhere along the way I missed a crucial pilgrim sign, failed to retrace my steps, and became completely lost. The pathways branched and branched again, sometimes looping back on themselves, and my response – rather than stop and try to reason my way out – was to walk faster and faster, increasingly frustrated. The ground was covered in loose scree, making every step a stumble, and dust clung to my trouser legs and worked its way inside my socks, creating an unpleasant paste that set between my toes. Then suddenly the trees cleared, and below me was the Rhône. It was a mixed panorama: between me and the river rose the belching cooling towers of a nuclear power station.

They were vast, clay-coloured things – with their simple curves and rounded mouths, they resembled Greek or Roman urns – massively disproportionate to everything around them. White vapour billowed vertically, angled by no wind. The hillside behind them had been quarried into enormous steps, like an amphitheatre for giants. And down there somewhere was Cruas, where I planned to spend the night.

All paths now led downhill. I emerged from the forest, tired and dazed, at another ruined château. Immediately below it lay the medieval remnants of the village, a craze of terracotta roofs at varying angles of collapse, part inhabited and part abandoned, with yellow flowers sprouting from walls and a pleasant smell of mould. My hopes of finding food died fast; rural France on a Sunday afternoon is never a good bet for opening hours, and Cruas slumbered in a siesta from another age. I approached a man and a woman on a bench by the church, and received a resounding *non* when I asked about a shop. But the woman, evidently noting my distress, led me to her car parked a little way down the road. Rummaging in the boot she conjured up a loaf of bread, cheese, bananas and a bottle of milk, and pressed them into my hands. When I thanked her she shook her head. '*C'est normal*. But why are you here?'

I invoked the Mistral's name, and two opposite reactions occurred. The woman sucked in her breath in horror, while her more elderly companion became tremendously animated, plunging into emphatic French while she did her best to translate. 'He says it begins at night . . . always three, six or nine days . . . south of Montélimar it gets stronger, in Avignon it never stops. It is not continuous, but like, like . . .' Here she struggled to find a word for what the old man was doing: violently sweeping his arms back and forth, making sounds like 'whooo, whooo!' Then they started shouting at each other, but what I took for argument was merely discussion of the Mistral's effect. 'It makes us nervous – angry, even. Yes, it makes us angry! He *enjoys* this! He likes the passion! Me, I *hate* it . . .' Both were throwing their arms about now, yelling, slapping themselves on the head, while I stood with my arms full of food wondering what I had unleashed. Apart from politics, it was hard to imagine any other topic producing such emotion.

And then there were the other winds, the old man wanted me to know: the Tramontana from the north-west, the Borle that brings snow to Ardèche, the generic *vent du sud*, south wind, that carries sand from *Afrique*. He was like a living weather vane, pivoting north, south, east and west, breathless in his urgency to orientate me. Towards the end a powerful gust – the first I'd felt that day – interrupted his monologue, and all of us froze. '*Pas le Mistral*', 'Not the Mistral,' he said after a moment's consideration, with a dismissive shrug. 'That one is not important, it has no name.'

The serendipity grew from there. After saying goodbye, I carried my food up the Rue Jean Jaurès, following the directions in my Chemin de Saint-Jacques guidebook. Past a long-defunct cement works – built in the days when they made factories more beautifully than most modern houses – I came to a dusty courtyard lined with brightly painted doors. I kicked away a breezeblock holding shut the second door from the left, which revealed, most improbably, a tiny studio complete with bunk bed, kitchenette and a stack of celebrity gossip magazines; my instructions were to leave twenty euros on the table when I left. This was modern-day pilgrims' accommodation – well-thumbed Michael Crichton thrillers took the place of the Bible – but operating on the same assumptions of trust and decency. I sat outside in a shrinking sliver of golden evening light, eating my gifts of bread and cheese while the night closed in around me.

The morning brought an ominous rent to the sky, as if it had been cleaved. Purple clouds hung in heavy bags, and the wind in the trees roared as loud as a motorway, a build-up of driving force with no beginning or end. Replacing the breezeblock in front of the door, I found an open shop at last and fell upon glistening pastries like a hungry dog. Then I traced the path to the Rhône, and turned south again.

The embankment led past the nuclear plant, and on the side of one of the towers I was startled to see a mural perhaps a hundred feet tall, painted in faded blues and browns: a naked child pouring water from a shell, a weirdly New Age design to decorate nuclear brutalism. The tower's mouth huffed steam while below, through a forest of supporting struts, gushed waterfalls of high-pressure mist drawn from the river nearby, a hint of the enormous forces channelled inside those walls. The wind bellowed, as if in answer to a rival power.

It was the south wind, not the Mistral, that gave its character to the day. In contrast to the steady flow that I had grown accustomed to, this came in short, ragged bursts, driving dust and dandelion seeds, making the trees along the river do Mexican waves with each gust. The pilgrim signs beckoned me down the Rhône to Rochemaure and Le Teil – across the bridge sprawled Montélimar, a diversion too far for aching feet – past junkyards and railway sidings, a Roma encampment with white horses tethered to rusting tractor parts. It was a scrappy, marginal day, full of fitful breezes. I stopped at a restaurant for the *plat du jour*, the first proper meal I'd eaten since leaving Geneva, and could almost feel the strength returning to my body.

Pleasantly dulled from food and wine, I let the trail carry me on, past lavender in long pillowy rows, through uncultivated meadows hissing with a thousand breaths. I was high above the river, descending to distant Viviers. Near a cul-de-sac called Impasse du Mistral a dreadlocked girl with heavy jade earrings was swinging a mattock at a pile of earth; she stopped work to say hello, and once again the Masterly was the topic of conversation. 'I travel a lot, I never stay long – maybe only the people who stay a long time get affected. Did you talk to other people here? There are many mad ones.' Ten minutes later I met a couple of mad ones on the Pont Romain, the beautiful arched Roman bridge spanning the River Escoutay: two teenaged boys leaping, rolling and howling, flailing their arms in the air. The wind covered the sound of my footsteps and they didn't see me until I was upon them; then they offered embarrassed *bonjours*, as if I'd stumbled on a secret ritual that wasn't meant for my eyes.

I slept that night in Viviers, an ancient bishopric of crumbling stone and sagging plaster walls. Largely intact from the thirteenth century, the walled city escaped destruction through generations of regional conflict; during the Second World War the Resistance destroyed its bridge – the city's sole strategic asset

– so it would not be targeted by bombers of either side. Despite its worn medieval beauty it retained a tough, working-class feel; teenagers huddled in clouds of hashish smoke, and stubble-headed men leaned from windows, watching nothing happen in the alleyways below.

Once the upper part of town was reserved exclusively for clergy – the lower level was for artisans, merchants and the *nouveau riche* – and I followed the waft of frankincense up to the ancient Canons Quarter, where the Cathédrale Saint-Vincent thrust its gargoyle-plugged crenellations. For a Catholic temple it was plain inside, with unadorned whitewashed walls that allowed for the slow progression of light, and this relative austerity made sense with the region's religious past: the convulsions of the Reformation had spread from Geneva to here, and the city was a Protestant bastion from the sixteenth century. During the brutal Wars of Religion the Ardèche became a battleground between Protestant Huguenot forces and the Catholic armies of the House of Bourbon, determined to purge the kingdom of Calvinist heresy. Several battles were fought near here, and the bloodshed reached a peak with the St Bartholomew's Day massacre of 1572, when thousands of Huguenots were murdered by mobs in the streets of Paris. Despite the signing of the Edict of Nantes, which granted Protestants the right to practise their religion in peace, the violence rolled on for another century; in 1629 the city of Privas was burned to the ground following an unsuccessful revolt against royal authority, and in 1685 the Sun King Louis XIV tore up the edict and instituted a policy called *dragonnades*, which terrorised Huguenot families by billeting unruly government soldiers in their homes. Hundreds of thousands of Protestants fled this persecution, and this depopulation is still evident in Ardèche today: Viviers, once a thriving city of 30,000 people, is now almost ten times smaller.

I sat down on a pew. The Virgin Mary had been reinstated, and the saints replaced on the walls, but under that vault of stone I was aware of a different spirit: outside the cathedral's hollow shell, the wind sobbed like a child. Divorced from trees, and leaves, and grass, and from its feeling on my skin, it was an immensely lonely sound – it brought to mind great distances and cold, empty spaces, a painful longing for people I loved who were far away – and its sadness was too much. I couldn't bear it long. I left the building in a kind of horror, thinking that churches are places of death. Stepping outside, into moving air, was like life returning.

From a vantage point on the city wall, looking down on terracotta tiles and cypresses taller than steeples, I forgot my loneliness in exchanging breaths with the wind. The Rhône flowed hazily below, and I had a view to Châteauneuf and the cliffs of the Donzère Gorge. On a distant rise a statue of the Archangel Michael stood poised, tentatively spreading his wings as if preparing for his first flight. I was emotional, and my feet hurt. It struck me as one of the most beautiful places I'd ever seen.

No pilgrim's shack for me that night; I was lucky enough to find a room in a house of amazing antiquity, opposite the Renaissance façade of the Maison des Chevaliers – with its frieze of busty ladies, charging horses and bearded men – back in the commoners' quarter of town, where I felt more comfortable. The house was owned by Mairie and Richard, a French couple of East Asian descent, whose humanity and warmth were diametric opposites to the cathedral's granite void. They invited me to join them for dinner, and over stew and local wine told me stories of the Ardèche and the character of its people; still marked, they said, by the shadow of religious conflict. The Ardèchois were inward-looking, independent, suspicious of strangers, which was hardly surprising considering the massacres that took place here. While the Rhône is a great natural connector – and may have been one of the routes by which humans first migrated into Europe – the hills and valleys on its western bank have always repelled outsiders. Doubly protected by geography and solid stone walls, the towns, like the *mas* farmsteads, functioned self-sufficiently, built to withstand storm and siege. Again I had the impression that people had been here a very long time, heaping stone on top of stone, grubbing themselves down into the soil.

Mairie and Richard were newcomers, from Marseille and Paris respectively. Richard was a cycling nut – he proudly showed me his collection of vintage racing bikes in the cellar – and he understood the Mistral as a sailor knows winds at sea. 'There is a town north-west of here called Aubenas, deeper in Ardèche. The old people say that until fifteen years ago, they had never known Mistral. Now it blows there frequently, very strong, only in the last two decades. No one knows why.'

This was not the first time I'd heard of winds changing their patterns – in Croatia people had argued incessantly over whether the Bora was stronger or weaker than before – but it was a topic I had mostly steered clear of. The complexity of meteorological science had been impressed on me early on, and statements like 'the winds are changing' are impossible to back up without meticulous data and computer modelling. Anecdotal evidence is equally dodgy territory, because people's memories of what the wind was like fifty years ago, or twenty, or two, relies on their subjective state, which can change as dramatically as the winds they are trying to remember. As every poet knows, the boundary between weather and mood is infinitely porous.

However, it seems clear enough that if Europe's climate is changing, the time-worn pathways of its winds eventually will too. If the climate changes the temperature changes, which means the atmospheric pressure changes; if the atmospheric pressure changes air will be forced along different routes, adapting to environmental shifts as species do. In fifty or a hundred years perhaps the Mistral will have migrated further to the east or west, rendering those blank north-facing walls obsolete technology. Perhaps the Helm will be displaced from its redoubt on Cross Fell – the demons finally exorcised for good – and the Bora, Foehn, Tramontana and Bise channelled into different territories, like climate refugees.

Viviers, it turned out, was a fitting place for such thoughts: a local legend warns of the perils of the wind changing its pattern. According to this origin myth the Mistral rises not far from here, in an area of marsh, pouring through the open mouth of an enormous cave. After years of suffering, the people living in its path devised a method of stifling it; they constructed a great wooden door, reinforced with iron bands, and nailed it swiftly into place to take the wind by surprise. The Masterly howled its discontent, cursing and threatening, but was trapped inside the rock with no hope of escape.

That winter was the mildest the Rhône Valley had ever known, untroubled by frost or snow, and the people were glad of what they'd done. When summer came, however, everything started to go wrong. The air was humid and unhealthy, causing sickness and disease. With no wind to dry the fields the grass grew lank, the ground became boggy and the crops developed mould; the countryside sweltered, and was plagued by insects. Unable to bear these conditions any longer the people decided to free the wind, nominating the nearest village to prise open the door. Before they did so, the locals made the Mistral promise to behave more gently, to stop flattening their crops and tearing down their barns. The Mistral kept its word, but – like any deal with the devil – acted to the letter rather than the spirit of the pact, sparing the immediate environs but not the countryside beyond; once released it howled to the south, frustrated from its captivity, and raged with a violence even greater than before. The moral of this environmental fable is very clear: don't mess with forces you don't understand. The cold north wind, for all its discomfort, brings blessings to the land.

The next day's walk was my last in Ardèche, and the wildest. After leaving Mairie and Richard I returned to the Pont Romain – yesterday's mad ones were nowhere to be seen – and followed the trail of *coquilles* through the Gorge de l'Enfer, the Gorge of Hell, a steep ravine that must have been the course of an ancient river. Beyond the gorge a narrow pathway burrowed into deeper woods, then out again through wind-smoothed fields, finally twisting back downhill to the castle village of Saint-Montan. Its alleyways were like the internal windings of a giant shell, a structure calcified by time, which grew around me as I walked, enclosing me on all sides; level on level of packed lanes that no cartographer could map. The impenetrability of the streets, which repelled my every attempt at navigation, was an effective defence against invasion, reminding me once again of the Reformation's wars. On arrival I had seen the prominent iron crucifix, which Richard had said was common to the region, like a territorial marker, erected by victorious Catholics when the apostates were crushed. Now gentrification had filtered in, and many of the ancient houses were given over to crêperies, ateliers and galleries displaying wishy-washy art, but underneath the prettiness was a hint of the savagery once enacted here.

Beyond the labyrinthine streets the trail plunged into the equally tangled pathways of Laoul, a sprawling acacia forest that swallowed me for the rest of the day. It felt like a purgatorial repetition of two days before, on the pathways of the Massif de Barre: the same stifling heat, the same dusty trees, and once again – I cursed my stupidity – no food and not enough water. In the airless trenches of the hills my sweat ran uncontrollably, and I learned to dread the yellow glare of an unshaded path ahead, always winding ever so slightly upward, sappingly out of reach. The wind might well create craziness, but the truly maddening thing that afternoon was the lack of it; in those slyly endless hills I imagined how madness might emerge, a mean, scratchy sort of madness filled with mosquitoes. A downhill slope, or the faintest breeze – the cooling zephyrs that came and went so quickly, refreshing my skin – lifted my spirits out of all proportion. The sweet-smelling herbs along the way, sage and purple-flowering thyme, reminded me that I was now officially in the Mediterranean; but mostly it was the dizzying heat that emphasised the climate.

Finally the forest released me, and at the bottom of the slope flowed grey fields of olive trees and ranks of maguey cactus. The tiles on the farmhouse roofs were weighed down with little doves, the same as in Slovenia – did they call them *petites colombes* here? – but no Mistral stirred today. The land opened out – my heart opened with it – and to the east I had a clear view of Mont Ventoux.

The name says it all: Windy Mountain, otherwise known as the Beast of Provence, the highest point from horizon to horizon, rising unexpectedly from an otherwise level plain. In a strong Mistral, so they say, you can see Corsica from its summit; they also say this has never been proved, because, in a strong Mistral, nobody can stand up there. Wind speeds of 200 miles per hour have been recorded on top, and the mountain road through the aptly named Col des Tempêtes, Storm Pass, is frequently closed to traffic. YouTube clips show climbers practically blown horizontal, in conditions that resemble the surface of another planet.

YouTube was the closest I'd get; I was not bound for that peak. Diverting to the mountain and back would take me days off course, and my ambition lay elsewhere. Over the last few weeks I had become obsessed with a little-known region further south, where the Rhône empties into the sea: on the other side of the river from the photogenic wetlands of the Camargue – famous for their flamingo flocks, white horses and *gardian* cowboys – lies the desolate and mysterious Plain of the Crau.

Various forces were aligning to carry me there. It marked the end of the Rhône Valley, the logical geographical conclusion to the distance I'd walked, and the forecasts were promising: in the next few days powerful northerlies and north-westerlies were predicted, and the Crau – which I'd been thrilled to discover is considered western Europe's only steppe – is notoriously exposed. In stripping away the complexities of hills, valleys and villages, I would encounter the Mistral with no distraction or defence. My decision to reach this empty place was clinched when I read *In Troubadour-Land: A Ramble in Provence and Languedoc*, by the roving Victorian vicar Sabine Baring-Gould, in which he christens the Crau the 'Home of the Winds'.

Cultures throughout history have believed in versions of this idea, often supposing the wind to inhabit caves or mountains. Xan Fielding describes an account by the Greek poet Aristeas of journeying to the Scythian steppes – inhabited by one-eyed horsemen and griffins guarding gold – to find 'a chasm called the Home of the Wind in a mountain range darkened by a perpetual rain of feathers'. This might refer to a location known as the Dzungarian Gate, between Central Asia and China, which – like the mouths of the Bora in the Dinaric Alps – is the only pass for hundreds of miles through which the wind can blow. Lyall Watson writes that peoples as far-flung as the Maori of New Zealand, the Algonquin and Iroquois of North America and the Batek Negrito of Malaysia all believed the winds dwelled in high mountain caves – so often considered the abodes of gods – while the Bakitara of Uganda thought they lived in a sacred hill, 'and pointed out that it had four holes from which the breezes blew'. In seeking the Home of the Mistral I had a choice between the mountain and the desert, the vertical and the horizontal, and I chose the latter. I had spent much time in high places during my wind-walks so far, and the aesthetic simplicity of level ground was more powerful than another climb. So I continued down the river, leaving Windy Mountain to its own devices.

In Saint-Martin-d'Ardèche I found accommodation in a pilgrims' hostel maintained by the tourist office; for a small donation I was given the key to a clean, simple room in the centre of the village, complete with fridge and cooker. It overlooked the river – not the Rhône but the Ardèche, for which the region is named – which came as a cool relief after the formlessness of those hills, its waters deep emerald green, meandering from its gorge past stony islets thick with trees, draped by weeping willows. Above smooth cliffs on the opposite bank Saint-Martin's sister-village, Aiguèze, thrust its turrets and spires; the church bells clanged every quarter-hour and were answered a second behind, as if the two communities were exchanging reassurances. A lozenge of pink cloud squatted over Mont Ventoux, and a heron flapped ponderously downriver. Reeling with happy exhaustion, I collapsed on the nearest bench.

'*Pèlerin?*' asked an old man, shifting seats to talk to me. He had intense, trustful eyes, a moustache, a grubby waistcoat. *Pèlerin* means 'pilgrim' so I answered noncommittally – although I was walking the Chemin I was not 'officially' a pilgrim, which requires documentation, and I didn't want to blow my cover – but the answer appeared to satisfy him. He gestured enthusiastically at the statue of St Martin, a bearded chap with a crosier, and launched into a stream of French. Realising I understood little, he reached for my notebook. In a shaky hand he wrote '*Je recherche initiation contre la sorcellerie,*' which I translated, in growing confusion, as 'I'm researching initiation against witchcraft.' There were many witches in Ardèche, I gathered from what he said next; they were everywhere, and he was trying to fight them. Were there witches in England also? '*Oui*,' I replied, not knowing what other answer to give. He seemed unsurprised. There were many in Germany too, he said darkly, especially in Bavaria. Austria, Italy; it was a Europe-wide problem. He finished making what was clearly a pitch – an appeal for help of some kind, spiritual assistance from a fellow believer – and stared at me with an expectancy I didn't know how to answer. '*Je recherche le Mistral*,' I told him, hoping it would get me off the hook. We each seemed as confused as the other. Looking back, I'm not sure which of our quests was the weirder.

It isn't by any means unusual to meet eccentrics on a walk; walkers are marginal figures, always between one thing and another, to whom eccentrics are drawn with magnetic inevitability. But during my time in the Midi I seemed to have met more than usual. Fixated on the Mistral as I was, it was impossible not to see links between the people I encountered and the wind believed to cause craziness; whether it was positive ions, malevolent spirits that dwell in the air or the relentless howling cold that doesn't let up for odd numbers of days, insanity was the connecting theme. As in Switzerland, people had told me that in the unspecified past judges would sentence more leniently during high winds – if the Mistral blew for nine days, a crime committed on the ninth day was considered a *crime passionnel* rather than a premeditated act – though once again, evidence for this was hard to find. And I was intrigued to discover that an old Provençal term for the Mistral is *le vent du fada*, which means 'the idiot wind'. Bob Dylan wrote a song of that name, on his 1975 album *Blood on the Tracks*, the repetitive, grinding tune of which – delivered in Dylan's most scathing snarl, shot through with bitterness – looped inside my head as I walked for the next few days.

I crossed the bridge from Ardèche to Gard – on a road sign *À Bientôt* had been changed to *À Bientae*, presumably by Provençal nationalists – and finally stepped off the breadcrumb trail of the Chemin de Saint-Jacques. The pilgrim path and I parted ways almost without me noticing, like the slipping away of an old friend who doesn't like making a fuss. The road led past potato fields, worked by gangs of Roma women in headscarves and bright, flowing clothes, and back over the Rhône at Pont-Saint-Esprit. This hardscrabble farming town, so different from the villages I had walked through in the last week – pick-up trucks and motorbikes, jug-eared, slightly moronic faces, cigarettes hanging from gendarmes' lips – had a peculiar edginess, an indefinable sense of threat. I couldn't put my finger on it but something felt disturbed, as if some quiet dysfunction worked beneath its surface.

It was only later that I discovered the town is chiefly known for the mass poisoning episode that occurred in August 1951. According to the *British Medical Journal* symptoms included hot and cold flushes, insomnia, nausea, vertigo, intense sweating and salivation, muscular spasms and 'mystical or macabre' hallucinations often involving animals and flames. *Time* magazine reported that 'patients thrashed wildly on their beds, screaming that red flowers were blossoming from their bodies, that their heads had turned to molten lead.' A postman was overwhelmed with the conviction that his body was shrinking, and fire and serpents were coiling around his arms. One man attempted to drown himself, believing that snakes were in his belly, another leapt from a second-floor window yelling 'I am a plane', and an eleven-year-old boy tried to strangle his grandmother. It was as if the entire town went mad on one hot summer day. Hundreds of people were affected, fifty ended up in asylums, several attempted suicide, and half a dozen died. Theories range from mercury poisoning to nefarious CIA research into the effects of LSD (this isn't as crazy as it sounds; during the Cold War the agency carried out extensive and well-documented experiments on unwitting participants as part of its investigations into mind control). But the most widely accepted explanation is *pain maudit*, 'cursed bread': it is thought that the rye in the flour was contaminated by ergot mould, which has similar properties to lysergic acid.

That would explain the spasms, the fits, the terrifying delusions. Might it also explain the man I'd met the evening before? Throughout history, from medieval Europe to seventeenth-century Salem, Massachusetts, outbreaks of ergot poisoning have been linked to witch hysteria; before the existence of ergot was known, afflicted rural populations blamed their inexplicable symptoms – which included everything from foaming at the mouth to uncontrollable dancing – on demonic possession, scapegoating members of the community thought to be in league with the devil. To people who believed in the literal existence of demons trying to seize their souls, the onset of these epidemics must have been petrifying. Was it possible the old eccentric had eaten the bread in Pont-Saint-Esprit, and seen witches ever since? Once again, stories of lunacy threaded through this land. Between the madness of bread and the Mistral, the sanity of these benighted people hardly stood a chance.

After Pont-Saint-Esprit came Vaucluse, the department on the Rhône's eastern bank, and I followed a tedious riverside path for hours without seeing a soul. The fields were wider, the sky was higher, white butterflies did drunken pirouettes, and occasionally a snake rustled in dry yellow grass. My body became coated in dust that mixed with the suncream and sweat to form a kind of roux, reminding me of Michael's soufflé lesson back in Geneva. But change was in the air: the grass was swishing to the north, an advance breath of the *vent du sud*, and rain pattered mysteriously out of a bright blue sky. The feel of it was delicious, but I knew something big was coming. Sitting down to rest my feet, I watched an old-fashioned wind turbine, like something from the American Midwest, suddenly revolve on its axis and spin with a mournful creak. The south wind was in full flow, with clouds surging northwards. It was like watching a tidal wave coming. Within seconds the sky was dark.

I hurried on, reaching country roads as the first heavy drops slapped down, bringing a spreading green smell that made me nostalgic for England. The tarmac darkened, puddles ran together, and just as I managed to find my umbrella there was a shocking roll of thunder and a whump of white light, followed by rain so intense it was like being hosed. My boots were quickly swimming in water, my lower body soaked. Thrashed and battered by the wind, I waded through white noise. My hands lost grip on the bucking umbrella, which turned itself inside out and leapt into a nearby field, and by the time I had climbed the fence, ripping my trousers on barbed wire, my upper body was soaked as well. Incredibly the volume of water increased; the road looked like it was being machine-gunned. Each lightning crack bleached the world, causing a moment's trauma. Then suddenly the violence slumped, and the downpour became a drizzle. Thunder still growled warily, but it had travelled far away. Cautious birds began to sing. I wrung out my socks beneath a railway bridge and tramped on, just as wet.

'Orange?' called a man from a passing car, slowing in a hiss of water. For a second I thought he was offering me an orange, but then my mind clicked back to sense: Orange was the town I was heading for, my only hope of dryness. My saviour whisked me in ten minutes down a road that would have taken an hour, and before I knew it I was drinking hot chocolate in a hotel bar. When I stepped back outside, leaving puddles on the floor, the sky was blindingly blue again. The colours leapt out sharp and clear, and only the overflowing drains, and the slosh of my waterlogged boots, seemed to hold a memory of what had just occurred.

In Orange the Mistral is said to blow for one in three days of the year, and famously in 2004 it blew for sixteen days straight. I had arrived on a *vent du sud* day, but already I saw the mud-eater's touch in the counterattack of dazzling sunlight, which made the town feel like the axis between two poles. I slept in a cheap bed and breakfast, and by the morning the sultriness had seemingly been banished for good: the air was crisp, golden light turned faces into radiant statues, and shadows strutted longer than the pigeons on the pavements. Street markets were setting up for the day – mounds of potatoes and runner beans, *saucisson sec* like artillery shells, tomatoes red enough to burst – and sunbeams poured through cigarette smoke, illuminating amber beer in early morning glasses.

One wall in particular glowed like a honeycomb, vaster and more venerable than anything else in sight. The centre of town was dominated by the Théâtre Antique, an ancient Roman theatre built in the time of Emperor Augustus, fronted by an intact façade 120 feet high. Louis XIV egotistically called it 'the finest wall in my kingdom', but it was nothing to do with him; pitted and corroded by time, alien in its massiveness, it threw history back to an age before French was spoken in France, making the châteaux and cathedrals feel like the recent past. And yet some things had stayed the same. The needle of my compass confirmed that the giant, windowless façade, a solid two millennia old, was angled squarely north-north-west, leaving the concentric seats of the amphitheatre behind protected from the chill of what its builders would have called the *magistralis*. The same wind that caused the people of Orange to zip up their anoraks today once ruffled togas on these streets, and whipped the feathery crests on centurions' helmets.

Eyes shaded by a Provençal straw hat bought from a market stall – of a type I immediately suspected is worn by no one under seventy – I left my Roman fantasies and followed country roads out of town, heading back to the riverbank and the trail south.

The monotonous track along the Rhône was much the same as the day before, but rather than being soaked by the rain I was seared by the sun. Despite the cool wind at my back the midday heat was fearsome, radiating in hostile waves from the baked dirt of the path. It was a slog of fifteen miles, and before I'd even got halfway the weight of my rucksack – always too heavy no matter how much I jettisoned from it – caused twisted agonies in my back, and the soles of my feet felt like they'd been beaten with hot iron. The pain grew worse with every mile, knotting my shoulders and frequently forcing me to stop, seeking shade wherever I could, and despite my hat I was reeling with sunstroke by the time I crossed the final bridge to Avignon. The sight of the city was unreal – ramparts of ethereal grey stone, a gilded statue of the Virgin Mary gleaming on top of the cathedral – and I entered through the ancient gateway of the Porte de l'Oulle stumbling giddily, tapping my way with a walking stick I had found beside the road.

According to John Murray's *Handbook* a medieval Latin proverb said: '*Avenie ventosa, sine vento venenosa, cum vento fastidiosa*', which roughly translates as 'Windy Avignon, poisonous without wind, disgusting with wind'. Dazed and sunstruck as I was, Avignon felt poisonous and disgusting both together. One of the most beautiful cities in France, I hated it at first. Through a mist of nauseousness I only saw the fashion boutiques, the jewellery stores, the crêperies, the men in shorts and sunglasses, and heard nothing but sleazy hip hop bumping out of gelato shops. But my room for the night was cool and airy, with billowing curtains and crisp white sheets, at the top of a tall tenement overlooking the city. My host was a French-Algerian man who gave me oranges and iced lemonade for the heat exhaustion; slowly the vertigo subsided, and relief took its place. He had lived in England for a year, 'by the sea in a house which was called Mistral. This is a French word for the wind . . .' I nodded and said nothing. 'In that house I felt at home. I felt so free in England. You can go to a nightclub wearing what you like, you can even go in your pyjamas, no one will stare at you. In France it's different. Especially in the Midi, they will not let me into a nightclub even if I put on a suit, because of my skin. They see my clothes, they say "come in", they see my face, they say "no thanks". People in Provence are very small in the mind.'

As he spoke he was crumbling fragments of hashish between finger and thumb, and the effects of this, combined with the sunstroke and fatigue, made my brain pleasantly creamy by the time I stepped outside again. It was late afternoon and the streets were in shadow, massaged by gentle breezes. I immediately got disorientated, walking in an anaesthetised daze through branching lanes and shaded squares, emerging without meaning to at the foot of the Palais des Papes, the gigantic palace in the centre of the city which, for much of the fourteenth century, was the residence of no fewer than nine popes.

Or, to be more accurate, seven officially recognised popes and two illegitimate antipopes, condemned as Babylonian impostors by their Vatican rivals. During the almost seventy years of the breakaway Avignon Papacy this vast Gothic edifice, more a fortress than a palace, was the capital of Christendom, the French crown's attempt to wrest spiritual authority from Rome. With its squared defensive towers and three-metre-thick walls it was almost too huge to take in, a presence to be absorbed rather than looked at, and in my reduced state of mind I concentrated on the smaller details: the impromptu picnics beneath its walls, the buskers and the street performers, the groves of selfie-sticks. It didn't take long to plunge from the sacred to the profane: a dog had just shat massively on the doorstep of a souvenir shop, and its owner, a living statue coated in silver greasepaint, was attempting, with furious curses, to scrape it up with scraps of cardboard held between shining silver fingers, which struck me as the funniest thing I'd seen for a long time. Chuckling away on my bench, ragged and sunburned as I was, I must have looked as crazy as him. For the first time I wondered if the madness had touched me as well.

The following day I returned to seek out something that Avignon, and Provence as a whole, was especially famous for: the clay figurines known as *santons* that appear in Nativity scenes, which depict stock characters from local life. I found them in the same souvenir shop the silver man's dog had defiled, a brightly painted population of farmers with sheep slung over their shoulders, rustic types holding staffs and lanterns, vagrants, paupers, dandies, milkmaids, pail-bearing yokels, firemen, priests, old women with chickens and ducks at their feet, their fashion caught in some pastoral eighteenth-century idyll. And there was the one I was searching for: the white-bearded man holding down his hat, his cape flying out behind him, stooped against the bitter north wind. As I walked on from Avignon I carried him in my top pocket, a talisman of the Mistral. The Plain of the Crau lay ahead, and it sounded like the kind of place I might need company in.

I arrived in Arles the next day, which felt like the last homely house before the wilderness.

The Rhône was broader than ever here – so broad it had picked up an adjective and become the Grand Rhône – flowing with a greasy pulse southwards towards its mouth. The wetlands of the Camargue lay somewhere to my right, while the arid waste of the Crau lay somewhere to my left; the river was the stark divide between two separate biomes. Its banks were flanked by lion-topped plinths that marked the span of an old railway bridge, demolished by wartime bombs; another bridge, which I had passed ten miles upriver at Tarascon, was a replacement for one destroyed by powerful winds in 1845. As if to commemorate that event, a ferryboat named *Mistral* was attempting to turn in the surging current, furiously gunning its engines and clearly losing the struggle. If the composition of the wide, flat river and the curved embankment looked familiar that's because it was: a sign indicated this was the spot where Vincent Van Gogh painted *Starry Night Over the Rhône*.

It wasn't the first time in the Midi that I'd experienced this effect, a slightly uncanny hunch of recognition. Somehow I'd seen it before, as if in a recurring dream: its landscapes, its colours, its tones, but most of all its light. The purifying action of the Mistral – which sweeps the air clean of water vapour, pollution and other diluting haze – creates the famously vibrant light that, along with cheap living and bohemian attitudes, attracted generations of artists to the south of France. Impressionists and Post-Impressionists in particular flourished here: Claude Monet, Édouard Manet, Pierre-Auguste Renoir, Henri Matisse, Paul Cézanne, Paul Gauguin, Pablo Picasso and dozens of others were drawn to the clarity of Provence as astronomers are drawn to that of the Atacama Desert. All of them painted the famous light, and some directly the wind's effects: Monet's seascapes at Cap d'Antibes show trees thrashing in the Mistral, the sea so violently blue it almost hurts the eyes. But no artist is more enmeshed with the 'wind of madness' than Van Gogh, who lived in Arles from 1888 to 1889, the year before his suicide.

The subjects of the 200 paintings that Van Gogh produced in this town encompass almost everything – he painted himself, landscapes, trees, scenes from town and country life, still lifes, portraits, peasants, flowers – but perhaps what his brushwork captures best is the restlessness of the air. David Abram puts it well: 'Even in self portraits the air is never still around Vincent – the characteristic brush strokes flex and flow around his head like moving air, which can then be seen seeping into his clothes, his features. The air bends and flows in disturbed eddies and swirls, never resting.' This produces, he suggests, an animistic quality:

In Vincent van Gogh's canvases there is nothing that is not alive. There is no point in the light-filled plenum of sky that does not have its own temporal dynamism, its own rhythm, its pulse. The landscape breathes. And each presence, each clump of soil, each stone and stalk of wheat is in vibrant dialogue with the beings around it.

As the wind seeps into the paintings, the paintings seep back into Arles; the sense of *déjà vu* was impossible to escape. On my wanderings through town, once away from the old Roman centre – with its shops selling *santons*, olive oil soap and Provençal lavender products in a uniform purple shade – it was impossible not to see Van Gogh everywhere. He was there in the mad blue of the sky, the leaping pines and cypresses, the shutters striped yellow and black like oil paint smeared on thick; in the way the sunlight halved the walls, in the shadows blacker than crows. Every flaking window frame seemed to conceal a wicker chair and a vase of sunflowers. My drifting took me to the Yellow House, where his relationship with Gauguin had fallen apart in a screaming row – Gauguin claimed he rushed towards him brandishing a razor-blade – and where, shortly afterwards, he sliced off a sizeable chunk of his left ear.

There are as many theories for Van Gogh's insanity as there are for the mass hallucination at Pont-Saint-Esprit: from tinnitus, epilepsy and bipolar disorder to the lead in his paints and the wormwood in his absinthe. But here at the mouth of the Rhône, where the Mistral finally breaks free of the restricting valley walls and surges down the coast – where it is at its most intense – the wind surely played a part. 'I have been for several walks in the country hereabouts but it is quite impossible to do anything in this wind,' he writes to his brother Theo in a letter from 9 March 1888, shortly after arriving in Arles. 'The sky is a hard blue with a great bright sun which has melted almost all the snow, but the wind is cold and so dry that it gives you goose-flesh.' And in a letter from 4 May: 'I very often think of Renoir here and his pure, clean drawing. That's just the way objects or figures are here, in the clear light. We have a tremendous amount of wind and mistral here, 3 days out of four at the moment, always with sunshine, though, but then it's difficult to work out of doors.' Mentioned over forty times in his correspondence to family and friends, he calls the Mistral 'a nagging malice', 'wicked', 'pestering', 'merciless', 'evil-minded' and 'the devil', and its howling forms a soundtrack to his increasing deprivation: 'These four days I have lived mainly on 23 cups of coffee, with bread which I still have to pay for . . . there is a merciless mistral furiously sweeping along the dead leaves.'

On 28 September he complains it interferes with his painting technique: 'this blasted mistral is very bothersome to do brush-strokes that hold and are well interwoven, with a feeling like music played with emotion.' But at other times it appears to drive some of his greatest creative bursts. 'Town violet, star yellow, sky blue-green; the wheatfields have all the tones: old gold, copper, green gold, red gold, yellow gold, green, red and yellow bronze. Square no. 30 canvas,' he writes in a letter to his fellow Post-Impressionist Émile Bernard. 'I painted it out in the mistral. My easel was fixed in the ground with iron pegs, a method that I recommend to you. You shove the feet of the easel in and then you push a 50-centimetre-long iron peg in beside them. You tie everything together with ropes; that way you can work in the wind.'

That ingenious trick with the easel, which allowed him to continue painting during the most violent winds – he also devised a method of weighing it down with heavy rocks – reminded me of the story of Turner lashed to a steamship's bridge in a gale; another Odyssean figure exposing himself to the elements, attempting to capture beauty without being blown away. Van Gogh walked this line, but could not maintain it long. After a year struggling with extreme poverty, bouts of depression and alcoholism, he was hospitalised following the self-mutilation of his ear – which he claimed he could not remember – in December 1888, and never saw Gauguin again. After being discharged he returned to the Yellow House, but was forced to leave after a local petition called for the eviction of *le fou roux*, 'the redheaded madman'; two months later he committed himself to the asylum in Saint-Rémy-de-Provence. During his year-long treatment there he continued to paint prolifically, becoming obsessed with cypress trees and developing the expressive swirls that appear in *A Wheatfield With Cypresses* and *The Starry Night*; with its wind-tormented clouds, its sky that leaps and twists with life, its enormous spinning yellow stars, it's a vision of reality that's too intense to bear. Soon after completing that work he suffered a major breakdown. 'Does the mistral blow at St. Rémy as it does in Arles?' writes Theo in November 1889, and he may as well have been asking: 'Are you mad there too?'

In May 1890 Van Gogh left the Midi and moved to a village north of Paris to be closer to his brother. Two months later he completed his famous *Wheatfield With Crows* – with its darkening sky and carrion birds it has been interpreted as a suicide note – and shortly afterwards took a revolver and shot himself in the chest. He died in a hospital bed on the morning of 29 July;

according to Theo his final words were '*La tristesse durera toujours*', 'The sadness will last for ever'.

As evening fell I found myself at the Place du Forum, where he painted *Café Terrace at Night*; now inevitably renamed the Café Van Gogh. Apart from the name change they'd done their best to keep the premises like the painting – the same long yellow awning hung over tables and chairs outside – and devotees with postcards in their hands were trying to align themselves precisely where his easel had stood, to take the exact same photograph. It seemed a meaningless endeavour; the whole point of Van Gogh's work is not what is found on the surface of things but in the seething life below, which a camera phone can never capture. Attempting a literal recreation of the vivid impressions in his mind could only invite disappointment; their purpose baffled me. As if to emphasise the contrast, the bars all closed before midnight. A lot had changed since Van Gogh's time: the prostitutes had vanished from the streets, and the wormwood from the absinthe. I departed down silent alleyways. It was a starry night, but not in the way he'd seen it.

I slept in the Maison des Pèlerins, the pilgrims' hostel marking the end of the Chemin de Saint-Jacques – Arles had brought the trail and me together for one last time – before the route branched west to merge with Spain's Camino. Again I expected rosaries, Bibles, scallop shells and discarded boots, but my two-bunk room felt more like the cabin of an overnight train. It was a short, functional sleep, and I had no dreams. Soon after dawn the next day, I was on the road to the Crau.

At first it was only straggling houses, villas tucked behind cypress trees, suburbs segueing into fields. But there were other clues. For a mile the eastbound road paralleled an aqueduct, long fallen into disrepair, and at the village of Pont-de-Crau I followed the Canal de Craponne, which was still very much in use, the main artery of an intricate network of smaller canals and sub-canals branching to the left and right, regulated by iron watergates that could be raised or lowered. This irrigation system was the legacy of Adam de Craponne, a sixteenth-century engineer tasked with turning what was considered a useless, unproductive desert into some of the most fertile farmland in Europe. Diverted from the Durance River and channelled into scores of tributary canals, the water divided the great plain into two uncompromising halves: the Crau Humide and the Crau Sèche, the Wet Crau and the Dry.

The former is famous for its hay, which is sold all over Europe and especially prized by Saudi and Emirati princes who import it for their racehorses; again the Mistral plays a part, drying the grass and eliminating microbes, meaning no preservatives or pesticides are required. It's wind-certified organic. This was the harvest of the squared fields appearing either side of the road, glowing almost luminous green in the clear light. But I was heading for the Crau Sèche, where Craponne's irrigation never reached. Satellite pictures show it as a threadbare yellow stain.

The attempt to stamp human authority on any patch of 'useless' land invariably involves straight lines, and the Crau Humide was no different. The landscape was becoming increasingly regular, the canals and fields arranged at right angles, a grid pattern on an enormous scale. The effect was emphasised by the cypresses planted in long, repetitive rows, always on an east–west axis to break the Mistral's northerly blasts; these swaying green-black barricades demarcated the borders of orchards, hayfields and the compounds of *mas* houses, and followed the course of the railway line that ploughed towards Aix-en-Provence. The sense of linearity – that everything in this landscape had been scored with a metre-rule – was suggested also by the Alpilles, the undulating blue hills to the north, the only feature even remotely resembling high ground. Once again I had seen them before: they appear in the background of *The Starry Night, A*

Wheatfield With Cypresses and many more of Van Gogh's works. He came to the Crau Humide to paint, his easel pegged into the earth. Beyond the hills lay the asylum where he was incarcerated.

I stopped in the village of Moules to buy coffee in a tobacconist called the Tabac Mistral. A television above the counter showed clouds of teargas, choking protesters, riot police swinging their batons; it was a crackdown on demonstrations against labour reforms in Paris. Next on the news was Marine Le Pen, leader of the National Front, polling well for elections in departments in the south of France. Traumatic events were under way, but it all felt very distant.

Around midday I came to the region's main town, Saint-Martin-de-Crau. There was a church, a *boulangerie*, a row of empty café-bars. Avenues of pale planes created shimmying shadows on the pavements, but other than that play of light nothing moved in the streets. If I had come on a different day it might have teemed with animals: once a year the Crau shepherds drive their flocks to church for *Pastrage*, a dedicated shepherds' mass to bless the newborn lambs, and in summer black bulls from the Camargue are stampeded into town by a phalanx of *gardians* – Provençal cowboys on white horses, wearing wide-brimmed black hats and brandishing long herding sticks – an injection of wild romance into the idle streets. Young men in bright white clothes play daredevils ahead of the horns, vaulting barriers at the last moment to avoid being trampled or gored; back in Arles, the Roman arena hosts an annual *corrida*, a Spanish-style bullfight complete with matadors, silver swords and blood on the sand. These festivals are vestigial links to ancient Mediterranean bull-cults, their participants distant descendants of the bull-leapers on 4,000-year-old Minoan frescoes; another reminder that the land I was walking through is closer to Spain than it is to Paris, both in geography and spirit.

I stayed long enough to stock up on supplies – bread, salami, cheese, fruit and as much water as I could heft – then continued south. Through an interzone of suburbs, train tracks, industrial units and hemmed squares of marsh I followed another small canal, threading through yellow rushes and outcrops of bamboo. The country grew ever lusher, the fig trees either side of the road bulging suggestively with fruit, and clover, poppies and wildflowers stippled the fields. But street signs for the Rue du Mérinos and the Rue de la Transhumance hinted at the change to come: the first referred to the breed of sheep, the second to the ancient seasonal practice of moving the flocks to high pastures in summer, and back to low ground in winter. This semi-nomadic droving rhythm is still maintained on the Crau Sèche – though when the grass shrivels up the flocks are trucked to the Alps in a day, rather than driven for weeks on foot – a way of life once known across Europe from the Pyrenees to the Caucasus. That day's walk was a transition from the agricultural to the pastoral, a duality that has underscored much of human existence; from the Roman Empire to the barbarian frontier, from the Middle Kingdom's paddy-fields to the Central Asian steppes, from Cain – the prototype farmer as well as the proto-type murderer – to his herding brother Abel. Once again the path of the wind led, quite literally, away from civilisation.

> *Parlement, Mistral et Durance*
> *Sont les troix fléaux de Provence*

> Parliament, Mistral and Durance
> Are the three plagues of Provence

This nursery rhyme appears in Baring-Gould's travelogue of 1890 – where I'd first read of the 'Home of the Winds' – and it lodged in my brain as I walked. I felt a proprietorial touch of pride that of the three Provençal plagues, the Mistral was the only one to have stood the test of time: 'Parlement exists no longer, or rather is expanded into a National Assembly that is a discredit to all France, and not Provence alone; the Durance has become, thanks to Adam de Craponne, an agent of fertilisation and wealth. But the *mistral* . . . still scourges the delta of the Rhone.' While parliaments have their mandates stripped and rivers are harnessed to human needs, the Masterly has reigned on as undefeated champion.

As if to emphasise this point the cultivated fields began to give way – somewhere along the road leading past the lagoon called Étang des Aulnes – to rougher grass interspersed with stones, unpenetrated by canals. As the water ran out the greenness turned, by steady degrees, to yellow and tan. At the same time the ranks of cypress became muddled by irregular trees that looked like harbingers of disorder: lone pines twisting south, with trunks at forty-five-degree angles and skewed, lopsided crowns, permanently disfigured by perennial wind-abuse. I started to see the crinkled bark of holm oaks, lichen-specked, and encroaching plants that looked like a cross between thistles and giant cabbages. From far away a donkey brayed with a sound like a rusty water-pump. And then abruptly the road ended, and the Crau Sèche began.

There was a car park without any cars, a dirt track leading nowhere. A noticeboard said this was Peau de Meau, derived from the Provençal Pau de Mau, meaning 'Well of Evil'. Even an evil well would have been a reassurance, for the yellow vastness ahead was like a painting entitled *Thirst*. This was western Europe's only steppe, but it looked more like a desert.

'Then was revealed La Crau, the bare, the waste,/The rough

with stones, the ancient, and the vast', Frédéric Mistral wrote. I was staring at a featureless and perfectly level plain of stones reaching as far as I could see, thousands upon thousands of them, with no deviation. The stones were pale and regular, spaced evenly apart from each other as if they had been carefully placed; the earth between them was parched, baked solid by the sun. Peculiar grasses gripped the ground – rare species with names like hairy feather grass, ramified falsebroom and cypress spurge – and here and there a struggling holm oak broke the horizon's monotony. But otherwise it was just stones. Stones and silence.

I prised one up with the tip of my boot, leaving a hollow in the ground. The stone was rounded on all sides, smoothed like a river pebble, which – if you go back far enough – is precisely what it was. Millennia ago the Durance River, a greater force than it is today, rolled these rocks along its bed to deposit them in what was then an enormous delta, fanning out towards the sea. I was walking into the dried-out mouth of an ancient waterway, which must have irrigated this land long before Craponne.

That was one account, at least. The Greek tragedian Aeschylus relates another origin myth, linking this uncanny terrain to the hero Heracles. After slaying the Nemean lion and the Lernaean hydra, capturing the Ceryneian hind and the Erymanthian boar, mucking out the Augean stables, driving away the Stymphalian birds, subduing the Cretan bull, taming the mares of Diomedes, retrieving the belt of Hippolyta and rustling Geryon's cattle, Heracles passed this way en route to stealing the golden apples from the Garden of the Hesperides at the edge of the known world. Ambushed by Ligurians, the barbarians who lived in these parts, he fought until he was out of arrows and nearing defeat, which would have been a disappointing death after all those labours. He was saved, in time-honoured fashion, by divine intervention: his father happened to be Zeus, and the king of the gods sent down a hail of rocks to crush his son's attackers. The Ligurians were destroyed and the barrage has lain there ever since, forming the rubble of the Crau. Squinting in the arid light, I could see how the rounded rocks – spaced and sized with a regularity that was oddly hypnotic – might be taken for headstones in a vast burial ground, each marking the grave of a fallen warrior.

This myth, recorded in 500 BC, is a good indication of how little the land has changed, and the passage of the wind has remained as fixed as the stones. Five centuries later the geographer Strabo, another Greek commentator, referred to the Crau as 'the stony plain', describing 'an impetuous and terrible wind which displaces rocks, hurls men from their chariots, breaks their limbs and strips them of their clothes and weapons'. From the start of recorded history the Crau and the Mistral have gone together, each lending terrible strength to the other in a positive feedback loop: the treeless expanse of the plain exaggerates the effects of the wind, and the effects of the wind prevent the trees from growing.

I hadn't moved from Peau de Meau. My feet were reluctant. There was something fundamentally frightening about the shapeless land ahead, its lack of visible boundaries; I seemed to have stepped out of France and into two dimensions. For ten minutes I paced back and forth, shading my eyes and kicking up dust, intermittently checking my map, which was next to useless. The Crau was depicted as a white space, devoid of definition. The night before, with the internet's help, I had pencilled in the rough approximations of what I'd assumed were roads, but these sketches bore no resemblance to anything I could see. It seemed a new level of foolhardiness, walking into a blank space following lines I had drawn myself, with no idea what they were meant to symbolise in the first place.

After some time had elapsed my vision became sharper. I had

thought the plain empty; now, screwing my eyes up tight, I spotted details I had missed. To the north a wall of cypresses protected a railway or a road – the heat haze made it quiver and bend, and sometimes vanish altogether – and to the south I could make out a plume of industrial smoke, which I guessed must be the port and refinery at Fos-sur-Mer. Somewhere in the milky vastness between that point and where I stood rose the shallow roof of a barn. And near that barn was a shimmering line that looked like a column of dirty ants: a flock of sheep, the other reason that trees don't grow on the plain.

It gave me a point to fix on, at least, and I started walking. As I moved the Mistral stirred, swelling from the north-west, and with the flatness of the land and the blank horizon ahead I felt like a ship setting sail into a yellow sea. Perspective had no meaning here – the barn could have been any size, or any distance away – and the repetition of stones produced a magic eye effect, an illusion of restless motion, like television static. It was a feeling, a little like vertigo. I had the funny sensation that the Mistral was the only thing, in this fathomlessness, that I could be sure of.

Another noticeboard loomed up. It seemed I was walking the Draille des Troupeaux, an old drovers' road based on an even older Roman road between Arles and Istres. Under my boots harvester ants were using the same beaten track as me, dragging along scraps of leaves or the body parts of larger insects, making me constantly shorten or lengthen my stride to avoid crushing them. Glancing from the tiny world at my feet to the enormity of space surrounding me was disorientating – the bigness was starting to get to me – and I was relieved to reach solid walls. As it turned out, the building hadn't been far away at all.

It was a sheep-barn, long and low, angled into the wind. Its construction followed an ancient design: excavations from Roman times have revealed that barns were built like ships, their prows pointing to the north, landlocked arks that could shelter up to 600 sheep. In the distance I made out others, lying far across the plain like becalmed barges. The flock I had seen was far away now, camouflaged among the stones – dogs prowled its peripheries, channelling it like liquid – and I had just decided that I was alone when a brown, weather-beaten man appeared in the doorway.

He greeted me with a friendly smile, the gleam of a gold tooth. But my attempts at French were met with embarrassed silence. '*Español?*' he asked hopefully, luckily the one other language I speak. But he wasn't from Spain at all; he was Romanian. '*Buna ziua,*' I was able to say, remembering greetings from a previous walk, and he was so delighted he invited me for coffee.

Inside was a very comfortable hovel, somehow spartan and homely at the same time. There was a camp bed covered in blankets, a gas hob and a tin kettle, an old water-pump and a large stone basin, a table heaped with packets of pasta, tins of vegetables, instant noodles and overflowing ashtrays. Everything stank of wool and manure, a reek I found strangely comforting. It felt good to be enclosed by walls; I had the sudden realisation that humans are house-dwelling animals, unable to cope with spaces as large as the one outside.

While the water boiled he told me his story in patchy Spanish. It was a familiar complaint: there was no money in his country, the people were good but the system was rotten, the wages were dismal, politicians cheated you every chance they got. Here he was paid a decent wage, and given accommodation. He was not the only Romanian working as a shepherd on the Crau. 'French people do not want this work. Maybe they have forgotten how to do it.'

'How long have you been here?' I asked.

'Four days.'

'Do you speak any French?'

'Not a word! I understand sheep better than French.' There were over 200 in his flock; the breed was Arles Merino, famed for their high-quality wool and enormous horns, spiralling either side of their heads in ludicrous arabesques. The castrated males – who acted as guides for the other sheep – were shaved, bar four dreadlocked tufts to set them apart from the rest. He would stay with them here until the grass died, and then move to pastures in the Alps until the winter.

'Is there a lot of wind on the Crau?'

'*Si, muy fuerte!* Very strong! Every day it's been blowing. They call it Mistral, it's a famous wind. Apart from *mouton* and *bonjour*, it's the only French word I know.'

I drank two cups of coffee with him and accepted his cigarettes. Leaving plunged me from comfortable darkness into blinding sunlight; the Mistral had chased the cloud away and the Plain of the Crau was spotlit, the horizon bouncing in the heat with a bilious motion. As I followed the drovers' road – no more than a trail of stones between stones – the wind pushed steadily at my back, steering me south-east.

Lost in the monotony, it was impossible to tell how fast I was moving, how far I had come, or how far I still had to walk until the edge. When I looked back the Romanian's barn had shrunk to the size of similar barns, indistinguishable from half a dozen others scattered at measureless intervals. Flocks of sheep materialised and disappeared again, herded by slinking dogs that eyed me warily. Once a white car rolled past on a dusty parallel track, and when I next looked up it had stopped and a woman was standing on the roof. I carried on walking, looked up again, and the vehicle had vanished. Why had she come here? What was she doing? It was a region of lost souls.

Now I started to see that in some places stones had been piled into metre-high cairns, not unlike the curricks I had seen on Cross Fell. Their purpose, though, was not to guide the lost but to cripple the landing gear of aircraft in the Second World War. As the Allies invaded southern Europe in 1944, the Germans became concerned that the flat, practically treeless Crau could be used as a landing ground, and dragooned the local population into heaping stones into obstacles scattered across the plain. I recalled the roadside memorial I had passed earlier, a sudden crop of British names – Cunningham, Miller, Howard, Smith – RAF pilots who had been shot down in aerial battles nearby. The German plan worked, more or less, as planes never invaded the Crau, but it didn't help them for long; the final invasion was launched at Le Muy, about a hundred miles east, and the Germans retreated up the Rhône towards Montélimar. Like Zeus's rocks that rained from the sky to crush the Ligurian warriors, the cairns remain to this day, testament to old conflict. Now these structures are used by grassland birds to build their nests in.

Kestrels, little owls, little bustards and pin-tailed sandgrouse make their homes among the stones, hiding in plain sight – on a couple of occasions grouse burst into the air with a flurry of wings – and migrants like the Egyptian vulture, the snake eagle and the red-footed falcon arrive here periodically, practising their own avian version of transhumance. As for endemic species, I looked in vain for the endangered Crau grasshopper and Crau jewel beetle, and for banded centipedes, which, I'd been warned in advance, have a painful sting. For many rare species, whose habitats have been compromised or destroyed elsewhere, this desolate plain provides a refuge. More lost souls, I thought as I tramped on, going nowhere.

I had been walking for several hours when there was a crack and boom from above. It was not a storm this time, but military jets sallying in evil pairs from an airfield to the east – I could make out the high wire fence that marked its perimeter – fiends travelling in their own thunder, ricocheting through the lower air where demons dwell. This, and the strengthening of the Mistral, pulled my mind towards shelter again. I was, as far as I could tell, in the centre now. My horizons were bordered by strips of green marking the start of irrigation, or else by the distant flares of the oil refineries to the south; I was roughly equidistant from them all. I turned a slow circle, dragging my eyes along the horizon. In the middle of the emptiness thrust a single tree – the only one I'd seen for miles that stood any taller than me – and instinctively I made my way towards it. Its presence drew me like a magnet. Here, I knew before I reached it, I would spend the night.

A hare broke for cover – no chance of that – and galloped thumpingly away. Other than that nothing moved except the rattling branches. It was a twisted and stubborn holm oak, throwing shade across the pebbles. My feet stopped quite naturally. This would be my anchor.

Mindful of banded centipedes, I spent half an hour clearing stones to make space for my tent, causing mass evacuations of ants, leaving the ground dimpled with fist-sized holes like meteorite craters. I built my own small cairn while warplanes rocked the sky. When the area was long enough for my body, I lay down in it. The tent could wait; it was still a long time until dark.

Why had I stopped in this place? Green fields were on the horizon, orchards, tended countryside; the town of Istres lay beyond, with restaurants and hotels. But I didn't want any of that. There was a reason I was here, in this land beyond the pale, long cursed by the civilised for its sheer oddness. Agriculture and industry had encroached on every side, as they have with all remaining scraps of wildness in the world, but the wild endured somehow; the preserve of gold-toothed shepherds, endangered species and the wandering lost. I had stopped here, simply enough, because it was a place where the world was reduced to its basic elements, stripped of complicating factors: there was only earth and sky, and the rushing air between. Here, more than anywhere else, the point of my journey revealed itself. I had caught the idiot wind in the open, where neither of us could hide.

It was answering my call, ravaging Strabo's stony plain, bending the grasses all the same way, worrying the shade. It was doing what it has done for thousands of years without respite, and what it will continue doing until the climate changes. I lay there long enough to grow used to its battering on my ears, its cool friction on my skin, until it almost felt like the way my body had always been. When I sat up, the arid land – which had looked so dead to me before – had been transformed by that motion into an animate entity, its million grasses on high alert, its stalks waggling like antennae, attuned to every signal. Like Van Gogh's paintings each stone, each shadow, sang with energy. The wind made the land alive; made *me* alive.

Dinner was *saucisson sec* and apples, wine instead of water. The sun went down a millimetre at a time, and the colours crept from variegated greys and browns to an extraordinary desert pink; shadows leapt eastwards hundreds of feet, and the individual grasses blazed like copper wires. After a sunset soaked in blood, the horizon flooded black. Darkness spread across the plain, and with it came the warbles, shrills and throaty grunts of roosting birds hidden among the pebbles, as if the rocks were singing.

Deprived of sight, I could only feel. The world was simplified even more. It was just the Mistral and me.

That dry tide ebbed towards the sea, and I was just another rock caught within its current. For the first time on these walks I understood – for a second, at least – what was actually going on around my body, under my skin: the molecules of air rushing from high pressure to low pressure, with their cargo of charged ions, righting an atmospheric balance knocked off kilter. What felt like violent, tearing force was really the restoration of peace; what felt like furious motion an attempt to reach a stillness.

Where does wind actually go? Where does it end or begin? It travels but it never arrives; it goes everywhere and nowhere. We swim in an invisible sea of atoms, and asking where one wind ends and another begins is like asking to see the point where two oceans meet. In this way winds are unlike walks, for which endings and beginnings are fundamental dividing lines. And yet, in another sense, winds are like walkers. Walkers find themselves drawn through the world – not so much pushed from behind, but pulled by the mysterious voids of understanding that lie ahead – often without being aware of the pressures that compel them. They travel from one place to the next, until those pressures balance out. Until they arrive on the darkened plain. Until they reach a stillness.

EPILOGUE
THE BAR IS UP

I take the Corpse Road up Cross Fell, ascending to a ragged sky. The sparse fellside is peat-brown, lichen-yellow, gritstone-grey, seething with the hiss of rushes in dried-out bogs. The late afternoon sunlight is fierce, and cloud shadows chase each other across vast swathes of moorland, plunging the land into darkness before it leaps back into light. The anemometer purrs in my hand. After eighteen months and three other winds, I am chasing the Helm again.

There have been missed opportunities, each of them agonising. Over the past year and a half I have heard reports of a barn full of cows demolished by wind near High Cup Nick; a farmer in Renwick who complained it was blowing so strongly he hadn't been able to open the door of his shed for three days; 200-year-old trees brought down in Skirwirth and Milburn. Each time the news arrived too late: the Helm, like a hit-and-run raider, vanished before I could travel north. On a freezing day in October I clambered up Great Dun Fell into a wet, howling cloud to experience what I later heard referred to as a Grey Helm – dark and rainy instead of dry, a bastardised, corrupted form of the pure 'White' variant – but in place of the famous Bar was only murk and splatter. I was begrudgingly reconciled to never finding the real thing. My final wind, I told myself, would be the one that got away, its elusive spirit remaining mysterious to the end.

But now it is the beginning of May, and bitter north-easterlies have been blowing for the past few days. At the start of the week two emails arrived simultaneously, one from Geoff Monk and one from Peter Brown. 'Are you still looking for Helm events?' wrote the meteorologist. 'Prolonged easterly this week. At present mixed signals in terms of its strength, although some consensus of strong easterlies around Thursday or Friday. There may well be an inversion above the summits and "correct" temperature profile.' And then a message from the ex-bobby: 'You could be in luck!' On Wednesday morning I packed my rucksack and drove north in a borrowed car – M4, M5, M6, leaving the dreary south and the Midlands sprawl behind – until the whaleback of Cross Fell loomed on the horizon.

After leaving the motorway I crossed the ridge of Orton Scar, passed through the old county town of Appleby-in-Westmorland – where sunlight dazzled off the River Eden, seagulls clustered on the banks and the air swirled with pink blossom torn from riverside trees – and once again came to a halt outside the Masons Arms in Long Marton. Peter and Anne were waiting at home with dinner and a bed for the night, regaling me with tales of rural policing in the 1970s – 'It was more fun back then' – and the next morning, fed and rested, I set out for the fells.

From Dufton I followed the Pennine Way down avenues of blowing oaks, under thorn-snagged plastic bags fluttering like pennants. In a holloway between twisted trees I came upon two lambs attempting to suckle a dead ewe who lay on her side, her eyes pecked out, blood congealed on the dusty earth. The lambs hid when I approached, peeking from the undergrowth. As soon as I began to climb, the early summer ended.

An icy breath streamed from the fells, and every time I reached a crest the temperature plunged a few more degrees; soon I was reaching for my scarf and hat. No old man offered me tea at Knock Old Man on this occasion, so I made a brew myself, and when I emerged from the lee of the currick the wind was strong enough to unfoot me, pushing me backwards several steps. It was intensifying by the minute. I needed no compass to know its direction: it thundered from the north-east.

It took several hours to traverse Great Dun Fell, Little Dun Fell and Cross Fell itself, making for the familiar bothy below the eastern screes. I wanted to stow my rucksack before returning to the summit – I had come prepared this time, loaded with logs and kindling – and found the little stone house as empty as I'd left it, though the visitors' book recorded the many comings and goings since then. I stacked the stove, swept the flagstone floors, hung my food on a nail beyond the reach of mice. I told myself I would remain until the Helm had come.

And so now I am here, retracing my steps to the exposed summit again, following the tottering curricks of the Pennine Way. The cold is almost too much to bear – the wind chill is minus nine degrees – and the north-easterly flow is too strong to stand against. Ghostly vapours whip across the moor at incredible speed, a torrent that drives across the fell and is sucked into the valley. Through the clouds, which surge above my head in a steady westward stream, the sun recurrently shrinks to a dot and then explodes to bleach the sky with a blinding amber glow. It feels as if a plug has been opened and a terrible coldness is draining away. The demons of the air are loose. But where is the Bar?

Thoroughly chilled and blasted now, I take shelter, as before, between the protective arms of the cruciform windbreak. I know this sensation well by now; I have been attuned. In these months of following wind my skin and my senses have been washed, scoured, scrubbed, frozen, heated, pummelled, pounded, exhilarated, enervated, downcast and uplifted; *animated*, in the deepest understanding of the word. The invisible alleyways of the air have twisted through mythology, in and out of landscapes and cultures, from zephyrs to howling gales. I have met the characters of the winds, and know the qualities they bring: the Bora strength and clarity; the Foehn destruction and depression; the Sirocco debilitation; the Mistral beauty and madness. Now it seems, hoping against hope, I am about to know the Helm – if only the Bar will come – and the wildness of the chase fills me, pulls me on.

It could pull me further, across the windy world. There are innumerable other wind-ways threading through the continents: the Rashabar of Kurdistan, the Lodos and the Karaburan, the Shamal of the Persian Gulf, the Sarma of Siberia, the Squamish, the Tehuano, the Puelche, the Harmattan of West Africa, the diminutive Sz, the preposterous Bad-i-sad-o-bist-roz. Each name is a fairy tale, an invitation to a quest, somewhere far beyond this streaming cloud.

I am walking again, driven west by the wind, and find myself on the edge of the scree-covered drop that plunges into the valley. The vapour has been torn away, and as I watch a higher veil of cloud unpeels from the troposphere, revealing an immaculate blue sky. And suddenly, there it is. It has been there all along.

The Helm Bar lolls above the fells. Vast, marble-smooth. Because of its superior height, and the position of the sun, its upper side glowers grey while its underneath shines white, a reversal of the travelling lawyer's observation from 1797 – 'tinged with white by the sun's rays that strike the upper parts, and spreading like a gloom below . . . like the shadows of night' – but the manifestation is just as 'awful and solemn' as he described. It hangs absolutely motionless, undisturbed by the wind below, an alien presence in the sky, jutting over Eden. From its lucent underbelly hang what look like long white hairs, a mane of wispy filaments – later on, Geoff will identify them as 'fall streaks', trails of tiny ice particles falling from the bottom of the cloud before evaporating – which give it the appearance of some great sea-mammal wallowing in the depthless blue. This is the helmet of the wind, the symbol of my journey's end. The Bar is up.

Tomorrow I will read reports in the local news: 'Stunning and unusual cloud sighted over Cumbria'; 'A rare form of the Helm Bar'; 'Striking tube-shaped cloud'. It seems this Bar, with its tendrils of ice, its strangely squared southern tip, and its unusual position – not lying parallel to the fells but shunted to the south-west, as if about to launch an invasion over the Lake District – is particularly outlandish, and has turned faces to the sky up and down the county. Soon it will untether itself and drift out above the valley – even crossing the River Eden, which, according to local lore, marks the westernmost limit of the Helm's effective range – to be sighted everywhere from Coniston to Keswick. It will lumber magnificently off into the west, while the wind that sculpted it still roars above the fells.

But for now it hangs without moving, a solid object in the sky. I watch until the cold becomes too much, then turn for shelter.

Not far now. I am almost done. One boot at a time. The Helm cannonades against me, slams me with powerful random blasts, and walking a hundred metres takes too long to feel real, as if time is being sucked away as well as air. It freezes the tunnels of my ears. Clumsy and slow with cold, my hands are pink lobster claws. I stop and turn for one last look, but the Bar is veiled again. I turn back into the wind and carry on.

Acknowledgements

Thanks to Anne and Peter Brown in Long Marton, Geoff Monk at the Mountain Weather Information Service, Vladimir Janković at the University of Manchester, Lionel Playford in Garrigill, Ruth Allgäuer and Markus Burgmeier in Balzers, Hans Richner, Patrick Hächler and Daniel Gerstgrasser in Switzerland, Jonathan Ruffer and Janin Eberhardt for their help with Rilke translations, Louis Porter, Baz Nicholas, Tomaš who helped me in the mountains, and everyone who freely offered stories and weather forecasts on the way, whether or not they turned out to be accurate.

The walking and writing of this book was enabled by a generous Authors' Foundation grant from the Society of Authors. It could not have been written or published without the support, enthusiasm and dedication of Nicholas Brealey, Nick Davies, Ben Slight, Louise Richardson, Caroline Westmore, Morag Lyall, Hannah Corbett, Yassine Belkacemi and Rosie Gailer. Thanks also to my inspiring friends and colleagues at the Dark Mountain Project.

Finally, love and thanks to the grand aeolian forces that move and shape my life: Caroline Williams, Caroline Hunt, Ron, Alisa and Isabella Hutchinson, and to all my friends.

The author and publisher would like to thank the following for permission to reproduce quotations. Excerpts from *The Weather in the Imagination* by Lucian Boia, translated by Roger Leverdier, are reprinted by kind permission of Reaktion Books. Excerpts from *Aeolus Displayed*, by Xan Fielding, are reprinted by kind permission of Terry Risk at Typographeum. The excerpt from Robert Harrison's translation of 'Letter from Vincent van Gogh to Theo van Gogh,' 28 September 1888', is reprinted by kind permission of WebExhibits. 'A Walk' from *Selected Poems of Rainer Maria Rilke, A Translation from the German and Commentary* by Robert Bly, copyright © 1981 by Robert Bly, is reprinted by permission of HarperCollins Publishers. Excerpts from *Peter Camenzind* by Hermann Hesse, translated by W.J. Strachan, are reprinted by kind permission of Peter Owen Publishers, London. Excerpts from *Becoming Animal* by David Abram are reprinted by kind permission of Penguin Random House. Excerpts from *Trieste and the Meaning of Nowhere* by Jan Morris, copyright © 2001 by Jan Morris, are reprinted by permission of Simon & Schuster, Inc., and by Faber and Faber Ltd. Excerpts from 'Los Angeles Notebook' from *Slouching Towards Bethlehem* by Joan Didion, copyright © 1966, 1968, renewed 1996 by Joan Didion, are reprinted by permission of Farrar, Straus and Giroux, and by Janklow & Nesbit Associates. Excerpts from Lyall Watson's *Heaven's Breath: A Natural History of the Wind* (pages 116, 117, 277, 301 and 304) are reprinted by kind permission of Adams & Adams.

Bibliography

Abram, David, *Becoming Animal: An Earthly Cosmology*, Vintage Books, 2011

Barcala, Rogelio Garcia, *The Doldrums, Christ, and the Plantanism*, Xlibris Corporation, 2003

Baring-Gould, Sabine, *In Troubadour-Land: A Ramble in Provence and Languedoc*, W.H. Allen & Company, 1891

Boia, Lucian, *The Weather in the Imagination*, Reaktion Books, 2005

Bouvier, Nicolas, Gordon A. Craig and Lionel Gossman, *Geneva, Zurich, Basel: History, Culture, and National Identity*, Princeton University Press, 1994

Camus, Albert, 'The Wind at Djemila', *Lyrical and Critical Essays*, Vintage Books, 1985

Chandler, Raymond, 'Red Wind', *Trouble is My Business*, Penguin, 2013

Didion, Joan, 'Los Angeles Notebook', *Slouching Towards Bethlehem*, Farrar, Straus & Giroux, 1968

Doumer, Michael, ed., *Van Gogh's Letters, Unabridged & Annotated*, WebExhibits

Endfield, Georgina, Lucy Veale and Simon Naylor, 'Knowing weather in place: the Helm Wind of Cross Fell', *Journal of Historical Geography*, 2014

Fielding, Xan, *Aeolus Displayed*, Typographeum, 1992

Gooley, Tristan, *The Natural Navigator Pocket Guide*, Virgin Books, 2011

Harris, Alexandra, *Weatherland: Writers and Artists under English Skies*, Thames and Hudson, 2015

Hesse, Hermann, *Peter Camenzind*, Penguin, 1974

Hughes-Hallett, Lucy, *The Pike: Gabriele d'Annunzio: Poet, Seducer and Preacher of War*, Fourth Estate, 2013

Hutchinson, William, *The History of the County of Cumberland*, EP Publishing, 1974

Ingold, Tim, 'Footprints through the weather-world: walking, breathing, knowing', *Journal of the Royal Anthropological Institute*, 2010

Janković, Vladimir, 'Gruff boreas, deadly calms: a medical perspective on winds and the Victorians', *Journal of the Royal Anthropological Institute*, 2007

Manley, George, 'The helm wind of Cross Fell', *Quarterly Journal of the Royal Meteorological Society*, 1945

Márquez, Gabriel García, 'Tramontana', *Strange Pilgrims*, Penguin, 1994

Moore, Peter, *The Weather Experiment: The Pioneers Who Sought to See the Future*, Chatto & Windus, 2015

Morris, Jan, *Trieste and the Meaning of Nowhere*, Faber, 2001

Pretor-Pinney, Gavin, *The Cloudspotter's Guide: The Science, History, and Culture of Clouds*, TarcherPerigee, 2007

Schiller, Friedrich, *Wilhelm Tell*, 1803

Shaw, Trevor R., *Foreign Travellers in the Slovene Karst: 1486–1900*, Založba ZRC, 2008

Thomson, William, A.R., *A Change of Air: Climate and Health*, Scribner's, 1979

Uttley, David, *The Anatomy of the Helm Wind*, Bookcase, 2000

Wainwright, Alfred, *Pennine Way Companion*, Westmorland Gazette, 1968

Watson, Lyall, *Heaven's Breath: A Natural History of the Wind*, Hodder and Stoughton, 1984

West, Rebecca, *Black Lamb and Grey Falcon: A Journey Through Yugoslavia*, Macmillan, 1942